T0351637

THE IMPERATIVE OF DEVELOPMENT

THE IMPERATIVE

OF

DEVELOPMENT

THE WOLFENSOHN CENTER AT BROOKINGS

GEOFFREY GERTZ,

HOMI KHARAS,

and

JOHANNES F. LINN

EDITORS

BROOKINGS INSTITUTION PRESS

Washington, D.C.

The Brookings Institution is a private nonprofit organization devoted to research, education, and publication on important issues of domestic and foreign policy. Its principal purpose is to bring the highest quality independent research and analysis to bear on current and emerging policy problems. Interpretations or conclusions in Brookings publications should be understood to be solely those of the authors.

Library of Congress Cataloging-in-Publication data are available.
ISBN 978-0-8157-3255-6 (cloth : alk. paper)
ISBN 978-0-8157-3256-3 (ebook)

Typeset in Adobe Jenson Pro

Composition by Elliott Beard

Contents

Contents

7

Acknowledgments

This volume represents five years of research and engagement at the Wolfensohn Center for Development at Brookings, and it would not be possible without the many individuals and organizations that supported the Center. After ten years as president of the World Bank, James D. Wolfensohn created the Center to continue research on some of the issues that he considered most important to the betterment of the developing world: early child development, human development in the Middle East, and development aid that is more sustainable and effective.

Brookings would particularly like to recognize James D. Wolfensohn and the Wolfensohn family for their generous financial, intellectual, and strategic support of the Center. Brookings would like to thank Alfonso Romo Garza and Jacob Rothschild and the Saffery Champness Trust Corporation as Trustee of the Arrow Charitable Trust for their support, as well as the Bernard van Leer Foundation, Open Society Foundations, Tecovas Foundation, UNICEF, Victor Pinchuk Foundation, World Bank, Conrad N. Hilton Foundation, Dubai School of Government, Silatech, Asian Development Bank, two anonymous donors, and other supporters for their contributions and partnership, which significantly advanced the Center's research and expanded its impact. We would also like to thank all the employees, staff, and interns who contributed to the Center's research and activities throughout its history; this volume is truly a reflection of their collective efforts and accomplishments.

Acknowledgments

We would additionally like to thank all the authors of the chapters in this volume, as well as those researchers whose original work for the Wolfensohn Center for Development is reprinted here. Steven Bennett, Martin Indyk, and Strobe Talbott in the Brookings Executive Office offered helpful guidance and advice in putting together this book. Finally, Valentina Kalk and Janet Walker with Brookings Institution Press provided invaluable editorial and production support and guided us through the publication process.

Foreword

Since its founding in 1916, the Brookings Institution's mission has been to improve governance. In the early years, that meant helping the executive branch of the U.S. federal government become more efficient. Over the decades, our scholars broadened their scope to the Congress, as well as state capitals and city authorities around the country. Starting in the 1920s, they engaged foreign governments and international organizations, eventually including the United Nations.

At the beginning of the twenty-first century, we substituted the word *governance* for government, since our writ had expanded from political institutions to civil society, academe, and other stakeholders in communities at all levels—from local to national to regional to worldwide.

As a Brookings trustee starting in 1983, Jim Wolfensohn was a passionate advocate for this evolution. He believed that a peaceful and prosperous world depended largely on the developing countries. To him, "development" meant more than economic growth: it required educated citizens and civic progress.

"Global" has always been part of Jim's vocabulary, worldview, and eclectic and distinguished career. He titled his autobiography *A Global Life*. In 2005 Jim came to me with the initial idea of creating a new center at Brookings focused on global development; the following year, we formally launched the Wolfensohn Center within Brookings's new Global Economy and Development research program.

The Center's aspirations, guiding principles, and accomplishments ring throughout this volume. And at this moment in history, it is a message that is more urgent than ever. The last few years have seen a welter of threats to global development and governance: the rise of nationalism, protectionism, and isolationism, the return to zero-sum geopolitics and great-power spheres of influence, the fear of globalization itself, as though it were an ideology or a policy rather than a condition of modernity.

Developing countries can be part of the mitigation of these adverse trends. They are now core drivers of the world economy, sources of demand and innovation; rich and poor countries alike have an interest in promoting their continued growth. Similarly, we cannot wall ourselves off from security challenges arising in fragile states any more than we can ban pandemics from crossing borders. And, of course, the perils facing our planet's environment will not be solved by individual nations acting alone, but will require global cooperation.

The Wolfensohn Center not only stimulated constructive debate and policy brainstorming in Washington and around the world when it was in operation, but it left a body of first-rate analysis and prescriptions for dealing with these challenges when it completed its own mission six years ago.

The articles and chapters reprinted in this volume remain timely and relevant today. In fact, the need for the type of cooperative action they outline has only increased. Work at Brookings today is often enriched by the Center's products and scholars, who are still part of our community—as is Jim.

Jim's commitment allowed Brookings to make a step change in our analysis and engagement of the developing world, which I consider one of the most important advances this institution has achieved during the last fifteen years. In recognition of the substantial contributions the Wolfensohn family has made to Brookings, the publication of this book coincides with the formal dedication of the Wolfensohn Room at our headquarters.

Individually, the chapters that follow address a range of topics, including how to deliver development assistance more effectively, support the inclusion of burgeoning youth populations, and reform the institutions of global governance. Collectively, these chapters tell the story of how even a relatively small research center can achieve lasting real-world impact. It is a legacy worth celebrating.

Strobe Talbott
PRESIDENT, BROOKINGS INSTITUTION

1

Introduction

GEOFFREY GERTZ *and* JOHANNES F. LINN

From 2006 to 2011 the Wolfensohn Center for Development at the Brookings Institution sought to help identify effective solutions to key development challenges in order to create a more prosperous and stable world. Founded by James and Elaine Wolfensohn, the Center's mission was to "to create knowledge that leads to action with real, scaled-up, and lasting development impact." Now, some six years after the Center has completed its work, this current volume reviews achievements and the Wolfensohn Center's lasting legacy. Combining highlights of research with contemporary reflections on how this research agenda has evolved, *The Imperative of Development* reflects on the origins, evolution, and impact of Brookings's first home of development research.

When the Wolfensohn Center was initially conceived, in late 2005 and early 2006, the world looked very different than it does today. In many ways it was a time of optimism in the international development community. In the summer of 2005 the G-7—the grouping of the world's largest economies—had met in Gleneagles, Scotland, and promised to double aid to Africa by 2010. International civil society campaigns, such as Make Poverty History, had helped bring more popular attention to the challenge of global poverty than ever before, generating new momentum for both government and citizen actions. In the United

States, the George W. Bush administration was in the process of scaling up the President's Emergency Plan for AIDS Relief, or PEPFAR, launched in 2003 and the largest global health initiative dedicated to a single disease. Through the work of the United Nations, countries were coalescing around the Millennium Development Goals (MDGs) as a vision of transformative economic and social development.

Moreover, the development community was also beginning to get more serious about aid effectiveness and measurement of results, ensuring international assistance was driven not only by soft hearts but also hard heads. In February 2005 members of the Organization for Economic Cooperation and Development's Development Assistance Committee, the primary bilateral aid agencies, had signed the Paris Declaration on Aid Effectiveness, committing themselves to improve their aid delivery systems to maximize the impact of every dollar spent. Monitoring and evaluation efforts were gaining traction, and rigorous impact evaluations were increasingly helping shape budgets and agendas.

At the same time, tectonic shifts in the global economy were fundamentally restructuring international economic and political relations. Jim O'Neill of Goldman Sachs had coined the term "BRICs" a few years earlier, designating the rising economies of Brazil, Russia, India, and China. These so-called emerging economies were the darlings of investment asset managers around the globe, even as most politicians and pundits had yet to fully reckon with how much they could disrupt long-existing patterns in the world economy.

For the Wolfensohn family this was also a period of transition. After a long and successful career as an investment banker, James Wolfensohn completed ten years at the helm of the World Bank in 2005; at the time he was only the third World Bank president to serve more than one term. He then spent a year as the special envoy to the Middle East for the Quartet—the diplomatic grouping of the United States, European Union, Russia, and the United Nations—charged with advancing the peace process between the Israelis and Palestinians, and in particular trying to catalyze growth in the Gazan economy. After more than a decade in such high-profile and demanding international finance and diplomacy roles, James and his wife, Elaine, wanted a less stressful and chaotic life. But both also knew that their commitment to public service, and in particular to the interlinked challenges of global prosperity and stability, had not diminished. The Wolfensohns thus sought a new venture for channeling their efforts to help spur transformative and sustainable development.

They decided that one way they could do so was by helping to create a new research center specifically focused on the imperative of development. Given that Mr. Wolfensohn had just come from running a development institution with a staff of thousands and annual disbursements of around $23 billion, this was perhaps a curious choice. In a development landscape driven by big players such as the World Bank, USAID, the Gates Foundation, and others, what role was there for a small research center with just a handful of senior scholars?

Yet his time at the Bank had helped convince Mr. Wolfensohn that there were a number of crucial contributions research institutes and think tanks could make to the development community. Of course, such centers would not have the same direct influence as larger players disbursing grants or setting policies, but it was precisely this independence from funding agencies and policymakers that allowed research institutes to have impact. Independent research centers could be more nimble and define their own research agenda, helping bring innovative new ideas into development discussions. Moreover, since it would not be directly connected to a government or international institution, and without any specified ideological commitments beyond an interest in the fates of the world's poorest people, a new research center focused on development could avoid some of the politicized debates that took place in other contexts. It could be a constructive outside analyst and critic, informing and prodding officials and policymakers in both rich and poor countries to do better in promoting a stable and prosperous world. And it could play a valuable convening role, as a place for different stakeholders to come together and discuss and debate potentially contentious issues in a neutral environment.

For the Wolfensohns, the Brookings Institution was the logical organization to partner with to build such a center. Mr. Wolfensohn knew Brookings well, having served on its Board of Trustees since 1983. By embedding the new Center in an established institution, rather than creating a new organization from scratch, the Wolfensohn Center for Development could draw on Brookings's extensive network, reputation, and convening power, as well as its back-office capabilities. This would allow the Center to have a more immediate and wide-ranging impact.

Meanwhile from Brookings's point of view, the proposed Wolfensohn Center would allow the think tank to significantly advance its nascent research agenda on the world economy and international development. Historically Brookings had focused on the United States' economy, foreign policy, and governance, but in the mid-2000s, under the leadership of President Strobe Talbott, Brookings was in the midst of further internationalizing its outlook. In early 2006 it launched a new major research program called Global Economy and Development, headed by Vice President Lael Brainard. This program would become Brookings's home for analysis on international trade and finance, and it was looking to strengthen its emphasis on international development. The Wolfensohns' proposed initiative would be a perfect fit.

With a $10 million, five-year commitment from James and Elaine Wolfensohn, the Wolfensohn Center for Development officially opened in July 2006, with a skeletal staff of four.[1] From the beginning, the Center's overarching objective was to identify pressing challenges in international development that (a) would significantly influence development outcomes over the next five to ten years; (b) were currently being under-researched by the academic and think tank community; and (c) offered opportunities for the Center's scholars to transform research into impact. The Wolfensohns worked with the Center's research staff to identify six principal topics that met these criteria.

The first issue that emerged as a priority research topic was the shifting structure of the world economy in the twenty-first century, and in particular the increasing importance of developing and emerging economies. At the heart of this work was a recognition that long-standing patterns of the global economy, where a small group of rich countries dominated global production and wealth and a large group of poor countries languished on the periphery, were breaking down. Instead, the global economy seemed to be splitting into what Mr. Wolfensohn and the Center's scholars saw as a "four-speed world," divided between affluent countries, quickly growing emerging economies, countries stuck at middle-income levels, and the poorest countries beset by low productivity, conflict, and corruption. Whereas the twentieth century had been shaped by the growing divide between developed and developing countries, the twenty-first century would be defined by the interactions and interdependencies of these four groups of countries. Chapter 2 of this book discusses the Center's work on the shifting structure of the world economy and includes a memo by James Wolfensohn, written for the incoming Barack Obama administration on the implications of this four-speed-world framework for international development, trade, governance, and security, as well as an op-ed for Project Syndicate on the emerging global order.

A second key research topic for the Center was the challenge of scaling up the impact of development interventions. While a growing interest in the monitoring and evaluation of development programs was helping scholars and practitioners identify successful projects, too often these successful pilots were not then expanded and implemented at scale. Projects were reaching hundreds or thousands of beneficiaries, instead of the millions who were in need. To have real impact, development interventions needed to be scaled up. The Wolfensohn Center worked to develop an analytical framework for understanding how to expand, replicate, adapt, and sustain successful policies and programs in space and over time. This work focused on the political and organizational leadership required to ensure that scaling up was at the core of development efforts. Chapter 3 presents an overview of the Center's research and analysis on scaling up and includes the introductory chapter from the Brookings book *Getting to Scale*.

A third issue the Center focused on, related to the question of scaling up, was the need to improve the effectiveness of official development assistance (ODA). While there had long been a debate about increasing the overall *quantity* of aid spending—with countries striving, and mostly failing, to meet the international target of 0.7 percent of gross national income—new attention was being paid to the *quality* of aid, or how to get the greatest impact for each dollar. The development assistance landscape was becoming increasingly complex and crowded, with new donors, private philanthropists, mushrooming multilateral agencies, and traditional bilateral aid donors all operating alongside one another, raising the likelihood of costly overlap and waste. By the Center's estimates, of every $100 spent on aid in rich countries, only $19 finally made it to intended beneficiaries in poor countries. Chapter 4 examines the Center's research and impact on the issue of development effectiveness and includes a policy brief on measuring the quality of development aid and the introductory chapter of the book *Catalyzing Development*, originally produced by the Center to inform the Fourth High-Level Panel on Aid Effectiveness held in Busan, South Korea, in 2011.

A fourth issue the Center prioritized was the urgent need to provide jobs and opportunities for Middle Eastern youth. From his time as special envoy for the Quartet, Mr. Wolfensohn had gained an acute appreciation of this crucial challenge, given that almost two-thirds of the region's population is under the age of thirty. As youth transitioned into adulthood, many struggled to find well-paying jobs and a meaningful role in society. Working with partners in the region, the Center launched the Middle East Youth Initiative, a program devoted to studying social and economic exclusion of young people across the Middle East and North Africa. In many ways this research anticipated the forces and drivers that lay behind the "Arab Spring" revolutions of 2010–11, when populations across the region took to the streets to express their economic, social, and political grievances. Chapter 5 discusses the Center's work on Middle East youth and includes the introductory chapter of the book *Generation in Waiting*, an edited volume addressing the challenges of youth exclusion; the book was published just prior to the Arab Spring and played a crucial role in explaining the socioeconomic contexts of these protests that shocked the world. The chapter also includes a policy brief on how public sector employment policies in Syria hindered the country's transition to a market economy.

The fifth big topic the Center worked on was Early Child Development (ECD). This research focused on how investments made in health, nutrition, and education during the early years of a child's life, before the age of five, have crucial long-lasting impacts on life trajectories. Much of this work focused on convincing policymakers that spending on young children's development is, in the long run, an extremely cost-effective investment. This emerged as a priority issue for both James and Elaine Wolfensohn, and the two were tireless advocates for ECD in countless meetings with policymakers, private sector leaders, and nongovernmental organizations (NGOs) around the world. Building on the Center's established expertise in scaling up, research on ECD focused on how to take small, successful pilot early child programs and roll them out at a national level. To this end, the Center commissioned a series of working papers of country case studies in developing national ECD programs. Chapter 6 details the Center's research and advocacy in this area and includes an excerpt from a country case study on South Africa's pioneering ECD program.

The sixth and final major research topic of the Wolfensohn Center was global governance and reform of the multilateral system. The governance structures of the key international institutions of the global economy—including the G-7, the World Bank and IMF, and the United Nations—revealed their post-WWII origins, and by the early 2000s these structures were becoming increasingly ill-fitted to reality. These institutions needed to be updated to reflect changes in the world, especially with the rise of emerging economies. The Center's scholars spent many years making the case for reforming international institutions, explaining why such modernization was necessary to preserve their legitimacy and efficiency. In particular, the Center was an early advocate for replacing the more restrictive and limited G-8 grouping with a G-20 leaders' forum, a transformation finally achieved in late 2008, in the wake of the global financial crisis. Chapter 7 of this book examines the Wolfensohn Center's work on global governance reform and includes the concluding chapter from a 2007 edited volume on global governance reform, an op-ed written by James Wolfensohn for the *Washington Post* on the eve of the first G-20 leaders forum, and a policy brief on the future of global economic governance after the financial crisis.

In keeping with its mission, in all six of these research areas the Center persistently sought to bridge the gap between development theory and practice. In some instances this meant working directly with development agencies and practitioners; for example, the Center partnered closely with the International Fund for Agricultural Development (IFAD) to help it scale up programming; with the Korean official development agency, to improve aid effectiveness and prepare for the Fourth High-Level Forum on Aid Effectiveness at Busan; and with G-20 sherpas for the United Kingdom and South Korea, to help them prepare for the early G-20 summits. More generally, however, this meant engaging with key stakeholders—including politicians, international organizations, businesses, NGOs, and the media—to broaden the reach of the Center's research. Throughout this book, we highlight how and where the Center built and leveraged these partnerships to help translate research and analysis into concrete action.

This book is not designed to be an exhaustive anthology of research from the Wolfensohn Center at Brookings. Rather, its goal is, with the benefit of hindsight and some years' distance from the immediate day-to-day demands and stresses, to reflect back on the broader impact and legacy of the Center. In each chapter, a scholar associated with the particular research stream provides an overview of the issue and its broader context, before describing the Center's work on the topic and the influence and impact of these efforts in the years since. This book chronicles the growth and expansion of the first center for development research in Brookings's one-hundred-year history and traces how the seeds of this initiative continue to bear fruit. It serves as an example of the constructive role a small research center can play, even in a crowded development landscape.

2

Meeting the Challenge of Development

HOMI KHARAS

As president of the World Bank, James Wolfensohn had visited 120 countries and witnessed the diversity of their experiences and their needs. He saw first-hand the massive growth potential in many countries, notwithstanding the domestic challenges they faced, while also facing up to the abject poverty in other places. His deep belief was that what happened in developing countries would drive change in the global economy—both the upside of growth and the downside of terrorism, conflict, and the spread of infectious disease. His worry was that there was little awareness in the United States of the importance of developing countries, and he was determined to contribute to increasing such awareness.

Mr. Wolfensohn often used to comment on the fact that when he was growing up, he could rely on a simple rule of thumb: the major, rich economies of the world accounted for about 80 percent of global output but only 20 percent of world population, while developing countries had the reverse. He foresaw a rapid transition in this state of affairs, with the developed-country share of global output falling to 35 percent, largely on account of the rise of Asia. He consistently talked about the major implications of such a change, especially for international organizations with increasingly outdated governance structures.

It was not surprising, therefore, that Mr. Wolfensohn suggested that the Wolfensohn Center place a high priority on studying changes in the world economic structure and the contribution of developing countries to what was fast becoming a multipolar world. The centerpiece of the analysis in the Center came to be known as the "four-speed world." In this formulation, countries were divided into four groups. The first, a group of affluent countries, had high per capita income levels but modest and steady growth. They were still important for the global economy but no longer the major drivers of global economic change. This was left to a second group, the globalizers. Globalizers were defined as countries growing at more than 3.5 percent per capita per year over the long term, among whom were China and India. Because of their large populations (over 3 billion people), the globalizers were responsible for most global growth.

The third category of the four-speed world consisted of middle-income "rentiers," countries with significant natural resource wealth that allowed them to reach middle-income levels but that also contributed to Dutch disease and governance challenges that made them victims of the natural resource curse. Rounding out the framework were "survivors," a group of low-income countries beset by low productivity, conflict, corruption, or high debt levels that struggled to do more than simply survive.

Implementing the four-speed-world concept required detailed modeling on economic trajectories. Building specific country growth models for every country in the world was not feasible given the capacity of the Wolfensohn Center. Equally, it would not have been the Center's comparative advantage: the IMF and World Bank had the resources and expertise to do that far better. What the Center wanted to provide was a "big picture" view, an overall perspective that would illustrate the shifting contours of the world economy. Such a picture had to have numbers—Mr. Wolfensohn favored a quantitative approach—but the numbers were used for illustrative purposes to talk about global strategic issues, rather than being the focus of the discussions themselves. In this, the Wolfensohn Center was quite different from the major international institutions; scholars did not have to concern themselves with whether the forecast for a particular country—Ethiopia, for example—was right or wrong, but only with whether they were capturing the broad outlines of global development in a reasonable way.

By framing country characteristics and prospects around the four-speed world, it became possible to respect the diversity of developing countries while not moving all the way to country-by-country modeling. Instead, the underlying growth model was built around capital accumulation and labor force projections. The model also included a "convergence" parameter that could be turned on for globalizers but took the value of zero for rentiers and survivors.[1]

With this tool in hand, the Center was able to quantify the underlying tectonic shifts in the global economic structure taking place. In one early piece based on research done in the Center—reprinted in this chapter—James Wolfensohn outlined the key dimensions of this changing world in a memo for the incoming Barack Obama administration. The point was not to make predictions about how the world would evolve but to note that very deep changes were happening that forced people to ask uncomfortable questions that had been safely ignored for the previous fifty years of relative stability in the world economic order.

Some of these questions seem prescient today. Consider the following quote from this memo:

> The harsh truth of blue collar manufacturing job losses concentrated in some parts of the country, coupled with technological advances that have enabled outsourcing of white collar jobs, has resulted in large-scale anxiety about free trade and globalization. In a recent poll, 54 percent of Americans thought that economic globalization was moving too quickly for their liking. 52 percent thought that economic benefits and burdens were unfairly shared, as a result of globalization. Given the history of pro-trade sentiment in the U.S., these perceptions are a sign of caution.

Based on this assessment, the article goes on to advocate for domestic programs that pay attention to the plight of workers displaced by trade and technology in order to resist a populist backlash.

The same understanding that some people and countries were being left behind by the great forces of globalization and technology pushed Mr. Wolfensohn to ask:

> Are the inequalities in living standards between the haves and the have-nots sustainable? What might they mean for pressures on migration and the security of our borders?

Today, what is happening in developing countries dominates the economic discussion in advanced economies. Jobs, inequality, and migration are all linked to globalization. Globalization in turn is linked to the emergence of developing countries as key players in the global economy.

China, of course, is the largest of the developing economies and the one most responsible for the tectonic shifts that are taking place. Mr. Wolfensohn is a long-time keen observer of China. He understood that much of China's early growth success was based on one-off improvements: agricultural reforms through the household responsibility system, openness to world markets, expansion in investment and trade. But he urged China to also focus on more sustainable sources of growth, based on ideas and education, and advocated for these to be expanded in two areas: in the weakest parts of society, namely in rural areas, and in the strongest urban areas where innovation to improve the quality and sustainability of growth would be developed.[2]

The development of China's urban and coastal areas is the centerpiece of what has since become the largest, fastest expansion of the middle class that the world has ever seen. Mr. Wolfensohn devoted the World Bank to the cause of reducing poverty, but he also appreciated that the driver of global change—what would affect the economies of the advanced countries—was the growth in the middle classes of emerging economies like China. It would be growth in these places that would offer the opportunities for Western companies to trade and invest and take advantage of the growing division of labor made possible by globalization.

A case study of the development of China's middle class undertaken by scholars at the Wolfensohn Center showed how the basic four-speed-world model could be used to understand far-reaching trends in individual countries.[3]

The work on China proceeded in parallel with work being done by Center scholars who were collaborating with others on a larger Organization for Economic Cooperation and Development (OECD) study on shifting global wealth.[4] Such collaboration helped the Center to achieve its basic goal of building awareness about the importance of studying developing countries. It did this through a series of working papers, policy briefs, op-eds, and speeches that took advantage of the many invitations to Mr. Wolfensohn to offer his perspectives on global development. One such op-ed reprinted in this chapter—"Farewell to Development's Old Divides"—illustrates the new ideas coming out of the Center.[5] Work done by the Wolfensohn Center was even referenced by Jim Cramer on his popular "Mad Money" TV show.

The original memo on the implications of the four-speed-world paper highlighted three areas with specific policy implications: reforming international institutions, rethinking trade, and reinventing aid. The first and third issues were already taken up as specific work streams of the Wolfenshohn Center and are addressed in separate chapters in this volume. While trade was not a specific focus of the Center, colleagues in the Brookings Global Economy and Development (GED) program addressed this issue, particularly related to the Africa Growth and Opportunity Act; important contributions were made by Brookings to shape its renewal in 2015.

But perhaps the most important legacy of the Wolfensohn Center's work on the shifting global economy has been the birth of a tradition of counting people across the world. GED's work on trends in the numbers living in poverty and numbers living in the middle class has been featured in *The Economist* magazine and other traditional and social media outlets.[6] It has resulted in major contributions to improved measurement of poverty and to the early identification of the coming concentration of global poverty in fragile states.[7] Meanwhile, the expansion of the middle class in developing countries is proceeding at an even faster pace than initially envisaged.[8] The work on this topic undertaken by GED continues to attract interest and attention from policymakers, as well as business and corporate strategists, and has been widely cited.

Within GED, research on implications of the global middle class has evolved. New areas have come into focus, most notably on climate change, sustainability, and urbanization.

The middle class has long presented a paradox for development practitioners. On one hand, expansion of the middle class represents, in large part, the ultimate success of development. On the other hand, it can potentially mean the end of development because of the potentially large expansion of energy and other material inputs that go into the products consumed by the middle class. Understanding and unpacking this paradox is one of the central challenges facing development policymakers today. Within GED, a new emphasis is being placed on understanding demographic change and its links to the middle class. If the middle class can contribute to reduced fertility rates, then it can also help global population stabilize at far lower levels. In fact, households in the middle class do have far lower fertility than poor households. Working women tend to delay childbirth and want fewer children. Educated women have far lower fertility rates; women who have completed secondary schooling have four to five fewer children than those with no education. If a fast expansion of the middle class takes hold everywhere, then the global population will stabilize at around 9 billion people by 2100 rather than 11 billion people. Unfortunately, at present, the most rapid expansion of population is in sub-Saharan Africa where the size and expansion rate of the middle class is still the smallest in the world.

A second strand of related current work in GED relates the middle class to urbanization. Most middle-class families live in urban areas because of the access to job opportunities available there. But the prosperity of the middle class depends on how urban spaces evolve. The current focus on dense cities does not always take into account the access to jobs and services that will be needed by the middle class and can give way to excessive gentrification and standardization that serves to exclude newcomers from joining the ranks of the middle class. Inclusive societies, another long-standing interest of James Wolfensohn, will depend on how cities manage access.

The Wolfensohn Center's work on meeting the challenge of development had two goals. First, it sought to build awareness, particularly in the United States, of how changes taking place in developing countries would have profound ramifications for understanding the economic, social, and political trajectories of advanced economies. Second, it sought to use this lens to highlight policy work in specific areas, starting with multilateral institutions, trade and aid, but now extending to climate change, sustainability, and urbanization. The Global Economy and Development program continues to build on this foundation.

The Imperative of Development

A Memo to the Next U.S. President

JAMES D. WOLFENSOHN

Wolfensohn Center for Development at Brookings

I. INTRODUCTION: A GLOBAL ELECTION DEMANDS A GLOBAL AGENDA

The 2008 U.S. presidential campaign is no longer a national election; it is a global one. Since the start of the campaign, I have traveled to many parts of the world. Whether I am in Sydney or Shanghai, or in Amman or Almaty, I encounter an unparalleled interest in the upcoming U.S. election. We in the U.S. may joke that we have perfected the art of mismanaging not only presidential elections, but also party primaries. The rest of the world, however, is serious, and anxiously awaits our electoral verdict this November.

As Americans, we may be frustrated by this: why should others care about who we elect as our chief executive? I believe this interest reflects the changing realities of our time. In a globalized world, the walls that divided the local from

Editors' Note: This is a memo originally prepared in October 2008 during the final weeks of the 2008 U.S. presidential election, which concluded in the election of Barack Obama.

the global have been shattered—this is a fact of life; it does not matter whether we like it or not. People outside America, particularly in the developing world, are much more cognizant of this emerging reality. In this new world we find that the U.S. is the most powerful nation, yet it is not omnipotent; this is made evident with the rise of a new set of powers, most notably China and India. We need new partners and allies—NATO no longer suffices—to confront key issues of our time, from combating climate change to managing globalization.

I find it unfortunate that the candidates have so far only paid lip service to these larger causes and have inordinately focused their attention on immediate crises like the ones in Iraq and Afghanistan. These are important concerns, and I appreciate their gravity. But in order to secure our long-term interests, we can no longer afford to equate "Iraq" with "international." We need to broaden our global engagement. The next president can do so by making "the imperative of development" a central platform of a global strategy. If the U.S. presidential race is a global election, then the imperative of development is a key issue for this race.

We need a comprehensive program to reduce global poverty and inequality, both because this is the right thing to do and because without such a program our own prosperity, based on globalization, is threatened. We can implement this through better leveraging traditional development instruments like aid and trade, and through global institutional reform. Pursuing the imperative of development would follow a noble tradition set by Roosevelt and Truman, when America led the creation of a liberal world order and commenced the reconstruction of Western Europe and Japan. Those visionary leaders realized that they "were present at the creation" of a new world—a world vastly different from the one they had known.

We stand at a similar point in human history. With global interdependence increasing daily and, in all spheres, from investment and trade to information and travel, our world is rapidly changing on an unprecedented scale. We are also "present at the creation of a new world" today. The question is will the next U.S. president have the boldness of vision to shape a positive future for all in coming decades? Will he or she ably carry the mantle of Roosevelt and Truman by successfully pursuing the imperative of development?

As a former World Bank president, I pen this article as a memo to the next occupant of the Oval Office to present an analysis of global development trends and why these matter for the future stability and prosperity of the United

States. The remainder of this memo lays out the tectonic shifts occurring in the global economy and proposes a "four-speed world" framework through which one can analyze the consequences of these shifts. I then go on to address the critical implications of a four-speed world. I end by proposing a set of recommendations on how to implement the imperative of development via a triad of smart power policies—by reforming institutions, rethinking trade, and reinventing aid. Even if the candidates and their campaigns disagree with my analysis and policy prescriptions, I hope that this memo will generate national debate on global development issues. It is my firm conviction that such a debate is vital in our political discourse, yet is woefully absent right now.

II. TECTONIC SHIFTS IN THE GLOBAL ECONOMY

Just over 50 years ago, geologists found evidence that the earth's crust moved on giant tectonic plates and that these movements could explain the mountains and valleys that characterize our physical landscape. Today, we find that the global economy also has its plates—groups of countries moving at different speeds in response to globalization.

These tectonic economic plates are shifting again and they will likely affect fundamental power transitions in the world, resulting in a very different geopolitical landscape in the next fifty years. The next president needs to understand and appreciate these global economic shifts and their potential impact on geopolitics. As the leading economy, the U.S. needs to act in concert with other major powers, both old and new, and through reinvigorated international institutions, to ensure that these shifts bring about peaceful and positive change.

What are these tectonic shifts in the global economy? At the end of the Second World War, the United States was the world's largest economy accounting for nearly half of world output. By 1965, the U.S. and six of its major allies accounted for 65 percent of global output (measured using market exchange rates) with just 17 percent of global population. In 2002 these advanced economies still dominated the world's economy, producing 65 percent of global output. In between, the share had varied slightly, reaching a low point of 61 percent in 1981 after the second oil price shock pushed the U.S. economy into recession, and a high point of 68 percent in 1993, when Japan's economy peaked. Today, that share has fallen to 56 percent and all projections suggest the fall will continue to accelerate. This decrease represents one of the tectonic shifts under way in the global economy.

The long period of U.S. leadership and its global influence was felt not just in economic output but in technology, higher education, medicine, finance, and capital investment. For fifty years after World War II, to safeguard prosperity, the U.S. and its key allies needed only to manage economic relations between themselves. Trade and investment mostly flowed among these advanced industrialized economies, with the rest of the world having only about a quarter of the world share. Most of the top universities were located in these nations, with the U.S. having about 7 out of the top 10 research institutions. Major Multinational Corporations (MNCs) were located in the U.S. All these facts symbolized the global economic might of the U.S. and its industrialized allies.

Over the past fifty years, there have been only two challenges to U.S. power. The most significant came from Communist countries, but their economic strengths were exaggerated and ultimately they imploded. A further challenge came from the cartel of oil exporters, but they too could not artificially sustain high prices, nor absorb their wealth into their own economies.*

Developing countries—the nations of the so called "South"—were not significant on the global scene and did not feature prominently—except for occasional spurts of interest—in U.S. policy circles. They were considered a homogeneous group of countries with common problems and a broadly standardized set of diagnostics and solutions that if properly implemented would suffice for growth. Their main contribution to the global economy was in the provision of natural resources and low-cost, labor-intensive manufactured goods, often in the factories of large multinationals. The prevailing expectation moreover was that capital and finance would flow from the rich to the poor countries in terms of private investment and aid transfers.

Today, this traditional view of the global economy has been stood on its head. Capital is flowing "uphill" from poor countries like China to rich countries like the U.S. China leads the world in terms of foreign exchange holdings, having $1.6 trillion in reserves. Many major multinationals have home bases outside the U.S., and others are so global that they can no longer be said to have any nationality at all. The acquisition of IBM's computer manufacturing

---

*Today we see these two challenges manifesting again, albeit in a different form: a strong and powerful Russia is increasing its influence on the global stage, and high oil prices are again giving the oil exporters more clout in the global economy.

division by the Chinese giant Lenovo, and the recent bid by the Indian conglomerate Tata—which may well be the new "West India Company"—to take over Ford's British units, Jaguar and Rover, are some striking examples of an emerging trend. Reliance is constructing the world's largest refinery in India. Developing countries are making their mark on the global stage with new technologies, capital, entrepreneurs, and businesses, and this represents another tectonic shift in the world economy.

When one looks at the global agenda of recent years, there is scarcely a topic on which it is conceivable to think of solutions which do not include developing countries. The global agendas, most evident in G-7/G-8 Summit communiqués, have covered trade, climate change and environment, terrorism and its financing, disease, financial stability, energy, labor standards, and economic and social development in a globalized world. All of these involve development. In many instances, like trade, climate change, and global imbalances, there has been miniscule progress on international rules of the game despite years of negotiation. Others, such as improved aid delivery and coordination, debt relief and efforts to deal with the threat of epidemics, drugs and failed states are at best moving very slowly. All these issues are closely related to U.S. national security and economic interests. That is why development—an understanding of the prospects and interests of developing countries in the context of a stable and equitable world —is a modern imperative, which we in America can no longer ignore.

III. A FOUR-SPEED WORLD, A NEW GLOBAL REALITY

In thinking about the tectonic shifts taking place in the world economy, I have found it useful to place countries into four groups, each moving with differing speeds and dynamics. Of course, I recognize that there are huge differences between countries within these groups, but to understand how the global economy might evolve it is useful to think about the common elements which shape country dynamics. I propose the analytic framework of a four-speed world as a device to understand the consequences of the changes under way in the global economy. The four-speed world provides a useful reference frame through which high level policymakers, like the U.S. president, may view global developments in a comprehensive, yet nuanced manner.

In this four-speed world we find a group of *affluents*, rich countries with mature economies and institutions which are experiencing steady per capita income growth at a modest rate of about 2 percent annually. The U.S. is the lead economy in this group, which has 33 countries, with per capita incomes ranging from $16,400 in Taiwan to almost $100,000 in Luxembourg. Outside of the U.S. and other G-7 economies, these countries are mostly in Europe, with a few Asian manufacturers and oil-exporting countries also in the mix. Countries in this group have 73 percent of global output and a population of 1 billion, or 15 percent of the world. By 2050, Wolfensohn Center estimates show that the global share of output of the affluents will likely have fallen to 32 percent, although their citizens will still enjoy the highest living standards in the world.

The eroding dominance of this group of countries is largely the result of growth in a second group, the *globalizers*, that have already managed to sustain per capita income growth of at least 3.5 percent per year over 25 years or more—a rate that is double that experienced by the United States—and in many cases are growing even more rapidly. Incomes in these countries are converging with those of the affluents. These countries have systematically leveraged the global economy to achieve rapid growth, but have formidable challenges in managing the internal stresses that fast growth can create. There are 30 such countries, mostly in East Asia and Eastern Europe. They accounted for 14.5 percent of global output last year, but half of global growth. 3.2 billion people—exactly half the world's population—live in these countries.

The most remarkable story within this group is the development of China and India, two countries which represented half of the world economy in 1820 (and for most of human history have been the leading economies, a fact which we tend to forget today), that are experiencing per capita growth rates of over 8 percent. As a result of rapid growth, their citizens are experiencing a 100-fold increase in their living standards over a single human lifespan. Larry Summers calls this the seminal event of our time.

I agree that an improvement in living standards of this scale is unprecedented in human history. My friend Vernon Jordan talks about how his grandfather, when asked what his last wish was, replied: "I wish I had a bathroom in my house." Now, less than a century later, every American home has a bathroom and much more—our life expectancy has doubled, we have achieved universal literacy, our incomes have grown nearly ten times, we have the largest consumer class and we lead the world in terms of innovation. If we accomplished this at a per capita growth rate that was nearly a fifth of what China and India are experiencing today, imagine what the giant globalizers will achieve in the next 50 years, when their per capita incomes are expected to rise forty-fold (India) and twenty-fold (China)?

It is inevitable that growth in these globalizers will slow down as they mature and get closer to the technological frontier of the affluents. With strong growth, these countries will also experience a slowdown in their population and labor force growth. This is already apparent in declining birth rates. But even taking these trends into account, Wolfensohn Center estimates show that the globalizers could account for 60 percent of global output by 2050. China is the only globalizer currently in the world's largest 10 economies. By 2050 it could be joined by India, Indonesia, and Vietnam.

The globalizers will drive economic growth for the next forty years. Some 5 percent of the world's middle class is in these countries, and that proportion may continue to grow to more than 50 percent in another generation. The globalizers will also become new centers of global wealth. Today, a tiny fraction of high-income families are outside the U.S. and "Western" countries. By 2050, perhaps one-half of all rich families will reside in globalizers. We already see this in the composition of the world's richest billionaires: five of the top ten billionaires are citizens of globalizer nations (and if you count Laxmi Mittal's Indian origins that number goes up to six).

A third group of countries has managed to develop into middle-income economies but has faltered in sustaining growth. Many oil and commodity producing countries fall into this category. They are essentially *rentier* economies that grow fast when commodity prices are high, but fall behind when the cycle swings. There are 49 countries with a combined population of 1.1 billion people in this group. They account for 11 percent of world output, the same level as in 1974 when oil prices were first raised by OPEC. Like the affluents, the share of rentiers in the global economy has been remarkably constant over time. They briefly reached a 12 percent share in the early 1980s, after the second oil price rise, but quickly saw their position deteriorate to 8 percent by 1988 as oil prices fell back only to recover to 11 percent today.

The rentiers are to be found mostly in Latin America and the Middle East. Individually, their growth has been volatile. They have vast natural resource wealth, perhaps half of total world oil deposits, for example. But they have been unable to translate this into sustained development, and indeed one can argue

21

that it is because of natural resource wealth that these economies never developed robust institutional structures that could promote private sector growth. These countries do not suffer from desperate poverty—indeed, their citizens are reasonably educated and healthy. But they lack jobs and have not developed the knowledge economy drivers required to move beyond middle income to rich country status. Instability in these countries—whether economic or political—is hugely important for the rest of the world because of the potential impact on commodity prices. The future stability of these nations forms a central pillar of U.S. national security since they are located in America's traditional sphere of influence—the Western Hemisphere—or in the case of Middle Eastern rentiers, an area that holds the highest concentration of the world's oil and gas supplies and is ground zero in the "war against terror."

The fourth group is comprised of countries struggling simply to survive. The *survivors* are poor, with per capita incomes under $1,000 a year. Their economies are stagnant, and sometimes even in decline. They are found mostly in sub-Saharan Africa and have been left behind by globalization. They account for less than 2 percent of global output, exports, and foreign direct investment. Yet they are home to more than 1 billion people—15 percent of the world's population. Survivor countries face crucial basic development challenges: expansion of quality primary education, decent health care, adequate nutrition, and essential infrastructure. The survivors are falling behind the rest of the world in relative terms. Each consumer in a survivor economy had eight and a half cents for every dollar of purchasing power of someone in a rich country in 1965. By 2007, this imbalance had widened dramatically—an average survivor had just one and a third cents per dollar spent by an affluent. Looking forward, the gap in living standards could increase still further. An additional challenge is that the population in survivor countries is expected to more than double to over 2.3 billion by 2050—this means that their share of global population goes to 25 percent from 16 percent today.

The scenario pictured above is one where today's economic features are scarcely recognizable. Total world output could increase sixfold from $50 trillion today to more than $300 trillion by 2050. The U.S. might for the first time lose its status as the preeminent economy and will likely be in third place, after India and China. Eighty percent of the growth in wealth may accrue to affluents and globalizers. Global population will increase from 6.4 billion to 9.1 billion, and two-thirds of this increase will be in the rentier and survivor nations, and less than 100 million will go to the affluent countries. This development divide characterized by low economic growth and lack of opportunities in areas with the highest demographic growth does not bode well for our future.

I must note here that there is nothing automatic or preordained about these estimates. They are based on scenarios where policies continue as they are today. In many countries, these may change. Some countries in the globalizer group might be unable to adapt rapidly enough and suffer a setback to growth. On the other hand, some of the survivors or rentiers could join the globalizers through domestic policy reform.

That said, what the scenario does show is that the world economy is moving into uncharted waters. Rarely have we seen global economic growth at this speed—average global growth from 2002 to 2007 was the highest since the start of World War I. Yet, as we grow more prosperous we also witness increasing inequities in our world. The four-speed world is replete with such paradoxes. It forces us to ask uncomfortable questions: Can the U.S. as the lead affluent nation accommodate the rise of giant globalizers, like China and India? Or will we see history repeat itself when changes in the economic balance of power resulted in violent political power transitions? Will we be able to sustain our recent remarkable global growth rate through greater economic integration or will there be a populist backlash against globalization? Will the scramble for access to raw materials, especially hydrocarbons, which literally fuel the global economy, destabilize the socio-political fabric of rentier nations? Or will high commodity prices provide adequate financing to encourage rentier states to change and modernize? Will energy security continue to remain the "albatross of our national security"? Are the inequalities in living standards between the haves and the have-nots sustainable? What might they mean for pressures on migration and the security of our borders?

IV. THE SECURITY TRIFECTA

I cannot answer these questions, but the four-speed-world scenario I have put forward has some clear implications. The global shape of economic security, energy security, and national security is rapidly changing, and this has important consequences for America's future prosperity.

Consider economic security. The U.S. economy needs to leverage the global economy to sustain its growth, which in turn enables higher living standards for us Americans. In order to do so, the next U.S. president will have to resist populist backlash at home and address the growing influence of globalizer nations in the world economy and build new alliances. This will require a careful balancing act.

The domestic political arena is fraught with populist sentiment that is stoking the protectionist fire. The harsh truth of blue collar manufacturing job losses concentrated in some parts of the country, coupled with technological advances that have enabled outsourcing of white collar jobs, has resulted in large-scale anxiety about free trade and globalization. In a recent poll, 54 percent of Americans thought that economic globalization was moving too quickly for their liking. And 52 percent thought that economic benefits and burdens were unfairly shared, as a result of globalization. Given the history of pro-trade sentiment in the U.S. these perceptions are a sign of caution. In the past we have seen how protectionist policies can threaten the entire liberal economic system, and we cannot afford a similar turn now. A protectionist policy limits our ability to raise productivity through a more efficient division of labor with the rest of the world. In such a scenario, we may end up in a situation that actualizes the worst public anxieties about globalization. In order to counter this dangerous trend, the next president must create domestic programs that ensure "optimal trajectories of transition" for displaced workers, which involve better social safety nets such as wage insurance, progressive health care subsidies for the unemployed, and job retraining opportunities.

The president must also recognize that major emerging markets have become the main engines for world growth. And that these countries must be engaged on an equal footing when it comes to economic globalization. Cooperation with globalizers increases our economic security because then we can all reap the benefits of free trade and a liberal economic order. China and India are making the largest country-level contributions to global growth. Yet, despite a long track record of success, it is unwise to believe that these globalizers will continue inexorably on their current trajectories, in a linear fashion, through 2050. There are likely to be stops and starts along the way. The current financial turmoil may be a major stop or a minor bump on this path. Another worry concerns the ability of these nations to handle domestic issues of inequity and environmental sustainability, thereby derailing them from their general growth trajectory.

There are many analysts who are skeptical about China's ability to sustain growth without democratization or India's ability to overcome its infrastructural bottlenecks. Both countries face major environmental challenges and huge domestic imbalances. The ratio between the incomes of people in the richest and poorest province in China reached 13.1 in 2005, and in India it reached 4.4. For comparison, the same ratio in the United States is just 2.1. In both countries, millions of people are migrating from the countryside to cities every year. Some of those cities provide jobs, services, and adequate housing, but others are swamped by the influx. Failure to deal with any of these issues could interrupt growth, possibly seriously. These globalizer nations need global trade and the revenues it brings to manage these domestic challenges. Thus, when it comes to economic security the fortunes of the U.S. and other affluents are intertwined with key globalizer nations—both need to cooperatively leverage the global economy to handle domestic challenges and increase their prosperity.

Next, look at energy security. Senator Lugar hit the nail on the head when he stated that "energy security is the albatross of our national security." With oil at over $120 per barrel, the hydrocarbon-fueled U.S. economy is under overwhelming pressure—as are the economies of other affluent and globalizer nations—to seek energy security. Energy security is about secure access to resources which are largely located in the rentier economies. These countries account for more than half of the world's proven oil reserves, so energy security is closely tied to stability in these countries. The main threat to these nations comes from internal implosion brewed from frustration, social immobility, and discontent.

Across Latin America and the Middle East, the rentier economies have huge concentrations of wealth and a growing gap between the aspirations of their young fast-growing populations and the policies of their rulers. From Venezuela to Iraq, we have seen ongoing political instability, with each episode prompting an immediate response in our energy markets. Unless we can bring economic opportunity and hope to these countries' populations, along with the vast wealth that is being transferred to them, it is unlikely that we will be able to ensure predictable access to energy resources to fuel our economies.

The U.S. will need to act cooperatively again with emerging powers such as China and India to ensure that the race for access to oil does not degenerate into hostile competition or even conflict in rentier nations. Perhaps more importantly, we will need to balance the democracy promotion agenda in rentier regions like the Middle East with a more proactive development strategy that seeks to meet the "revolution of expectations" of the young in these countries with a "revolution of satisfactions." This can be achieved by inclusive socio-economic programs that include suitable employment opportunities for their educated workforce and investment in areas that facilitate the creation of a knowledge economy. Of course, we need to realize that we cannot impose solutions from the outside, but rather create enabling environments and establish partnerships with domestic actors in rentier states to aid their path to sustainable development.

Finally, let me reflect on national security and the link with poverty. It is unimaginable that the world can prosper if one-quarter of its population—2.3 billion people in 2050—live in countries where poverty is rife. Poverty in survivor countries undermines state capacity to deliver even the most basic public services, including security and the exercise of the legitimate monopoly on the use of violence, to borrow a phrase from Weber. Without basic public health, the prospect for new diseases emerging out of survivor states rises. So the problem of poverty and instability abroad becomes a problem of security at home. In America, we were grimly reminded of this reality on September 11, 2001, when the image of a great big wall around our country protecting us against poverty and conflict in distant Kabul or Kandahar was decisively and tragically shattered.

Broad-based development is the only way to manage our world's codependency, and the U.S. needs to take a lead in realizing this goal. If a country or a group within a country falls behind, it can become a drag on nations and regions—distant or near, it does not matter. This is the new shape of a globalized world. This is why the pursuit of the imperative of development is essential. It is both a strategic imperative and a moral one.

V. A TRIAD OF SMART POWER

The long-term changes in the global economic landscape are not as immediately visible as the short-term issues of terrorism and war which currently preoccupy our presidential candidates and the national media. It takes visionary leadership to look beyond these immediate issues. The next president needs to realize that the past will not be a guide to our economic future. In the United States, there is little awareness about the importance of developing countries. We do not invest in understanding their cultures, their problems, and the options for solutions. In 2007 only 9 percent of American students studying abroad chose Asia as a destination, while 60 percent went to Europe. Remedying our education system to tackle the emerging global realities is a smart policy that we need to embark upon urgently.

In addition to education reform, I find that the United States has long used three instruments in its dealings with developing countries. It works with International Financial Institutions (IFIs), like the IMF and World Bank, which have mandates for promoting growth and stability, and reducing poverty. It has been a champion of free trade and globalization. And it has the world's largest foreign assistance program (although relative to the size of the economy, the United States ranks 21st out of 22 member countries of the Development Assistance Committee) to directly fund development in developing regions. I call these instruments the triad of smart power because, if used effectively, they can help shape the global economic landscape and aid the pursuit of the imperative of development. The problem is that none of these instruments is being used effectively today. The next U.S. president has the daunting task of making these instruments effective again by reforming institutions (particularly the IFIs), rethinking trade, and reinventing aid.

REFORMING INSTITUTIONS: The IFIs form the first pillar of the triad of smart power. Fortunately, with new leadership, they are recognizing the core problems of development in the rentier and globalizer countries that house most of the world's poor. Bob Zoellick's "inclusive and sustainable globalization agenda" is a step in the right direction. Key developing countries are asking for practical advice on how to manage issues such as decentralization, financial market reform, governance, inequality, social and environmental costs associated with rapid growth, and infrastructure development. They want to be engaged as equal partners. The World Bank, International Monetary Fund, and other multilateral development banks need to respond to these needs.

In addition to development advice and technical assistance, IFIs were a source of capital for developing nations. Today, globalizers and rentiers have ample access to private capital. In 2007 private capital flows to developing countries may have totaled $1 trillion, including remittances. The net non-concessional lending from international financial institutions to all countries totaled just $2.6 billion in 2007, and, over the last four years, the international financial institutions were paid back $100 billion more than they lent by developing countries. Of course, this reflects the booming global economy and hence a reduced need for funds, but it also shows that in financial terms the major institutions are less relevant than before. Their role needs to be recast to make them more relevant to developing countries.

As the largest shareholder in the IFIs the U.S. can recast these institutions by altering their fundamental mandates. First, I propose that the next U.S. president redefine what constitutes global poverty. If we are to counter deprivation, let us not have diminished expectations that set the bar of extreme poverty at $1 per day and poverty at $2 per day (PPP terms). We need to aim higher and have a bolder vision than the mere attainment of subsistence as a mark of human well-being. That bold vision would set the threshold of global poverty as people living on less than $10 a day (PPP terms), which is the lower spectrum poverty line among OECD countries. I choose this measure because it provides a safety-net for people who have a minimum wage job and are part of the modern economy. Under this definition, more than two-thirds of the world is poor today and the task of poverty reduction then cuts across the tiers of the four-speed world. This would make the IFIs more relevant in globalizer and rentier nations, as well as help widen the scope of their long-term strategy in survivor nations.

Second, I would urge the IFIs to capitalize on their near universal membership to help secure global public goods. The prime task here should be countering global climate change through better facilitation of knowledge dissemination and resource transfers to developing nations to help them in reducing their CO_2 emissions. In addition to climate change, the IFIs can help promote better financial stability and help counter the spread of pandemics, or secure other public goods according to their area of expertise.

Third, the IFIs should lead the way in accommodating globalizers in the international system. If we want the emerging powers to be responsible stakeholders, we must give them a stake in the system that is commensurate with their size. Some initial reforms to give these countries more voice in the IMF have been proposed, but these look to be completely inadequate to the task. China's quota share would only increase to 3.5 percent, for example. This needs to change. The U.S. can take a lead on this front by unilaterally proposing that it forgo its veto power in the IFIs and will abide by a new formula that weighs voting shares on the basis of economic strengths and global population shares.

At present the globalizers have little voice in setting the agenda for traditional global institutions like the IFIs and as a result are developing their own alliances and informal structures, like regular Quadrilateral Summits between Brazil, Russia, India, and China. Similarly, the G-8 have invited five major developing countries to attend as observers—Brazil, China, India, Mexico, and South Africa—but this does not recognize the fact that, as President Lula of Brazil is said to have remarked during the Evian Summit, five of the G-8 countries may not be in the world's top eight list in 20 years. We risk creating competing institutions and informal summits in the global system, and complicating an already fractured system, unless we reform existing institutions.

RETHINKING TRADE: Trade is the second pillar in the triad, and here too the international system has stalled. The new round of trade liberalization under the WTO had a rocky birth, and an agreement to even start negotiating had to be postponed by two years after a deadlock in Seattle in 1999. The Doha Development Round had the welcome objective of creating a more inclusive trading system by giving greater emphasis to the voice of developing countries, as well as a potential annual $460 billion benefit to them. But it has bogged down and is now entering its seventh year of negotiations.

The U.S. is not doing much to help move Doha forward, largely due to an impasse over agricultural subsidies, and has chosen to pursue bilateral free trade agreements leaving the multilateral trading system in a precarious balance. It is time for the U.S. to rethink its trade policy and jump-start Doha. The next president must be willing to take on domestic lobbies that prevent further trade liberalization and also rationalize U.S. trade policies so that they do not hurt the poorest in the world.

The problem with our current policy is that trade is still viewed as a zero sum game. Even after trade barriers are formally reduced in an agreement, many obstacles are created in implementing complex rules-of-origin. These mostly affect developing countries that often have poor institutional support mechanisms and cannot easily "prove" that goods indeed originated in their country and are eligible for reduced tariffs. This results in an absurd situation where we levy $14 billion in tariffs on imports of around $500 billion from low income and lower middle income countries, while we only levy $11 billion in tariffs on imports worth about $1,350 billion from upper middle income and high income countries. If one were to take a concrete country-level example, we find that the U.S. receives more tariff revenue from Cambodia than it does from Great Britain, despite the fact that its trade with Great Britain is 50 times larger than with Cambodia. America needs to renew efforts at deeper and fairer trade rules, beginning by rethinking its own skewed tariff structure, and then rethinking multilateral rules, which will enable developing countries to create the jobs and pathways to social mobility that are needed for stability in their rapidly growing populations.

REINVENTING AID: Official Development Assistance (ODA) could be used to bring opportunity to the survivor nations. As the largest ODA provider the U.S. can help survivor nations overcome their binding growth constraints. A historic agreement at Gleneagles among the G-8 countries, supported by President Bush, promised a significant increase in aid, especially to Africa, to help countries achieve the Millennium Development Goals. Sadly, it looks increasingly unlikely that those promises can be kept. Aid was increased temporarily, through a process of forgiving debts owed by developing countries, but now that process is over and aid is falling again. We need a new, effective aid plan for the poorest countries in the world, especially for the continent of Africa, that mirrors the Marshall Plan.

Moreover, the aid system itself is not efficient in terms of resource allocation. Total official development assistance from the rich countries today amounts to about $105 billion. But less than $40 billion of this actually flows to the programs and projects that developing countries themselves are trying to implement. The rest takes the form of free-standing technical assistance, debt relief, administrative costs in aid agencies, and other components which do not directly contribute to sustainable development.

Two years ago, the U.S. Congress established the Helping to Enhance the Livelihood of People around the Globe (HELP) Commission to study development and humanitarian assistance programs and make recommendations for improving their effectiveness in the 21st century. This bipartisan commission commented that "not one of the people that appeared before us (in 20 months of hearings) defended the status quo." They concluded that after 45 years, the framework for assistance and the modifications that have been introduced are obsolete. A fresh approach is needed to raise the level and improve the effectiveness of aid. The next president can implement the recommendations of the HELP commission and reinvent how the aid business is done. The U.S. could lead by example, and show other countries that face similar challenges how to improve the efficiency of their aid systems.

VI. CONCLUSION: EXERCISING PRESIDENTIAL DIPLOMACY TO FULFILL A GLOBAL MANDATE

International institutions, trade, and aid are instruments which can be used to shift us from a focus on immediate issues towards a balanced perspective on how our planet is going to develop. There is already an understanding of interdependence. Polls show that 85 percent of Americans worry a lot or somewhat about the way things are going for our country in world affairs. Only 25 percent think that the U.S. is doing a good or excellent job in creating a more peaceful and prosperous world. That level of awareness and realism is grounds for hope that we can overcome the challenges of the future if we debate the issues of global development and understand the long-term context in which development is taking place.

The next president can relieve the popular anxiety over America's place in the world by exercising presidential diplomacy in recognizing the emerging realities of a four-speed world. First and foremost is a need to acknowledge the importance of globalizer nations, by undertaking the first state visit to Beijing and New Delhi, instead of Brussels or London. After that promising symbolic start, a new president can proceed to substantively change the course of America's global engagements through the pursuit of the imperative of development. By doing so, he or she can help usher in a Global Century—one that truly reflects the interdependence of our time—and thereby fulfill the global mandate to shape a new world order.

Farewell to Development's Old Divides

JAMES D. WOLFENSOHN

*James Wolfensohn is Chairman of Wolfensohn & Co
and a former President of the World Bank.*

The notion of a divide between the rich north and the poor and developing south has long been a central concept among economists and policymakers. From 1950 to 1980, the north accounted for almost 80% of global GDP but only 22% of its population, and the south accounted for the remainder of global population and 20% global income.

But the north-south divide is now obsolete. The dynamic process of globalization has resulted in unprecedented levels of growth and interdependence. However, while this has blurred the old division, new ones have emerged, splintering today's world into four inter-connected tiers.

The first tier comprises the affluent countries, notably the United States, European nations, Australia, and Japan—with a combined population of around one billion and per capita incomes ranging from $79,000 (Luxembourg) to $16,000 (Republic of Korea). For the past 50 years, these affluent countries have dominated the global economy, producing four-fifths of its economic output. However, in recent years, a new set of economies has emerged that is contesting the affluent countries' economic dominance.

These emerging economies—call them the Globalizers—constitute a

Editors' Note: This op-ed was originally published on November 23, 2007, by Project Syndicate at www.project-syndicate.org. © Project Syndicate 2007.

second tier of about 30 poor and middle-income countries (including China and India), with per capita GDP growth rates of 3.5% or more, and a total population of 3.2 billion, or roughly 50% of the world's population. These countries have experienced unprecedented levels of sustained economic growth that may well enable them to replace the "Affluents" as engines of the world economy.

The Globalizers are a large and diverse group of countries—in size, geography, culture, and history—that have learned how to integrate optimally with, and leverage, the global economy to catalyze their development.

A third tier is made up of roughly 50 middle-income countries with a combined population of 1.1 billion. They are also home to many of the world's critical natural resources, possessing around 60% of proven oil reserves. But these "Rentiers" have not been able to translate the rents of their natural resource wealth into sustained economic growth.

The fourth tier comprises countries that are lagging behind—the world's poorest economies, with more than a billion people. They continue to stagnate or decline economically. Mostly located in sub-Saharan Africa, these "Laggards" are largely isolated from the global economy, and they face crucial development challenges.

This emerging four-tier world presents three key challenges.

First, we need to increase our efforts to ensure that the Laggards are no longer left behind. This requires policy changes as well as more generous and more effective aid. If one considers the issue of aid flows, one finds that though development aid rose in 2005 to $107 billion, most of the increase was geared towards "special circumstances," such as debt forgiveness and for Iraq and Afghanistan. The sad truth is that development aid to Africa has decreased from $49 per person in 1980 to $38 per person in 2005. The true development needs of Laggard countries and other parts of the world are not being met, despite the rhetoric of scaling up aid.

Second, the old powers need to accommodate the rise of Globalizer economies—particularly China and India—by reforming our international order. The Affluents will continue to be major global players, but as the Globalizers' relative economic power rises, they will demand a greater role in international affairs. Most Affluents seem unprepared for this change, but such demands will need to be accommodated.

Finally, while the Globalizers have lifted millions of people out of poverty and reduced global inequality, this has not resulted in a more equal world, because star economies like India and China are experiencing a rise in domestic inequity. Whether it is coastal versus inland or rural versus urban, these countries must tackle the widening disparities, because high inequality may well threaten their very ability to continue growing as they have.

If we are to create a more equitable world, then traditional levers of development such as trade, investment, aid, and migration need to be scaled up comprehensively and coherently, and global institutions must be reformed. This would improve our ability to address global challenges and better our prospects for building a more equitable world. Otherwise, we might bid farewell to old development divides only to welcome new ones.

3

Scaling Up Development Impact

JOHANNES F. LINN

"We have to discover how we move from our feel-good successes, how to scale up these initiatives to a depth and a breadth where we can really have an impact on poverty, where we can achieve the Millennium Development Goals."

—James Wolfensohn, in *Reducing Poverty on a Global Scale* (World Bank 2005)

In 1999, while serving as president of the World Bank, James Wolfensohn visited the Republic of Georgia. At that time I was the Bank's vice president for Europe and Central Asia. When we briefed Mr. Wolfensohn on a successful rural credit project financed by the Bank, he asked how many farmers would benefit from this project. We responded that thousands of farmers would, but he wanted to know how many farmers could in principle benefit from such an intervention. When we told him this was in the tens of thousands, he pressed on: "So what are we doing to make sure they also benefit from this intervention?" Our answer, mine included, was something along the lines of: "Well, somebody else will have to follow up on this good project, our pipeline is already fully programmed with other initiatives." Quite correctly, he was not very pleased with this response!

35

Throughout his decade at the World Bank, Mr. Wolfensohn had a pervasive interest in scaling up the impact of development. He was particularly impressed by the Chinese development approach of systematically piloting alternative approaches on a small scale, learning which ones worked, and then systematically scaling up those that did across the country. This led him to have the World Bank commission a series of collaborative studies on the scaling up experience in the developing world. This effort culminated in a high-level conference in Shanghai, China, in 2004, co-hosted by the Chinese government and the World Bank, at which political and thought leaders, experts, and practitioners from around the globe explored how best to scale up development impact for global poverty reduction and the achievement of the Millennium Development Goals. In 2005 the World Bank published the results of the background work and the key findings of the Shanghai forum in a volume entitled *Reducing Poverty on a Global Scale: Findings from the Shanghai Global Learning Initiative*.[1] Mr. Wolfensohn's foreword to that volume provides a convincing case for why scaling up matters and what are some essential elements in the systematic pursuit of scaling up development impact.

It was then a natural next step for James Wolfensohn, when setting up the Wolfensohn Center for Development, to place the idea of scaling up at the core of the Center's agenda. Indeed, the Center's mission statement highlighted the priority of scaling up: "to create knowledge that leads to action with real, scaled-up and lasting development impact."[2] This principle was reflected both in cross-cutting work on how to make scaling happen as well as in the design of all aspects of the Center's work.

In the search for an effective approach to scaling up, the Center took a multipronged pathway. In a book commissioned early on by the Center, Santiago Levy explored in depth a highly successful case of scaling up, the Progresa-Oportunidades program in Mexico.[3] This program provided conditional cash transfers to poor people and became the model for worldwide adoption of conditional transfer programs as a key instrument for reducing poverty. In a Wolfensohn Center working paper, Raj Desai focused on the political economy of scaling up antipoverty programs, a key determinant of success or failure in scaling.[4] Clifford Zinnes provided an in-depth assessment of competitions and tournaments as an instrument to incentivize and support scaling up in a book and in a policy brief sponsored by the Center.[5] One particular form of the tournament approach, the so-called challenge funding method, has now been widely adopted by the development assistance community as a way to supporting innovation and scaling.[6]

Drawing on these initial efforts and a broader survey of the literature and practice of scaling up in development, Arntraud Hartmann and I developed a definition of scaling up development impact (that is, the expansion, replication, adaption, and sustaining of successful policies and programs in space and over time to reach a greater number of people) and a simple analytical framework to help assess scaling up pathways retrospectively and design suitable pathways looking forward. In a Wolfensohn Center working paper we explored "the possible approaches and paths to scaling up, the drivers of expansion and of replication, the space that has to be created for interventions to grow, and the role of evaluation and of careful planning and implementation," all elements well exemplified in Levy's account of the Progresa-Oportunidades design and implementation. We concluded that "more than anything else, scaling up is about political and organizational leadership, about vision, values, and mindset, and about incentives and accountability—all oriented to make scaling up a central element of individual, institutional, national, and international development."[7]

Based on the approach developed by Hartmann and myself, the Wolfensohn Center team developed further avenues of research and experimentation. Hartmann and I spelled out the implications of our research for donor agencies in a Brookings Global policy brief, concluding that donors had to develop a more systematic approach to support scaling up through the projects and programs that they finance and that a good first step is to carry out a scaling up review of their institutional practices and results.[8]

As a first experimental application of this approach, the Wolfensohn Center partnered with the International Fund for Agricultural Development (IFAD) and carried out a scaling up review for the agency. The review concluded that IFAD had successfully supported scaling up under some of its projects, but that a more systematic approach was required if IFAD wanted to implement its intention to make scaling up a central pillar of its operational engagement.[9] The review also successfully tested and further developed our scaling framework. Since then IFAD has taken on board the scaling up agenda and with continued help from Brookings has pushed ahead in operationalizing it systematically.[10] A recent independent evaluation of IFAD's scaling up effort shows substantial progress, but also noted that after ten years there is still a way to go in pushing the scaling up idea into the front lines of the organization's operational work.[11]

In parallel I explored in greater depth the operational practices of donor agencies with regard to scaling up, as an input to the Wolfensohn Center's work on aid effectiveness for the Fourth ODA International Conference held in Seoul, Korea, on November 29, 2010.[12] This review found that while scaling up had become increasingly more recognized as an important ingredient of the development agenda, donor agencies had a long way to go in incorporating scaling up in their operational practices. The review concluded with specific recommendations for the donor community as it prepared for the Fourth High-Level Forum on Aid Effectiveness in Busan, Republic of Korea; they found an echo in the statement on the Busan Partnership for Effective Development Cooperation.[13]

With support from the Australian government, the Center also focused on the role of scaling up in fragile and conflict-affected areas. Laurence Chandy and I reviewed the experience of humanitarian and development programs in fragile states, adopting the framework developed by Hartmann and myself described above. We found that, contrary to expectations, there are compelling examples of successful scaling in such settings. And we concluded that a scaling up focus is as important in fragile environments as it is in more stable contexts, but that the challenges and risks are generally higher in the former and need to be explicitly considered in developing scaling pathways.[14] As a side benefit of our work, the Australian aid agency took the scaling framework on board and reflected it in a set of scaling guidelines.[15]

By the end of 2010, as the Wolfensohn Center's effort to incubate a new global focus on scaling up development impact was coming to a close, the participants in this undertaking—Laurence Chandy, Homi Kharas, and myself—had learned to appreciate that as do most scaling up initiatives, this ambitious task required more than five years to come to fruition. If we wanted to have sustained impact at scale, we had to "stick with it" and had to reach beyond the Brookings Global Economy and Development (GED) program to form lasting partnerships with other like-minded development actors. So we continued with research, advisory work, and outreach on the scaling up agenda on multiple fronts.

In partnership with the Japan International Cooperation Agency (JICA), the Brookings GED scaling team assembled a group of international development experts in 2012, with the goal to bring together the experience from specific cases of scaling and insights on important crosscutting dimensions and factors shaping scaling pathways. A key conclusion, reflected in the Brookings book *Getting to Scale: How to Bring Development Solutions to Millions of Poor People,* was that successful scaling requires joint efforts by public, private, and civil society actors, with the careful design of programs and interventions that involve innovative policy design, financing, partnerships, and incentives.[16] (The volume's introduction is reprinted in this chapter.) Subsequent work with the World Bank on the role of social enterprise innovation further deepened our understanding of how to scale up the delivery of social services at the base of the pyramid in a delivery chain involving social enterprises, in collaboration with government and private business.[17]

In 2014, under the auspices of Brookings's Center for Universal Education, Brookings experts Jenny Perlman Robinson, Rebecca Winthrop, and Eileen McGivney initiated a major research study on "Millions Learning," which explored the experience with scaling up of educational programs in developing countries.[18] Their analytical approach drew on the work of the Wolfensohn Center and serves as the basis for the design of a second phase of work that aims to assist education practitioners in scaling up educational innovations.

In promoting the practical implementation of the scaling agenda, I engaged intensively with various development actors with the objective of more widely sharing the Wolfensohn Center's and IFAD's scaling up approach and experience, and learning more about how to integrate the scaling up perspective in operational work. Multilateral partners included the African Development Bank,[19] United Nations Development Program,[20] and the World Bank;[21] bilateral partners were the German development agency GIZ and the U.S. Agency for International Development, and operating NGOs included Save the Children and Heifer International. In addition, I teamed up with the Results for Development Institute (R4D) in support of the International Development Innovation Alliance (IDIA), a group of eleven major development funding agencies (multi- and bilateral donor agencies, large foundations, and challenge funds) that aims to develop a shared systematic approach to scaling up successful development innovations.[22]

Finally, Brookings scholars engaged with other think tanks and consulting partners to develop learning products and platforms: with the International Food Policy Research Institute (IFPRI) in the production of a set of policy briefs on scaling up in agriculture and rural development;[23] with Management Systems International (MSI) on a joint paper reviewing analytical approaches and practical experience in scaling up;[24] with the Organization for Economic Cooperation and Development (OECD) in the establishment of the DAC Prize "Taking Development Innovation to Scale,"[25] and with R4D and MSI in setting up a Scaling Up Community of Practice, which brings together some forty experts from various partner institutions to share scaling experience and lessons across sectors and disciplines through workshop, working groups, and newsletters.[26]

Today, scaling has become the watchword for many development agencies and actors around the globe. Fifteen years ago, when James Wolfensohn took up the cause of championing the idea and practice of systematically pursuing scale of development impact, few others did so. Mr. Wolfensohn helped seed the scaling up idea at the World Bank, though it failed to fully take hold under his successor. So James Wolfensohn then became an impact investor, willing to start up a small center of research and action at Brookings. The Wolfensohn Center for Development incubated the by now widely recognized development work of the Brookings Global Economy and Development program, itself a scaling up story. What is more, James Wolfensohn's vision of scaling up development impact and his readiness to assemble and support a team to focus specifically on the process and experience with scaling up pathways had a lasting impact on the development debate and practice of the last decade and likely beyond. While the idea of scaling up is now widely recognized, the practice remains sorely underdeveloped. Much remains to be done to turn the idea into action, but we now have a platform on which to build, thanks in part to the work of the Wolfensohn Center.

The Challenge of Reaching Scale

LAURENCE CHANDY, AKIO HOSONO, HOMI KHARAS, and JOHANNES LINN

*Laurence Chandy is Fellow, Global Economy
and Development, Brookings Institution*

Akio Hosono is Director, JICA Research Institute

*Homi Kharas is Senior Fellow and Deputy Director, Global
Economy and Development, Brookings Institution*

*Johannes F. Linn is Senior Resident Scholar, Emerging
Markets Forum, and Nonresident Senior Fellow, Global
Economy and Development, Brookings Institution*

The challenges of global development can be counted in millions, if not billions: 2 million preventable infant deaths a year from pneumonia and diarrhea, 61 million children out of school, 850 million malnourished people, a billion people living in city slums, 1.3 billion people without access to electricity, 1.5 billion people living in conflict-affected states, 2.5 billion people without access to formal financial services. Meeting these challenges hinges on finding sustainable solutions that can have a transformational impact on the lives of millions of the world's poorest people.

Developed countries have, by definition, solved these problems.[1] These countries are identifiable by both their superior level of income and the insti-

Editors' Note: This is the introductory chapter from the book *Getting to Scale: How to Bring Development Solutions to Millions of Poor People*, edited by Laurence Chandy, Akio Hosono, Homi Kharas, and Johannes F. Linn, published by Brookings Institution Press in 2013.

tutions through which their societies and politics are organized, which enable their living standards to be sustained. Over the last half century, a handful of countries have succeeded in making the transition from developing to developed, and the hope is that many more will do so in the next.

However, such transitions are extremely hard to pull off. Using past performance as a guide, it would take nearly 6,000 years for the poorest countries to reach the level of income currently enjoyed by the United States of America.[2] Similarly, improvement in the capacity of poor countries to deliver basic public services to their citizens is proceeding at a glacial pace. Extremely optimistic estimates, using the performance of the fastest-improving countries as a yardstick for what is possible, suggest that the waiting time to eradicate extreme poverty and deprivation should still be measured in generations. For instance, were Haiti to somehow adopt the rate of progress in government quality of the twenty fastest-improving countries in the world, it would be another twenty-six years before it reached the current standard of Malawi.

To speed up this process for today's poor countries would require a recipe for development—something that after years of looking has not yet been found, and maybe never will be. Countless studies have been undertaken examining what countries such as Japan and Korea did to advance so quickly. But it is quite another thing to translate these studies into a meaningful plan for today's poor countries. This explains much of the skepticism around foreign aid. If the role of aid is to encourage countries to grow faster and to accelerate up the development ladder, then it is easy to conclude that the mission has been a failure and is probably futile.

There is an alternative and more hopeful view. It submits that there is much that can be done to address global development challenges without altogether altering the trajectories of poor countries. A number of targeted solutions have been found that can solve specific challenges: vaccines and water treatment to prevent child death; conditional cash transfers to nudge parents to encourage school attendance; micronutrient supplements and the promotion of breast-feeding to vanquish malnourishment. These solutions can permit poor countries today to overcome many of the deprivations associated with their low levels of income and to improve the lives of their people.

To succeed, however, these solutions need to be scaled up to reach poor people everywhere. Herein lies the problem.

REACHING SCALE

There are certainly examples of scale being reached in a developing country context. Mexico rolled out its Oportunidades program, a conditional cash transfer scheme, to all of its regions, reaching around one-quarter of the entire population with cash incentives designed to improve health and educational attainment among poor families.[3] Brazil dramatically reduced poverty with its Bolsa Família program, which today reaches 12 million families.[4] Indonesia's Kecamatan Development Program provides grants to half of all villages in the country for small infrastructure projects chosen by the community. Oral rehydration therapy, introduced by UNICEF, has almost halved deaths from diarrhea, cholera, and related diseases. Long-lasting insecticide-treated bed nets have dramatically reduced malaria. China has initiated vast poverty reduction programs, including those affecting millions of poor farmers of the Loess Plateau.

Yet these examples are the exception as opposed to the rule. Many development solutions create more of a whimper than a wave. This is surprising when one considers that scaling up is at the core of the development model that donor agencies purport to follow. They regularly develop pilot projects with the supposed intention of replicating or expanding successes, or handing them over to developing country governments to do the same. But only a small share makes it beyond a pilot phase. This is why donors are more likely to report one-time, localized success stories than examples of transformative wide-reaching progress.

Even when a dedicated effort is made to transition from pilot to program, scale is rarely achieved. The use of fuel-efficient cooking stoves in India, for example, has proceeded very slowly. Ten years after their introduction through the National Improved Stoves Program, improved stoves accounted for less than 7 percent of all stoves in use.[5]

We believe this deserves a full inquiry. Remarkably little is understood about how to design scalable projects, the impediments to reaching scale, and the most appropriate pathways for getting there. Despite its centrality to development, scaling up is rarely studied in its own right and has undergone little scrutiny.[6] Scaling up has been treated as something that occurs spontaneously and organically when successful development interventions are identified rather than as a challenge in and of itself.

This book is about increasing the number of people who are assisted through development programs so they can be counted in the hundreds of millions and in a time frame that is measured in decades rather than centuries. It asks what could be done to improve living conditions in poor countries in a way that is financially affordable and technically feasible. It is the contention of this book that scaling up is mission critical if extreme poverty is to be vanquished in our lifetime.[7]

Already, the idea of accelerating poverty reduction is taking root among development practitioners. This is evidenced by the Millennium Development Goals (MDGs), which are expressed in terms of the pursuit of results at scale, reflecting the desire to transform lives and to bring about far-reaching, sustainable change. In 2011 the international development community congregated in Busan, Korea, at the High Level Forum on Aid Effectiveness, to discuss how approaches to development need to change if accelerated results are to be achieved. The outcome document for the meeting concludes, "We recognize that progress has been uneven and neither fast nor far-reaching enough. . . . We reaffirm our commitment to scale up development cooperation . . . scaling up our support of development results . . . scaling up the use of triangular approaches to development cooperation . . . and scaling up of efforts in support of development goals."[8] Easier said than done.

But perhaps such pledges are not so unrealistic. What if scaling up was being held back by some well-defined obstacles, which could be overcome through a dedicated effort? This claim has become associated with two schools of thought.

The first can be caricatured as a West Coast "Silicon Valley" perspective. It puts its emphasis on finding innovative technological solutions to development challenges through scientific advances and visionary entrepreneurship. From this perspective, the reason that scaling up rarely occurs in developing countries is the dearth of scalable opportunities. If scientists, engineers, and innovators focused on the problems of poor people, as opposed to those of the rich, new opportunities could be discovered. New vaccines and off-grid lighting solutions are examples of what can be achieved when innovators turn their attention to development problems.

The second camp is associated with what we call the East Coast "Kendall Square" perspective, named for the location of MIT's Abdul Latif Jameel Poverty Action Lab. Researchers there have organized a massive effort to compile compelling statistical evidence of what development interventions work best, based on randomized trials. Their aim is to equip policymakers with sufficient information to determine how resources can be efficiently allocated: in other words, what interventions should be taken to scale and what interventions should be discarded. A good example of the former is the Kenya National School-Based Deworming Program, which has treated millions of school children at modest cost, thereby substantially improving attendance rates and learning outcomes throughout the country. Public backing for the program followed the publication of an impact evaluation that demonstrated the intervention's unequivocal success when attempted on a small scale.[9]

This book argues that the challenges to scaling up are more complex and more numerous than either a lack of appropriate technology or a lack of evidence of what works. Without understating the importance of both technological innovation and rigorous evaluation for development and scaling up, we believe that neither can be viewed as the binding constraint for the failure of many existing successful interventions to reach scale.

Instead, the challenge of scaling up development impact cannot be reduced to a single constraint but is better approached as a process challenge. The business model—the specific combination and design of product, distribution, supply chain, financing, pricing, payment, and sales—is often far more important in determining success than a specific technology or piece of evidence. It is attention to the details of implementation at a large scale that makes the difference between successful and unsuccessful scaling up.

This poses a challenge for the development community. Donors have traditionally resolved implementation problems by breaking up projects into small and "doable" efforts, which they can supervise from abroad. Many governments of poor countries, meanwhile, have limited capacity for scaling interventions competently. The private sector has enjoyed more success when interventions have been proven to have a commercial return—witness the explosion of microfinance through the private sector—but is rarely involved in development activities affecting poor people.

Given this reality, it is useful to try and learn systematically how to scale up development impact by analyzing examples of success and failure. Each of the essays in this book documents one or more contemporary case studies or syntheses of cases, which together provide a body of evidence on the challenges, opportunities, risks, and rewards of pursuing a scaling agenda. Cases of scaling up by the private sector and by the public sector are included. They reveal some hard truths. Scaling up is difficult to plan because it involves transformational change. Tools like cost-benefit analysis, the workhorse for analyzing development projects, are not helpful because scaling up often involves changing cost curves, altering beneficiary behavior, and an endogenous policy environment. Business models to implement scaled solutions cannot be taken off the shelf or easily replicated from one context to another—what is called external validity—but need to be designed and fine-tuned for scale over many years.

There are high risks to trying to reach scale, with more failures than successes. That is typical of most innovations, as entrepreneurs can attest. According to one estimate, it takes an average of fifty-eight new product ideas to deliver one that is viable.[10] This is enough to scare off bureaucrats, whether in donor agencies or governments, whose expected rates of success are set impossibly high. (For instance, the World Bank aims for a project success rate of 85 percent.) Their strategy has been to seek modest impacts across many small interventions, rather than attempting to scale their best investments. By contrast, corporations are usually willing to take on risks, as huge returns from a few successes can compensate for the financial losses of failures, so long as the latter are truncated efficiently. But the same calculus doesn't apply when corporations operate in the development sphere. There, the returns to a successful scaled-up intervention may be large in terms of development impact but are typically small in terms of profits. The financial returns, therefore, do not compensate for the costs incurred in failed pilots.

In each of the cases in this book, we show that the scaling-up challenge can be divided into two. There is the challenge of financing scaled-up interventions, because poor people cannot afford to pay full cost for many services. These costs can be especially high when new markets or products, like solar power, are being introduced. The second challenge is managing delivery to large numbers of beneficiaries. The logistics, training, recruitment, and systems needed to deliver goods and services efficiently to poor people spread out throughout a country are incredibly complex and depend on a strong customer-oriented design. Very few actors—whether governments, donors, nonprofits, charities, or corporations—have the management ability to operate efficiently at scale. Large corporations are most adept at handling this challenge, but development activities are not at the top of their priorities. In every case, scaling up requires sustained commitment from top leadership, something that can be hard to achieve in most environments.

Scaling Definitions

In this book, we are particularly interested in the range of interventions that can transform the lives of poor people. Transformation may entail providing them with goods and services to which they otherwise have no access, such as education, health, finance, and energy, or involving them directly in the design or implementation of development projects, making them partners and providers as well as potential beneficiaries. For example, when poor farmers are linked into commercial agricultural value chains, they can achieve unprecedented improvements in income. Or when children are enrolled in schools that teach them literacy and numeracy skills to a minimum standard, their lifetime earnings opportunities are expanded hugely. When lives are saved through medical attention at birth, and illnesses avoided by reducing indoor air pollution or improving nutrition, the development benefits are startling.

In other words, we define scaling-up development impact in terms of not just reaching large numbers of poor people but doing so with interventions that transform their lives. These interventions often lead to behavioral changes in poor households that trigger further innovations and development: poor families invest more in their children when they are more likely to survive; they save more when they see opportunities for further income advancement; they work more when they are not sick; their children go on to higher education when they excel at the basics.

What constitutes scale can differ according to circumstances. Scale may be defined in terms of the level at which objectives are set: for instance, a mayor's pledge to a city, a government's national development strategy, or the global MDGs. We do not limit ourselves to a rigid definition of scale here, but the case studies are principally oriented to experiences where the goal is transformational impact at the country level. With this definition, we exclude the activities of many small social enterprises and nonprofit organizations, which can have enormous transformational impact on the lives of those they reach but do not have the resources or capacity to implement national programs. However, we do include so-called franchise models, where many of these entities replicate a similar business model and thereby achieve scale in aggregate. In other words, we do not restrict ourselves to scaling up through a single program or organization. Sometimes, a successful business model leads to imitation and replication, and that becomes the process for reaching scale. That has been true for the microfinance and the mobile phone industries, for example.

Although our interest is in understanding how to transform the lives of poor people, we do not focus only on scaling up interventions that reach the poorest of the poor. For the most part, poor people are not a well-defined, static group. Poor families may have good years, when they would be classified as near poor, and bad years, when they fall back into poverty. But if they benefit from a scaled-up intervention when they are just above the poverty threshold, they are far less likely to fall back into poverty at a later stage. Hence the impact on poverty reduction over time can be just as large by including the near poor in the target group compared to interventions that target only extremely poor populations. While the precise target group varies from organization to organization, most of the examples presented here are aimed at those individuals spending less than 4 dollars a day.

SCALING UP TODAY

Scaling up is an inherently complex process involving the management and organization of vast numbers of dollars and people: dollars, to cover the cost of establishing and running large-scale operations; and people, to manage those operations, serve as intermediaries in the delivery of interventions, and to interface with low-income beneficiaries. In other words, any attempt at getting to scale hinges on establishing a business model—the nexus of finance and delivery—that can support a scaled-up operation.

Figure 1-1 provides a stylized schematic of how this works in practice today. Development interventions are arranged according to whether they require subsidies or can be made profitable. Typically, when subsidies are needed, government, aid donors, or large international NGOs take the lead. Examples range from vaccine programs to national employment guarantee schemes. When profits are feasible, it is the private business sector that undertakes scaling up. In the last decade, small sachet shampoos, community water, and biomass stoves have demonstrated market potential when poor households are viewed as a specific customer segment, while contract farming models show the commercial viability of viewing poor communities as low-cost producers.[11] Whether scaling up is financed through subsidies or on a commercial basis determines whether interventions are ultimately delivered through the public or private sector.

FIGURE 1   Scaling-Up Models: The Status Quo

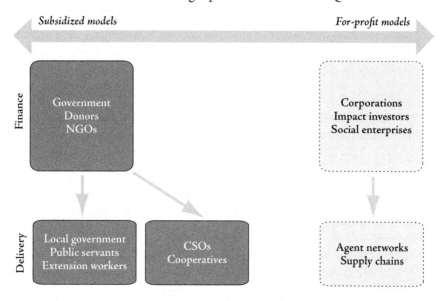

Subsidy Models

The financial challenge of scaling up subsidized interventions is straightforward enough: subsidies cost money. Even with the benefit of scale economies, total costs typically increase with the number of beneficiaries, so the availability of resources can determine the degree of scale that is ultimately achieved. Sustaining subsidized interventions at scale requires a long-term commitment, far beyond the duration of the domestic political cycle or a donor's strategy for a country. While governments, international NGOs (INGOs), and donors command large budgets, the number of interventions they can feasibly scale remains finite.

Take, for instance, the treatment of people living with HIV/AIDS in the developing world, which is considered to be one of the most comprehensive and successful examples of a subsidized model of scaling up in the development field. In 2011, 8 million individuals received antiretroviral therapy, at a cost of $16.8 billion: $8.6 billion collectively spent by developing country governments and $8.2 billion spent by the donor community.[12] The latter represents a sizable share of all foreign aid (6 percent). The goal of universal provision for all 34 million people living with HIV/AIDS—a number that is rising by 2.5 million a year—demands additional resources, despite a steep reduction in per person costs. Recent cost estimates for meeting global demand by 2015 indicate the need for an additional $7 billion of annual spending.[13] Critics question whether such large expenditure on HIV/AIDS crowds out spending on other diseases that can save lives at a lower cost.[14]

To be viable, a business model that relies on subsidies has to be narrowly focused on a specific issue. If the range of activities is too broad, resources must be thinly spread, and scale becomes unachievable. That forces a trade-off: scaling up can require taking a narrow approach, potentially limiting development impact, while the alternative of broadening the range of activities to encompass the multisectoral interventions that are often required for sustained development impact can make scaling up unaffordable. The United Nations' Millennium Villages project has been criticized for exactly these reasons. Its critics argue that it is too broad and expensive to be scalable.[15] On the other hand, when global education resources were channeled in a focused way for building new schools to meet the enrollment targets of the MDGs, school quality and learning outcomes fell in some countries, causing a backlash against such programs.[16] These examples show how difficult it can be to find the right balance between scaling up to reach more people—a public good imperative—and providing the range of services that truly achieve a transformational impact in beneficiaries' lives.

Subsidized models also have difficulty organizing efficient delivery. As an intervention's scale increases, so do logistical demands. Systems need to be developed to monitor effective implementation and to manage personnel. Even in the most easily mechanized activities, distribution models require the identification of reliable individuals and the development of their skills to perform different roles. With large numbers of people involved in a scaled-up operation, there is a premium on effective recruitment, training, and managing churn. The relationships between individuals along the distribution channel must be managed so as to provide the right incentives and to promote accountability and productivity.

Subsidized models rely on implementing organizations to provide these systems and manage personnel. Governments tend to work through ministries, subnational government, state-owned enterprises, and extension networks, whereas INGOs typically partner with local civil society organizations (CSOs) or cooperatives. These implementing organizations provide the networks for reaching poor populations, extending down to the level of individual villages and communities.

The difficulties of achieving scale with these delivery systems are well known. Government ministries and local authorities often lack the capability for effective administration, including financial management, procurement, and service delivery, and despite their public service mandate, struggle to foster a customer-service orientation and adopt a customer-driven design.

Few countries have meritocratic-based civil services that reward employees for the efficiency and effectiveness of their performance. Hiring is as likely to be based on patronage as on merit. In developing countries, government information and payroll systems, structured learning, willingness to innovate and experiment to fine-tune delivery, and training programs for employees are notoriously poor. Corruption, absenteeism, and theft can be widespread. In India and Uganda, for example, teacher absenteeism in public schools still reaches over 25 percent.[17]

When programs are administered by local CSOs, results tend to be better, but few of these organizations have national reach. Indeed, in some cases their effectiveness is a consequence of their small size, and their organizational systems are not capable of expansion. A franchise model, involving multiple CSOs, may provide a path to scale but can imply higher transaction costs and greater variability in quality.

Donor agencies are acutely aware of these weaknesses and have oscillated between establishing their own delivery systems and working through government or CSO delivery channels. Over the last decade, donors have made commitments to working through government in recognition that long-term sustainable development depends on countries being in control and having viable institutions of their own, consistent with the principle of ownership. Despite this rhetoric, donors have made less progress in practice. Less than half of all aid is channeled through government systems, and less than half employs programmatic approaches, which pool government and donor efforts around government-led plans.

Large donor investments have focused on boosting governments' capacity to deliver and on improving government systems, from public financial management to procurement to sector policy, planning, and evaluation. But achieving progress in these areas has proven to be much harder than expected. Civil service reform and public capacity building are among the least well performing and most challenging of all development cooperation efforts.[18]

Taken together, the obstacles to financing sustained large-scale subsidies and building efficient and effective delivery systems are daunting. Developing country governments have no choice but to muddle through and to provide interventions at scale to the extent and to a standard that fiscal and capacity constraints allow. Scale, in a literal sense, is often achieved, but poor quality of delivery and an inappropriate level of focus constrains impact. Few NGOs have the resources and interest in sustaining large-scale subsidized interventions, although there are some notable exceptions (box 1-1).

What about donors? Their best chance for achieving scale is to play a catalytic role, with a focus typically on supporting government or NGO efforts. In practice, however, donors have often favored more modest interventions, diversifying their investments widely and avoiding working through others where this weakens their ability to account for money spent. Interventions are favored that can generate immediate results, with little consideration given to the fact that development impact rarely unfolds in a linear and monotonic fashion.[19] This is reflected in the characteristics commonly associated with today's aid investments, characteristics that emerge from the peculiar set of factors that shape donor choices (box 1-2). Incentives such as short termism and an extreme aversion to institutional risk inform aid allocations and modalities and permeate agency culture.

For-Profit Models

It used to be thought that subsidized models presented the most, and possibly only, viable way of delivering development solutions at scale to poor people. But this idea was challenged with the 2004 publication of C. K. Prahalad's *The Fortune at the Bottom of the Pyramid*. Prahalad argues that there exist significant, untapped profitable opportunities in low-income—or base of the pyramid (BoP)—markets, which can be seized if businesses adjust for the circumstances, preferences, and behavior of low-income customers.

This concept offers a radical, alternative route to scaling up development impact. Whereas subsidized models depend on government planning to spur the transition to scale, for-profit models harness market forces and the univer-

BOX 1 Lessons from BRAC

Over the course of forty years, BRAC has evolved from an organization dedicated to relief and rehabilitation in the wake of Bangladesh's independence to the world's largest development NGO. Its presence in Asia, Africa, and the Caribbean benefits an estimated 126 million people. BRAC's growth reflects a strong focus on bringing successful interventions to scale, which it has achieved in a variety of areas, including income generation, health, education, agriculture, food security, water, and sanitation.

BRAC's visionary founder, Fazle Hasan Abed, identifies a number of factors to which the organization's success in scaling up can be attributed.[a] First, BRAC has the goal of achieving scale engendered in all its activities from the outset. This vision informs its choice and pursuit of business models. Second, BRAC adopts a well-trodden pathway in getting to scale: demonstrating the *effectiveness* of a given intervention, then achieving *efficiency* by lowering cost, and finally *expanding* to reach large numbers of beneficiaries. This sequence is crucial in giving BRAC the confidence to invest in the right interventions. Third, BRAC puts an emphasis on strong internal systems to support operations at scale. These include a focus on human resources, management, monitoring, performance metrics, financial accounting, and delivery.

a. Abed (2012).

sal motivation to make profits. (In fact, Prahalad argues that being profitable in low-income markets relies more on turnover than margins, providing a further spur to the achievement of scale.) Private corporations replace governments, donors, and INGOs as the investors behind these ventures. Corporations are joined by a growing cadre of social enterprises committed to using market-based solutions to address development goals. Meanwhile, private networks of agents and supply chains provide a delivery route to beneficiaries.

For-profit models of scaling up face an immediate problem: achieving a financially attractive rate of return. Margins at the base of the pyramid are very low—some 3 to 10 percent, compared to an opportunity cost of capital for most multinationals of 20 percent or more.[20] Further, the upfront costs of penetrating or sometimes creating those markets are high. In the first instance, funding is needed to finance research and development, to design and refine consumer products, to test consumer interest among low-income households, and to iden-

BOX 2 Aid Characteristics

An analysis of aid interventions reveals three salient characteristics.

First, they are typically very *small*. In 2010, $133.5 billion was spent on foreign aid by the OECD Development Assistance Committee (DAC) countries and multilateral agencies on 19,186 projects.[a] This was broken up further into 139,832 activities, giving a mean activity size of approximately $1 million. Half of these activities had a value of under $50,000. Given that there can be no rigorous definition of a *project* or an *activity*—essentially, there are no limits on the degree to which interventions are bundled together—these figures can give only a rough indication of the degree of atomization within the official aid system. Nevertheless, official data point to a steady fall in the average size of activities over time. It seems fair to assume that the typical aid intervention is dwarfed in size by the development challenge (or challenges) it is intended to address.

Second, interventions tend to have a *short* duration. Those same 19,186 projects had a mean length of 613 days from start to expected completion, with half occurring within a single year. Given such a fast rate of turnover, less than one in ten of the 19,186 projects in 2010 will still be running in 2014.[b] Again, this seems at odds with the type of problems facing the world's poor, problems that are often deeply rooted and persistent. While it is possible that a series of short interventions may succeed at overturning persistent challenges, it is hard to marry this approach to the challenge of achieving structural improvements in developing economies, such as institution building and developing skills.

tify ways to lower unit costs. If this stage is successful, additional investments can be required to lay the groundwork for expansion. This may include building a business infrastructure, institutions, or skills, where the enabling environment is otherwise deficient, and generating demand for products through marketing and educational campaigns.

A key feature of for-profit models is that they take considerable time to reach scale, and firms must be willing to absorb losses over this trial period. For some products, low-income consumers are already active purchasers even when these markets are informal, expensive, and unregulated. For these market-entry and "pull" products, the time to reach a scaled-up sales volume for better or cheaper products is two to five years. But it can be considerably longer when

Third, interventions are largely *discrete*, in the sense that they are disconnected from each other both within and across time. This is partly a result of fragmentation; with hundreds of actors delivering hundreds of brief, small-scale interventions, coordination is hard to pull off. However, the problem runs deeper than this. Interventions are supposed to serve a common, focused agenda as defined by national development strategies. But in reality, strategy documents perform the opposite role: defining objectives in the broadest possible terms and providing justification for interventions regardless of how tenuous and superficial their link is to others.

Interventions that are mostly small, short, and discrete can still have a positive impact on the world's poor, albeit one that is below the aid system's potential.[c]

a. There is no standardized way of measuring a project size. We adopt the methodology used by Birdsall and Kharas (2010) in which activities reported to DAC's creditor reporting system database are collapsed into a single project if they have the same donor name, agency name, recipient name, project title, and expected start date. Small projects (those with less than $250,000 in funding) are excluded, as they often represent line-item adjustments to existing projects rather than new projects. For a detailed account of this methodology, see www.cgdev.org/userfiles/quoda/QuODA%20Second%20Edition%20Report.pdf.

b. Calculations based on those projects of known duration.

c. Linn (2011).

poor people are being introduced to new market-creation and "push" products, even if buying these has a major social benefit. In these cases, time is required to build beneficiaries' trust of a new product or to induce behavioral change. BoP markets like microfinance and contract farming are still maturing after thirty and fifty years, respectively.

The time and money spent on nurturing the market for push products are a public good. They benefit not only the first mover, who incurs the expense, but also all other potential suppliers. For that reason, individual companies are often unwilling to take on the burden themselves, preferring to wait until another firm covers the initial costs.

For-profit actors are well suited to building efficient delivery systems at scale. Private companies have a strong pedigree in product-testing and customer-oriented design. They are free to hire and fire and to experiment with different delivery models. Building networks of agents or supply chains to reach poor beneficiaries is still a challenge, but these can often piggyback onto existing structures. For example, MicroEnsure, a company that seeks to provide a safety net to reduce economic setbacks for those living on less than 4 dollars a day, uses the customer network of existing microfinance enterprises for selling its products.

Of all private sector actors, large, multinational (or at least national-scale) companies are best placed to build the systems required for scale. They have experience with logistics, personnel, information technology, and other back-office functions. But they also have alternative priorities. For now, the BoP space is dominated by social enterprises with hybrid profit and development motives. These enterprises are small and thus have a hard time developing the institutional wherewithal for large-scale delivery.

Thus for all the enthusiasm that for-profit models have generated, there have been disappointingly few examples of their interventions reaching scale. In some cases, market fragmentation or poor market linkages have inhibited growth by forcing prices too high for large numbers of low-income customers to afford. More often, ventures have never even gotten off the ground, as the fixed costs incurred in early discovery and pilot phases, or in creating a new market, cannot be met. Potential financiers are put off by the anticipation of high-risk, low-return, and long-term investments. Patient capital for development does not exist as an asset class. Social enterprises have shown glimmers of promise but remain too small in number and size to make a difference. Some view the failure of for-profit models as a saving grace, protecting poor consumers from exploitation at the hands of powerful corporations, which they cannot hope to hold to account.

REVOLUTIONS IN FINANCE, DELIVERY, AND PARTNERSHIPS

Until now, the number of scaling-up success stories is relatively small, reflecting the limitations of existing business models.

First, financial resources for development are not being effectively utilized. Public and NGO resources are thinly spread across the many challenges that confront poor people and lack a sufficient degree of focus. Donor resources, in particular, have struggled to perform a catalytic role. Significant additional resources for scaling up could be unleashed through private finance, but this has been constrained by the large up-front costs and low rates of return incurred in identifying and developing scalable commercial opportunities.

Second, systems for managing delivery at scale in developing countries have been found wanting. While succeeding at turning delivery at a small scale into an art, donors and NGOs have struggled to master the complexities of developing large-scale delivery operations that are sustainable, cost effective, and customer oriented. Government implementation capabilities are often especially weak and are undermined by inadequate information and communication technology and by poor internal incentive and accountability mechanisms. Private sector know-how in this area has yet to be successfully harnessed to serve the world's poor people. More fundamentally, many poor people remain hard to reach, and the high transaction costs incurred in connecting to them drive up the price of subsidy models and reduce the scope for identifying commercially feasible for-profit models. However, these structural factors are starting to shift, creating a sense of excitement about the possibilities for scaling up in the near future.

Among the drivers of change are the evolving roles of actors in the development community. A wave of successful entrepreneurs is entering the world of philanthropy, seeking to apply to social problems the calculated risk taking, discipline, and drive for scalable solutions that served them well in their for-profit ventures.[21] In addition, there has been a dramatic expansion in the number and range of social enterprises in advanced and developing countries, blurring the lines between traditional categories of profit and nonprofit actors. The official donor community has also expanded to include members from emerging economies who exhibit different ways of working. Traditional donors, meanwhile, are looking to leverage increasingly scarce aid dollars into greater value for money. Finally, developing country governments wish to translate greater domestic resources into stronger leadership and more effective service delivery.

Another driver is technological progress. A cluster of new technologies—identification, communication, payment, digitalization, and data processing—are being combined in ways that could alter how global efforts to tackle poverty are forged. For instance, mobile money promises to strengthen consumers' participation in markets and thus expand the scope for market-based service delivery. Improved targeting technology and real-time data collection and analysis can improve management capacity and strengthen systems for large-scale interventions. And the dramatic expansion of mass media has introduced transparency to all development efforts, which has given fresh confidence that partners with different agendas but shared goals can come together and be accountable to civil society at large.

As the case studies in this volume attest, these dynamics are generating innovative approaches to scaling up. They are still too few to yield a complete science of execution, but they offer tantalizing examples of how scaled-up development impact may soon become the norm rather than the exception.

We have organized the case studies into three groups, indicating the ways in which business models for scaling up are changing: finance, delivery, and partnerships.

Finance for Scale

The flows of official development assistance from OECD countries fell in 2011 for the first time since 1997, and projections of future aid levels up to 2015 indicate continued risks to the downside, resulting from the poor economic outlook in most donor countries. This prompted Oxfam to warn of "hundreds of thousands of poor people [going] without life-saving medicines and many more children [missing] out on school."[22] Given this backdrop, now seems a strange time to make the argument that the prospects for resources for scaling up are strong.

However, to focus exclusively on the value of official flows is to miss the forest for the trees. Aid flows have never been sufficient to meet all development challenges. In fact, they equate to only 30 cents a day, per poor person, after excluding aid devoted to extraneous issues beyond development programs and projects.

Instead, aid flows have to be looked at in the context of all resources available for development, both domestic and international. The significance of these additional resources has increased in recent years. Despite rising aid volumes over the past decade, average aid dependence in low-income countries has fallen sharply, with the number of governments relying on aid for at least 30 percent of their public expenditure falling from forty-two to thirty.[23] This is the result both of faster economic growth in the developing world and a dramatic expansion in government capacity to collect taxes. As a share of total international capital flows to developing countries, aid has fallen from 70 percent in the 1960s to 13 percent today, due to the takeoff in trade, remittances, equity, and foreign direct investment.

Of course, numbers alone cannot tell the whole story. Understanding the prospects of finance for scale requires an assessment not only of the size of resources but also of how resources are being applied: whether sufficient attention is given to the objective of scale, whether investments have an appropriate degree of focus, and whether specific resources succeed at crowding in others to support scalable programs.

One of the largest potential new sources of finance for development comes from the private corporate sector. This is distinct from the corporate social responsibility of charitable contributions, which large firms have long been making. Rather, it concerns the direct engagement of major corporations in development through their core business strategies. As economic growth in the advanced countries has slowed, multinational corporations are looking to developing countries for the bulk of their own growth. That has shifted the priority of development from an afterthought to a central priority of major business leaders.

Private financing offers the potential for significant expansion in capital flows to poor countries. The OECD's Development Assistance Committee reports $330 billion in such flows destined for low- and middle-income countries. This is mostly direct foreign investment and bank loans that are not directly related to development, although in many cases, such as infrastructure investments in telecommunications, toll roads, and power plants, the profit motive of the private sector is well aligned with the development motive of creating the enabling environment for growth and poverty reduction.

There are, however, the new phenomena of inclusive business and impact investing that promise to align incentives between private capital and the achievement of social impact more closely and in many more fields. Inclusive business is defined as a profitable core business activity that tangibly expands opportunities for the poor and disadvantaged as producers, employees, or consumers in formal markets and commercial value chains. Impact investments are investments made in companies, organizations, and funds with the intention of generating measurable social and environmental impact alongside financial return. While it is difficult to estimate the amount of money flowing into such efforts, the Global Impact Investing Network (GIIN) estimates that $50 billion has already been mobilized for impact investing (although largely in advanced countries) and that $9 billion in new commitments are expected in 2013 by respondents to their survey.[24] A recent J. P. Morgan report suggests that impact investing could emerge as an asset class with committed funds of $400 billion to $1 trillion within ten years, just counting five sectors: housing, rural water delivery, maternal health, primary education, and financial services.[25]

Can these new funds and business models make a material difference in developing countries? Mike Kubzansky explores the potential for private capital to contribute to scaling up development impact (chapter 2). He challenges the assumption that a single entity offers the best route to scale in all circumstances, whether through a multinational corporation or a social enterprise. He posits two alternative routes to scale using the for-profit model. One route is to replicate a proven business model through hundreds of small and medium enterprises, as has happened with microfinance and contract farming. The key to exploiting this route is the demonstration of effectiveness in transforming poor people's lives. The second route is to leverage existing informal providers, who are legion in developing countries, by organizing them, providing them with technical assistance, and improving and upgrading their services. This latter route is similar to a franchise model, and while examples are few, they indicate the potential for success. The Greenstar network in Pakistan, for example, a franchise of small clinics, has been shown to provide better quality health services, to poorer clients, at lower unit cost than either government health clinics or private for-profit clinics.

Kubzansky highlights the dearth of funding for early-stage investments to get good ideas off the ground and to test new business models before they can be taken to a growth and expansion phase. But he also points to constraints on the amount of grants for technical assistance, training, and the establishment of networks that franchising requires. If these gaps can be filled, Kubzansky believes that for-profit scaling up could take off. His suggestion: donors and philanthropists interested in scaling up should try to identify and fill key financing gaps in conjunction with for-profit businesses and social enterprises in new hybrid arrangements.

This leads to the question of whether donors can alter the way they work to achieve scaled-up development impact. Laurence Chandy (chapter 3) reviews the past decade of rising aid flows to explore how agencies made use of additional resources. He argues that growing aid budgets generate competing pressures within donor governments. In combination, these pressures produce an ambiguous effect in terms of whether donors strive for scale.

Chandy shows that to understand the success of subsidized models requires much more than a simple assessment of the volume of resources committed. He submits that few donors have an approach to aid management that is conducive to scaling up as it is classically conceived, whereby good ideas emerge from the field, are rigorously evaluated, and are ultimately propagated with support from donor headquarters. For other donors, the best opportunity for achieving scale is to choose development problems that lend themselves to more mechanized solutions, where the challenge consists mainly in overcoming logistic and resource constraints rather than institutional strengthening and sustainability challenges, and the drive for scale can come from the top. This suggests that donors could be much more effective in achieving scale if they were matched to particular development challenges based on their expertise. A division of labor, based on the operational models of different donors, offers the chance of greater impact without any growth in global aid budgets.

To be viable, a business model that relies on subsidies has to be narrowly focused on a specific issue. David Gartner and Homi Kharas (chapter 4) look at the efforts to scale up resources and impact through vertical funds: specialized aid agencies that adopt a strong focus by providing a critical mass of expertise, identifying results in measurable ways, and mobilizing highly targeted financial support. These organizations have been controversial among development practitioners because, while they scale up impact and results in one area, they may inadvertently dilute resources going into other areas.[26] If vertical funds are truly efficient, however, then the net impact on development by operating through vertical funds could potentially be larger.

Gartner and Kharas find that there is considerable variation in the practices of vertical funds. Some are highly successful, with considerable impact, while others have made less of a difference. They attribute this to the governance arrangements of the funds. Those with more independence, greater beneficiary involvement, and clear performance-based metrics do better in terms of impact, resource mobilization, and learning. These, they submit, are all attributes necessary for scaling up. The authors conclude that a vertical fund approach can lead to scaled-up impact, but only if management, governance, and implementation practices are properly designed.

Together, these three chapters demonstrate that resources for scale could be dramatically enhanced over the near future, by both unlocking pools of private finance for development and altering the way in which donor resources are utilized to derive greater impact.

Delivery at Scale

Earlier in this chapter we define delivery as being a problem about managing people. Delivery is what makes getting to scale not merely difficult but complex. Securing finance for scale may be extremely hard to achieve, but there is normally a clear vision from the outset as to what the end goal should look like. By contrast, successful delivery at scale is more an art than a science. This is especially apparent when operating at the base of the pyramid, where the last mile of delivery involves not merely a transaction but also obtaining beneficiaries' trust and understanding and often changing their behavior. A strong customer-oriented design can be of critical importance in shaping products, prices, distribution, marketing, and sales, which together create a viable business model.

The chapters in this section touch on many aspects of delivery: strategic, institutional, and administrative. It is no surprise that they put forward no silver bullet solutions. However, recent experimentation and learning from implementers justify optimism and indicate opportunities for progress in many areas.

Johannes Linn (chapter 5) examines incentives and accountability within and between governments and aid agencies as they grapple with scaling up. He frames the transition to scale as a classic principal-agent problem, where success hinges on the alignment of stakeholders' interests. In theory, he argues, all parties should share the goal of expanding the reach of successful public goods and services. Yet a collection of government and market failures results in a wedge being driven between parties. Moreover, the longer the chain of accountability between development planners and ultimate beneficiaries, the greater the likelihood that interests will diverge and that scaling up will not be pursued, or will fail.

Linn identifies a variety of instruments that can be deployed to better align incentives around the objectives of scaling up. These include ways to amplify the voice of beneficiaries, to unite donors and recipient governments behind shared strategies and approaches, and to introduce market mechanisms that induce competition around the achievement of specified goals. He views experimentation as a valuable path to innovation and improvement. However,

Linn's greatest interest is in opening the black box of government and donor agencies to shed light on internal institutional incentives. He argues that too often "internal management practices do not provide for effective incentives and accountability between top management and the front-line staff." Fixing these—to pinpoint aspects that discourage scaling up—requires top-to-bottom reviews of institutions to assess their corporate missions, strategies, operational policies, processes, and instrumentalities, and human resource and budget management. Linn makes the case that this more systematic approach to scaling up can identify small reforms that result in significantly improved institutional performance.

Chris West (chapter 6) is enthusiastic about the application of private sector know-how for delivering development solutions at scale. He calls this "business DNA," which he defines as an understanding of how "to develop and execute viable models to deliver products or services to customers in ways that they value." West's enthusiasm is informed by a decade of experience with the Shell Foundation, an angel investor committed to catalyzing scalable development solutions through supporting social enterprises. When the foundation focused narrowly on providing short-term grants, 80 percent of those enterprises failed to achieve any evidence of scalability. However, when grants were incorporated into long-term partnerships and coupled with hands-on business skills support and the identification of market linkages, the foundation's results turned around dramatically.

Through a collection of case studies, West highlights the wide variety of business skills required for scaling up social enterprises. The foundation supports its clients in project management competencies, such as developing operating systems and setting milestones, as well as in more specialized areas, such as product marketing and market analysis. In addition, by using its own network of partners, the foundation has been able to pair its clients with investors, sources of business, route-to-market partners, and others with close links to local communities. This testifies to the complexity of mastering delivery at scale, but it also highlights that typical efforts to support social enterprises are not sufficiently focused on building these critical skill sets. Greater attention to these weaknesses could help unleash the potential of social enterprises, which have traditionally been written off as unscalable.

The story of M-PESA, the mobile money service in Kenya, presents one of the most celebrated cases of scaled-up development impact and is quite possibly the quickest the world has seen. M-PESA offers a commercially viable business model for serving poor customers where traditional banking falls short. M-PESA overcomes the constraint of access by substituting mobile phone ownership and networks of agents for physical banks; and it allows small-value transfers and minimal fees by encouraging a shift away from cash to electronic money in which simple movements of money incur virtually no transaction costs. The adoption of mobile money by 73 percent of adults in Kenya—where 67 percent of the population lives below 2 dollars a day—suggests that it should be possible to conceive of a world where virtually all poor people are "banked."

Pauline Vaughan, Wolfgang Fengler, and Michael Joseph (chapter 7) provide a unique insiders' view on how M-PESA triumphed. They identify many contributing factors concerning the company's approach to management, design, and delivery. Robust internal processes, the setting of targets, and visionary leadership are all identified as important components of success, in which the objective of reaching scale was fully reflected. However, arguably the most ingenious aspect of the business model is the approach to reaching customers through the formation, training, and retention of a cadre of M-PESA agents.

M-PESA recognized from the outset that its success would critically depend on its agents. Agents would be the most visible element of the company and would have to earn the trust of potential customers to bring about the behavioral change required in the adoption of a new product. Rather than creating agents from scratch, M-PESA identified existing networks of competent operatives in the Kenyan economy, which they could readily employ. These included their own airtime dealers (sellers of prepaid mobile phone credit), the fuel retailer Caltex, Group 4 Securicor courier services, supermarket chains and other retailers, dry cleaners, and the Pesa Point ATM network. By the end of 2011 the number of agent outlets exceeded 35,000, or 1 for every 700 adult Kenyans. Regular interactions between M-PESA and its agents provided an opportunity for training (to ensure a high quality of service), information gathering (to identify possible improvements to the service), and instilling loyalty (to retain agents and avoid rehiring costs). From a scaling-up perspective, the virtue of this approach was to ensure that delivery could expand swiftly while transaction costs are kept low.

Inspirational though the story of M-PESA is, its consequences for scaling up go much further. The possibility of introducing poor people the world over into the banking system provides a route for engaging them in other and new

BoP markets. In Kenya today, over 500 organizations use M-PESA to pay bills and conduct transactions, including utilities, medical saving plans, crop insurance for smallholder farmers, and teacher payment programs (as an alternative to standard school fees). Of course, so long as poor people remain poor, their purchasing power in these markets will be limited. However, mobile banking services provide a means for governments, donors, and charities to give money directly to poor populations and allow them to buy the goods and services they seek, rather than attempting to supply these themselves. When poor people have access to funds, markets for goods and services spring up spontaneously. That has been the experience with schools in slums, rural water supply, health clinics, and a range of other products. Scaling up is most likely to take off by increasing the purchasing power of poor people rather than by organizing the delivery of specific goods and services.

Mobile money is one of a number of new technologies that can expand the scope for scaling up (box 3). The internet provides another fast track for reaching vast numbers of customers at low cost. This is demonstrated in one of two highly successful case studies examined by Hiroshi Kato and Akio Hosono (chapter 8) in which the private sector plays a leading role. The authors describe how the Micro Finance International Corporation (MFIC), a social enterprise, established a low-cost online facility to enable rapid and low-cost remittance transfers for "unbanked" migrant workers. The facility is supported by a new payment platform called Arias, which employs COBIS (core banking system) technology. This technology is associated with fast-speed intrabank transactions, as opposed to the more cumbersome traditional SWIFT technology. Recipients receive remittances via local microfinance branches that partner with MFIC. In 2010 MFIC and KDDI, one of the largest telecommunication companies in Japan, announced a new partnership to jointly promote a global remittance and payment platform for telecommunications carriers. This will allow users to make remittance payments using prepaid international telephone cards and prepaid mobile phones.

In their second case study, Kato and Hosono tell the story of the development and propagation of the Olyset net, a long-lasting insecticidal net created by the company Sumitomo Chemical to support the fight against malaria. Over the past decade, the Olyset net has been rapidly disseminated in sub-Saharan Africa, as a result of a unique approach to production and delivery supported by a diverse group of partners. The manufacture of the Olyset net has been trans-

BOX 3 Technological Innovations for Delivery

The creative application of modern technologies can push out the possibility frontier of future development efforts by enabling better targeting, real-time data collection and analysis, and responsiveness to beneficiary feedback.

Around half a billion people in the developing world have had their bio-metric identification recorded in a government database using fingerprint-ing, or iris or facial recognition, a number that is currently rising at an as-tounding 25 percent a year. As biometric identification expands, so does the possibility of more accurate programs to assist poor and vulnerable com-munities. Spatial identification and mapping can also enhance the targeting of programs. These technologies are increasingly being deployed to ensure equitable distribution across geographical areas and in supporting coordina-tion across donors and NGOs. Most recently, they have proven valuable in responding to crises such as the monitoring of violence in Nairobi and the search for missing earthquake victims in Haiti, both organized by the NGO Ushahidi.

Modern technologies allow data to be collected and analyzed in real time (or with drastically reduced lags), with greater reliability, at less cost, and in larger quantities. Cell phone surveys allow data collection to be conducted remotely in conflict-affected environments and to bypass weak institutions, which are often the underlying cause of low-quality data. Electronic plat-forms that manage finances create an auditable trail, typically running from the issuing agency all the way to ultimate beneficiaries. This trail can then be analyzed, helping to evaluate interventions and make them more effective.

Over the past decade, there has been growing interest in social ac-countability mechanisms, which strengthen citizens' ability to monitor and demand accountability from service providers and funders. Technologies can be employed to facilitate ex ante consultation of beneficiaries and sup-port ex post consultation, to strengthen the feedback loop from beneficiaries to service providers and aid agencies.

New media are transforming the way that citizens can hold governments and other development actors accountable for their efforts. Advocacy efforts can now be organized at speed and at low cost. Pressure for greater trans-parency has encouraged governments to simplify processes: Kenya's Revenue Authority has placed customs, excises, and value-added taxes on an elec-tronic portal, and Tanzania's mobile payments system permits taxes to be filed without citizens having to visit a government office. The accountability promoted by media access and scrutiny in developing countries extends to all development resources, not just aid, and to all development actors, not just governments. Donors, NGOs, and private corporations are subject to the same standards to promote development or at least avoid harm.

ferred to A to Z Textile Mills in Tanzania under a joint venture with Sumitomo Chemical, resulting in the elimination of shipping costs. Delivery is handled by a combination of local government, NGOs, and commercial retailers, depending on the terms of sale.

Partnerships for Scale

The Global Partnership for Effective Development Cooperation, which emerged from the Fourth High Level Forum on Aid Effectiveness, acknowledges the critical role of partnerships in supporting development and seeks to forge closer cooperation between the traditional development community, emerging economy donors, civil society, and corporations. Partnerships can expand the scope for achieving scale in two related ways: first, by pooling the resources and expertise of different parties to enable larger and more ambitious programs and goals; and second, by recognizing the strengths and weaknesses of different parties and effecting an appropriate division of labor.

It is this latter rationale that provides the motivation for the partnerships explored in this section of the book. The case studies promote alternative allocations of roles for tackling the twin challenges of finance and delivery from the organizational arrangements assumed by standard subsidized and for-profit models.

For all their promise, the case studies show that partnerships are much easier to conceive than to agree on, operate, and sustain. Working in partnership can involve large transaction costs, and when these exceed the benefits to individual parties of working with others, they will choose to go it alone. Another problem is overcoming the cultural differences associated with different institutions. Goals, time horizons, decisionmaking, risk tolerances, and commitments vary enormously from one party to another and can feed mistrust. This is especially apparent in public-private partnerships (PPPs), which have been experimented with for over fifty years. In spite of their long history, until recently only a few examples have delivered impact at scale. These constraints are important to keep in mind when assessing the feasibility of various partnership approaches.

One partnership structure that received significant acknowledgment at the Fourth High Level Forum on Aid Effectiveness was South-South cooperation, in which developing countries share know-how on solving common challenges. While this practice is growing fast, it typically involves only small, one-off projects, so the scope for scaled-up impact is limited. Akio Hosono (chapter 9) suggests that a slight modification of this type of partnership can radically alter the prospects for achieving scale. He advocates for what is called triangular cooperation, in which a traditional donor facilitates a South-South exchange. The role of the traditional donor is twofold: to complement knowledge exchange with assistance for capacity and institutional development; and to propagate South-South cooperation across countries by organizing, institutionalizing, and programming the replication of effective interventions.

Hosono's argument is backed by a number of case studies drawn from the Japan International Cooperation Agency's (JICA's) long-standing focus on capacity development and its creation of centers of excellence in developing countries. He draws an analogy between establishing these centers and the concept of training the trainers, in which a center provides a vehicle for reaching beneficiaries far beyond the number that JICA could feasibly reach directly. JICA views itself as a catalyst in enabling Southern partners to become donors and providing them with the institutions to assist others. Hosono uses the Brazilian Agricultural Research Corporation (Embrapa) as an example of an organization that reached global standards of excellence, thanks in part to collaboration with Japanese researchers, and that is now transferring this know-how to transform tropical agriculture in Mozambique. Japan complements these efforts with related investments in Mozambique to support the development of its agricultural export markets.

An honest assessment of the role of partnerships in getting to scale requires an understanding of the responsibilities and scope of different parties. Tessa Bold, Mwangi Kimenyi, Germano Mwabu, Alice Ng'ang'a, and Justin Sandefur (chapter 10) describe a fascinating experiment in Kenya to test the government's ability to implement and scale up an NGO intervention of proven effectiveness: a contract teacher program. The government was unable to replicate the success achieved by World Vision when it took responsibility for selecting, paying, and monitoring contract teachers. Since the government is the dominant actor in Kenya's education sector and the only party capable of scaling up education policies, this collaboration between the NGO and government failed to produce a truly scalable model.

The authors draw sharp conclusions from their work. While it is tempting to devise and study pilots as a way of understanding what might work at scale, the act of scaling up can pose political economy obstacles that a small pilot does not encounter. During the implementation of the contract teacher program, the government faced resistance from the teachers' union and committed to hiring all contract teachers into the regular civil service at the end of their contracts—a factor the authors cite as a possible cause of the intervention's failure. This case study is a reminder that scalable models are not just large, replicated pilots but often have their own unique characteristics. However, the experiment is one of the first to show how controlled trials can be used to inform a scaling-up operation, using similar techniques to those used to evaluate pilot interventions.

Shunichiro Honda and Hiroshi Kato (chapter 11) provide an account of the scaling up of another popular education reform, this time in Niger. Encouraged by experiences elsewhere, the Niger government mandated each primary school to establish a school management committee composed of the principal, a teacher, and representatives from parent-teacher and school mother associations. These committees were given extensive autonomy to manage community funds, monitor the performance of teachers, and procure supplies and basic infrastructure in a way that responded to local needs.

At the core of this program was a partnership between a weak government, donors, and civil society. Niger is one of the poorest countries in the world, and the government's strong focus on poverty reduction over the past decade could not make up for its very limited capacity. Sharing responsibility for school oversight with civil society, twinned with low-cost interventions to raise capacity, offered a way of leveraging community strength to improve education across the country quickly and to sustain improvements. Honda and Kato demonstrate that the program also displayed a high degree of cooperation among official and nongovernment donors as part of a sectorwide approach. This included joint evaluations of alternative models of school management, joint selection of the preferred model, and joint support for implementation.

Jane Nelson (chapter 12) documents the evolution of PPPs into new sectors and structures and asks what potential these have for driving scaled-up impact where traditional models fall short. She identifies four sectors where PPPs are demonstrating particular promise: health, nutrition, sustainable agriculture, and mining and energy. In these sectors, PPPs take on many forms, from project-based partnerships to country-based alliances and global multistakeholder platforms. She argues that effective scaling up often involves close linkages among these PPPs, providing a bridge between global resources, policymakers and decisionmakers, and local beneficiaries and knowledge.

Nelson offers some powerful recommendations for enabling PPPs to better support the scaling-up agenda. Among these is the establishment of large-scale replication funds that employ competitive bids (like today's challenge funds) and combine financial resources with technical advice, brokerage, and government policy dialogue. She also advocates the creation of joint investment networks for science and technology to identify breakthrough technologies and mobilize financing, research, development, and delivery through multistakeholder platforms.

A NEW FRAMEWORK FOR SCALING UP

The emergence of new approaches for tackling development problems calls into question traditional ways of conceptualizing the scaling-up challenge. The dichotomy of public-led and private-led efforts to reach scale makes less sense in an ecosystem containing hybrid actors and hybrid partnerships. We suggested earlier that development interventions are normally arranged according to whether they require subsidies or can be made profitable, but what happens if both are true at once? Almost all cases of successful scaling up, including those where the private sector led the charge, have involved some soft money.

We submit that a large number of scalable development solutions occupy the middle ground on the spectrum between subsidized and for-profit models. Delivering these solutions requires the promotion of new hybrid models.

Hybrid models would combine the development efforts of a government, donor, foundation, or INGO with the efforts of a private corporation under a joint venture, drawing on the financial strengths of the nonprofit sector and its accountability to citizens and on the management and delivery strengths of the private sector. These ventures offer most promise in those instances where the fixed costs associated with creating a new product or product market prohibit a commercial intervention from moving forward but where variable costs could feasibly be recovered through market-based delivery once scale economies are achieved.

Finance from the nonprofit actor would provide a temporary subsidy to support the intervention during the early stages of scaling up, to cover costs such as research and development, market testing, piloting and evaluations, and marketing and education campaigns. These costs may not be recoverable in a commercial sense but would have the potential to generate large social returns and serve the development objectives pursued by government, donors, or INGOs.

Another aspect of hybrid models is a clearer division of labor between those responsible for the finance aspects of scaling up and those responsible for the delivery aspects. Subsidized and for-profit models have usually paired up financing institutions and implementing organizations along traditional lines: government with government, NGOs with NGOs, corporations with other private actors. Under hybrid models, partnerships would be determined by best fit for the particular challenge. Witness, for instance, the growing interest of pharmaceutical and agribusiness companies in partnering with and training health care professionals and agricultural extension officers. This would drastically expand the possibilities for scaling up and lead to significant efficiency gains (figure 2).

M-PESA is an example of a hybrid model designed to solve a social problem: a technology developed with financial support from both the multinational corporation, Vodafone, and a challenge fund operated by the UK's Department for International Development; piloting conducted in collaboration with a microfinance institution, Faulu, to deepen understanding of the customer; exemplary customer-driven design, management, and execution, including the formation

FIGURE 2 A New Framework for Scaling Up

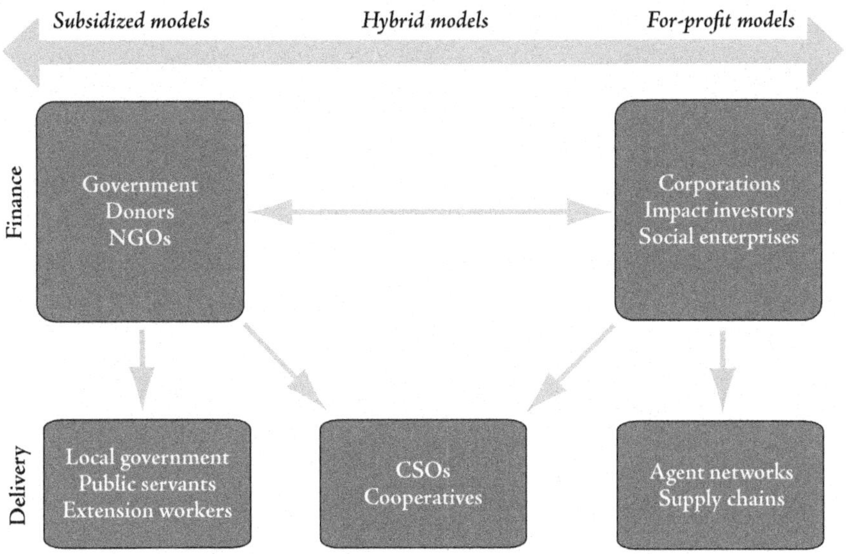

| Subsidized models | Hybrid models | For-profit models |

Finance		
Government Donors NGOs		Corporations Impact investors Social enterprises

Delivery		
Local government Public servants Extension workers	CSOs Cooperatives	Agent networks Supply chains

of a network of trusted agents by M-PESA; new public regulations to ensure no abuse of monopoly power despite a network covering most poor communities; and a further round of innovations by NGOs and social enterprises in response to the changed circumstances of "banked" poor people.

The role of the Kenyan government in this case is especially notable. Not only did it look to safeguard the rights and interests of users through consumer protection and market oversight, it also provided a supportive public policy and regulatory environment in which M-PESA could emerge and ultimately flourish. It should be noted that, at the time M-PESA was piloted, no regulations existed for e-money initiatives or for the involvement of mobile phone operators in any kind of financial transactions. The willingness of the government to allow regulation to follow innovation is an integral part of M-PESA's success story. This reinforces our belief that scaling up is fundamentally a process challenge. That process can entail identifying not only the right business model but policy reform and policy innovation. In a case such as M-PESA, it was the interaction between the new business model (notably its approach to financing, delivery, and partnerships) and the progressive and enabling policy environment that facilitated scaling up; both were necessary and neither was sufficient without the other.

The propagation of hybrid models starts with nonprofit actors and their investment choices. Altering these choices requires a fundamental change of culture for some organizations: one that accepts a higher frequency of failure, is comfortable with providing subsidies to profitable entities, and is sufficiently flexible to allow partners to operate freely rather than being excessively bound by the stipulations of an operational manual. A number of donor agencies are making efforts to move in this direction.

This emergence of hybrid models does not spell the end of traditional subsidized and for-profit models. The case studies suggest a number of ways in which these too can advance. Moreover, the typology of subsidized, for-profit, and hybrid models for scaling up is not mutually exclusive. An intervention that starts with a subsidy model, for instance, may metamorphose into a for-profit or hybrid model over time.

For subsidized models, new technologies offer great promise for overcoming long-standing weaknesses in delivery. However, these will be of little help unless organizations—donors especially—can tackle the perverse incentives that drive many away from the goal of achieving scale and lead instead to small, fragmented efforts. A stricter division of labor among nonprofit actors could advance scaling up but has proven hard to implement over the past decade. New approaches, such as triangular cooperation and vertical funds, offer promise but only if they are designed for scale; today, many are not.

The scope for growth in for-profit models could receive a major boost through the expansion of financial services to poor populations. Nevertheless, it remains unclear whether multinational corporations can be drawn into BoP markets. Social enterprises cannot be expected to completely fill their shoes, but they are capable of delivering at scale if they are supported with technical assistance and incorporated into market networks. Steps to leverage existing, informal providers into upgraded franchises offer an alternate route to scaling up impact. Ultimately, more information is needed on the unit costs of service provision in order to determine which sectors offer the most promise for BoP markets.

Any attempt to scale up encounters both opportunities and hurdles. The successful examples from our case studies took the commitment of leaders over long periods of time. These leaders were willing to take risks even when the business model remained unproven, because they understood the transformational impact of a scaled-up effort for the BoP market and the intangible value that could be generated in terms of a brand or an expanded network. They also demonstrated skill and empathy in understanding the perspective of their customers and earning their trust. In many cases, such trust is a prerequisite to the behavioral change required for new product markets to succeed.

Furthermore, effective partnerships are at the core of all successful scaling-up initiatives. Rarely can any one organization—public or private—tackle a major development challenge on its own. But partnerships do not happen without deliberate efforts on all sides to establish clear and transparent mechanisms of cooperation and a division of labor. Partnerships require a common vision, shared goals, and agreements over execution details, including resources, responsibilities, and risks. Sustained implementation of partnership agreements in turn requires institutional leadership, mutual trust, and staying power among the partners.

Are we at a tipping point in terms of the takeoff of scalable solutions for development? Some caution here may be prudent. Theory tells us that identifying a viable business model and reaching scale can take years but that, once a model is proven, it should be possible to replicate it quickly. Yet the case of mobile money doesn't seem to fit this model. M-PESA reached large scale in Kenya in only two to three years, but replication in many other countries has proven harder and slower.

It is unclear what can account for this. One explanation is that business models that appear replicable, like M-PESA's, may not be universally applicable after all. Safaricom saw M-PESA as a loyalty driver to protect and expand its market share in its core profitable mobile business; it did not need to turn a profit from mobile money. Furthermore, the main appeal of M-PESA to consumers was the ability to send money home, a practice that is less common in other countries. This is a reminder that external validity applies only weakly in scaling up.

Another explanation is that the demonstration effect can have a more insidious side. Kenyan regulators and policymakers may have played a less supportive role in the emergence of mobile money if they had known what a tremendous success it would turn out to be and the subsequent opportunities created for rent seeking. Officials in other countries are better prepared to seize such opportunities when mobile money offerings are launched, with potentially negative consequences for whether these offerings succeed. In some circumstances, then, scaling up could become its own worst enemy.

At the same time, M-PESA has developed a virtuous circle of scaling up. Other services that piggyback on M-PESA's infrastructure in Kenya are experiencing their own rapid transitions to scale. The propagation of hybrid models could trigger a similar effect. If corporations and other private sector actors (social enterprises, impact investors) can be drawn into BoP markets with the assistance of, and in partnership with, governments, donors, and INGOs, agent networks will expand, driving down unit costs and further increasing the number of market-based opportunities. This will broaden the scope of for-profit models in delivering development solutions, creating yet more momentum. The provision of cash transfers directly to poor populations by governments and donors, channeled through mobile money services, can enhance the participation of poor people in BoP markets, providing a further channel of reinforcement.

These opportunities for scaling up will not solve all development problems, but offer the best chance for improving the lives of millions of poor people. We hope through this book to encourage more development actors to think systematically about getting to scale.

REFERENCES

Abed, Fazle Hasan. 2012. Remarks. Asia Foundation, Washington, September 19.

ActionAid. 2011. "Real Aid 3."

Birdsall, Nancy, and Homi Kharas. 2010. "Quality of Official Development Assistance Assessment." Center for Global Development (www.cgdev.org/section/topics/aid_effectiveness/quoda).

Bishop, Matthew, and Michael Green. 2010. *Philanthrocapitalism: How Giving Can Save the World.* London: A and C Black.

Busan Partnership for Effective Development Cooperation. 2011. "Outcome Document, Fourth High-Level Forum on Aid Effectiveness" (www.aideffectiveness.org/busanhlf4/images/stories/hlf4/OUTCOME_DOCUMENT_-_FINAL_EN.pdf).

Duffy, Gary. 2010. "Family Friendly: Brazil's Scheme to Tackle Poverty." *BBC News,* May 25 (www.bbc.co.uk/news/10122754).

Hartmann, Arntraud, and Johannes Linn. 2008. "Scaling Up: A Framework and Lessons for Development Effectiveness from Literature and Practice." Working Paper 4. Wolfensohn Center, Brookings.

Isenman, Paul, and Alexander Shakow. 2010. "Donor Schizophrenia and Aid Effectiveness: The Role of Global Funds." Practice Paper 5. Institute of Development Studies (www.ids.ac.uk/files/dmfile/Pp5.pdf).

J. P. Morgan. 2010. "Impact Investments: An Emerging Asset Class" (www.rockefellerfoundation.org/uploads/files/2b053b2b-8feb-46ea-adbd-f89068d59785-impact.pdf).

Kenny, Charles. 2010. "Learning about Schools in Development." Working Paper 236. Center for Global Development (www.cgdev.org/files/1424678_file_Learning_About_Schools_in_Development_FINAL.pdf).

Kubzansky, Michael. 2010. "Inclusive Markets Report 2010." Monitor Group.

Levy, Santiago. 2006. *Progress against Poverty: Sustaining Mexico's Progresa-Oportunidades Program.* Brookings.

Lewin, Keith M. 2008. "Why Some Education for All and Millennium Development Goals Will Not Be Met: Difficulties with Goals and Targets." *Southern African Review of Education* 13, no. 2: 41–60.

Linn, Johannes F. 2011. "Scaling Up with Aid: The Institutional Dimension." In *Catalyzing Development: A New Vision for Aid,* edited by H. Kharas, K. Makino, and W. Jung. Brookings.

Miguel, Edward, and Michael Kremer. 2004. "Worms: Identifying Impacts on Education and Health in the Presence of Treatment Externalities." *Econometrica* 72, no. 1: 159–217.

Mullins, John, and Randy Komisar. 2009. *Getting to Plan B: Breaking through to a Better Business Model.* Harvard Business Press.

Oxfam. 2012. "First Global Aid Cut in 14 Years Will Cost Lives and Must Be Reversed" (www.oxfam.org/en/pressroom/pressrelease/2012-04-04/first-global-aid-cut-14-years-will-cost-lives-and-must-be-reversed).

Prahalad, C. K. 2004. *The Fortune at the Bottom of the Pyramid: Eradicating Poverty through Profits*. Wharton School Publishing.

Pritchett, Lant, Michael Woolcock, and Matt Andrews. 2010. "Capability Traps? The Mechanisms of Persistent Implementation Failure." Working Paper 234. Center for Global Development (www.cgdev.org/content/publications/detail/1424651).

Saltuk, Yasemin, Amit Bouri, Abhilash Mudaliar, and Min Pease. 2013. "Perspectives on Progress." January (www.thegiin.org/cgi-bin/iowa/download?row=489&field=gated_download_1;).

Stabile, Tom. 2010. "Architects of a 'Social Investment Data Engine.'" *Financial Times*, April 11 (www.ft.com/intl/cms/s/0/e297b7de-440b-11df-9235-00144feab49a.html#axzz27Oglc9xY).

UK DFID. 2008. "Capacity Building in Research." In Department for International Development, "Research Strategy 2008–2013 Working Paper Series" (www.dfid.gov.uk/r4d/PDF/Outputs/Consultation/ResearchStrategyWorkingPaperfinal_capacity_P1.pdf).

UNAIDS. 2012. "Factsheet: Getting to Zero" (www.unaids.org/en/media/unaids/contentassets/documents/epidemiology/2012/201207_FactSheet_Global_en.pdf).

Woolcock, Michael, Simon Szreter, and Vijayendra Rao, 2011. "How and Why Does History Matter for Development Policy?" *Journal of Development Studies* 47, no. 1: 70–96.

World Bank. 2011. "Household Cookstoves, Environment, Health and Climate Change. A New Look at an Old Problem." *World Bank Report*.

———. 2012. Nineteenth International AIDS Conference Debate (http://live.worldbank.org/debate-global-health-funding-hiv-aids-liveblog-webcast).

Worthington, Samuel A., and Tony Pipa. 2011. "Private Development Assistance: The Importance of International NGOs and Foundations in a New Aid Architecture." In *Catalyzing Development: A New Vision for Aid*, edited by Homi Kharas, Woojin Jung, and Koji Makino. Brookings.

4

The Effectiveness of Development Assistance

HOMI KHARAS

When James Wolfensohn took over as president of the World Bank, a long-running debate on aid effectiveness within the development community had failed to produce a concerted international effort to improve matters. A lack of coordination among aid agencies, overly ambitious targets, unrealistic timetables, and budget constraints prevented aid from being as effective as desired.[1] Indeed, given these shortcomings, a considerable lobby of NGOs actively campaigned against aid agencies; a coalition of some 200 U.S. grassroots agencies organized itself around the slogan "Fifty Years Is Enough" and advocated for closing down the World Bank in 1999. The case they made was that aid, as implemented by official agencies, was not effective.

During his time at the Bank Mr. Wolfensohn played a leading role in trying to enhance aid effectiveness, most notably as one of the leaders who brought about the Rome Declaration on Harmonization in 2003. This document committed aid agencies to simplify and harmonize their procedures while strengthening fiduciary oversight and focusing on results. Despite great initial hopes, progress on implementation by agencies turned out to be slow. A follow-up meeting, at Paris in February 2005, led to the Paris Declaration on Aid Effectiveness, an agreement among donors that established ownership, alignment, harmonization, results, and mutual accountability as the five core principles of effective aid.

When the Wolfensohn Center launched the year after the Paris Declaration, it was thus natural that one of its goals was to help realize the ideals of the Declaration. The Center's development effectiveness work program took on the challenge of how to speed up the reduction of unnecessary overlap, waste, and duplication in aid programs. The starting point was to recognize the complex range of authorizing environments of aid institutions, and the self-interest that lay at the heart of many institutions' mission-creep. An initial proposition was that little was likely to be accomplished without some effort at quantifying the size of the problem and measuring the speed of improvements. The use of metrics would become one of the most important contributions of the Center to the aid effectiveness debate.

An early effort was made to simply map the architecture and volume of the flows of official development assistance (ODA).[2] In its early years, ODA had had a relatively simple design. Large donor countries dominated. In fact, the United States, France, and the United Kingdom provided three-quarters of ODA through the 1970s, while a handful of multilateral agencies, principally the International Development Association (IDA), the soft credit arm of the World Bank, provided avenues for other countries to provide assistance. But by the turn of the century, there was a huge proliferation of donors. Almost every Organization for Economic Cooperation and Development (OECD) member had become a member of the OECD's Development Assistance Committee (DAC), each with its own aid program. There are now 30 members of the DAC, and together they disburse aid through 317 specific, named agencies, and a further 31 "miscellaneous" bodies. Additionally, many countries beyond the DAC provide aid: a further 21 countries formally share data on their aid program with the OECD even though they are not members of the DAC, and several other countries, including China and India, are known to have large foreign assistance programs even if there are little comparable data to properly measure their contributions.

There is an equivalent proliferation on the multilateral side. Today, some 220 multilateral institutions are formally approved to receive aid and disburse money or services-in-kind to recipients. This system has evolved in an idiosyncratic fashion rather than strategically. For a while, it seemed as if the solution to any large global meeting on a development problem was a decision to form a new global institution. The proliferation became so ubiquitous that, in the Accra Action Agenda on aid effectiveness in 2008, countries agreed to "look twice" before forming additional institutions. (Unfortunately, that advice has rarely been heeded.)

Adding to the complexity of the aid architecture is the growth of private philanthropy, now a $70 billion global enterprise, at times competing with, and at times collaborating with, official aid.

One implication of proliferation is that aid tends to become compartmentalized, fragmented into small projects and spread too thinly across a large number of beneficiaries. Bilateral donors, in particular, tend to have very small projects. But many multilateral agencies are under political pressure to distribute aid evenly, not to where it can do most good. In such an environment, administrative costs and overheads rise, there is more scope for diversion of funds from intended beneficiaries, and corruption is harder to control.

The conclusion of scholars at the Wolfensohn Center was that the structure of aid had become so complex that little was filtering down to poor people for actual projects and programs. Indeed, research by the Center showed that out of the headline figure of $100 in aid, on average only $19 actually made it to final beneficiaries—and for African beneficiaries, that figure was only $8.[3]

The Wolfensohn Center also tackled the issue of aid volatility. Donors feel the need to have a short leash on aid resources, reserving the right to withdraw or expand aid on an annual basis, often linked to the annual budget cycle. A multiyear commitment can be impossible to make when budgets are annually approved. At other times, however, aid is linked to the behavior of the recipient. "Conditionality," as this is termed, was a contentious issue between aid recipients and donors. Our work at the Center suggested that the volatility associated with conditionality reduced the value of aid by 20 percent.[4]

Identifying macro trends was one thing, but using data to drive changes in behavior was another thing entirely. Having demonstrated that the size of the losses associated with aid practices was substantial, it was necessary to break these down by agency and rank countries and agencies in terms of their contribution to the problem. This required a quite different approach and far more granular data about what countries and their aid agencies were doing in practice.

Fortunately, the Paris Declaration established a monitoring mechanism to assess progress on aid effectiveness practices, based on a biennial survey of donors and recipients. The survey provided indicators for a number of good practices to improve the quality of aid and its impact on development. Coupled with data on where aid was actually going, and how it was targeted, the Paris survey provided a rich source of quantitative material.

The Wolfensohn Center, working in collaboration with colleagues at another think tank, the Center for Global Development, processed all the available data into an index called the Quality of Official Development Assistance index, familiarly known by its acronym, QuODA.[5] Unlike other indexes that focused primarily on the volume of aid, QuODA focused squarely on the *quality* of assistance. All countries, large and small, could therefore be treated on an equal footing. A policy brief explaining QuODA is reprinted in this chapter.

QuODA was, by necessity, a crude index, but one that had significant impact. It had two components: a ranking by country and a ranking by agency. The first generated commentary, the second spurred action. Agency officials called to check on the methodology and the data lying behind the calculation of the metrics. Often, agency management was unaware of how its own institution compared to others. An easy-to-use tool was constructed so comparators could be flexibly chosen by each agency.

QuODA helped shine light on certain practices. Typically, agencies did well on some metrics but poorly on others. Some took transparency and learning seriously, doing rigorous evaluations. Others had little institutionalized learning. Some agencies focused squarely on poor countries and fragile states. Others avoided them and favored places in which it was easier to do business. Some agencies imposed a significant administrative burden on their clients. Others were more flexible and programmatic. For every agency, QuODA could help identify areas that could be improved to enhance aid effectiveness.

One interesting debate spurred by QuODA was how to address fragility. On the one hand, aid effectiveness indexes tended to favor giving aid to countries that already had administrative machinery in place to use aid effectively—then donors could more readily provide budget support, larger projects, and more sustained and programmed assistance, all ingredients of more effective aid. Yet at the same time, effective aid also needed to address the toughest challenges—those prevailing in poorly managed countries. Analysis at the Center had shown that a growing concentration of people live in poverty in fragile states, yet (aside from Iraq and Afghanistan) the amount of aid going to fragile states had not increased.[6] QuODA contributed to the debate on how to treat fragility in the context of the aid effectiveness discourse. It helped to balance the two perspectives of using aid in ways that were more likely to contribute to sustainable development outcomes, while also giving credit to those prepared to take on more difficult challenges.

QuODA was able to provide an objective assessment of some dimensions of aid effectiveness where none had existed before. It continued as a series for three editions, until the OECD stopped conducting the Paris Survey, removing the main data for the calculations. Following QuODA, several bilateral agencies started to do their own agency reviews, especially of multilaterals, as a way of identifying to whom they should give support. In parallel, a number of OECD countries banded together to form a Multilateral Organization Performance Assessment Network. After considerable debate, MOPAN has now started to use quantitative, comparative data in its reports, drawing its inspiration from QuODA.

The Center was able to engage on aid effectiveness at many levels thanks to Mr. Wolfensohn's personal engagement on this topic as president of the World Bank. One significant achievement was to help the Republic of Korea with its preparations for the Fourth High-Level Forum on Aid Effectiveness at Busan, scheduled for the end of 2011. This forum, a follow-up to earlier meetings at Rome, Paris, and Accra, was to shape the aid effectiveness agenda.

The government of Korea took preparations very seriously. Ambassador Kang-ho Park was seconded to the Wolfensohn Center to work on aid effectiveness from 2009 to 2010. Through his efforts, and in collaboration with the Korean International Cooperation Agency (KOICA) and the Japan International Cooperation Agency (JICA), the Wolfensohn Center engaged with a number of experts on concrete measures to improve aid effectiveness. The resulting book, *Catalyzing Development: A New Vision for Aid*—the introduction of which is reprinted in this chapter—was used by the Korean government as a blueprint for the Busan meeting.[7]

The book analyzed the new players, challenges, and approaches to aid effectiveness. Today development assistance, once the primary domain of a few rich country governments, has spread to become far more inclusive. Non-DAC development partners, private philanthropy, and even business, both through corporate social responsibility (CSR) efforts and increasingly through mainstreaming sustainability into core business practices, have become large players.

The High-Level Forum at Busan also recognized that development challenges have shifted. Some core issues, such as vaccinating children and managing communicable diseases, have had great success, with new funding sources and institutional arrangements contributing to better development results. But other issues, such as breaking the cycle of conflict and poverty, mobilizing climate finance, and building human and institutional capacity to permit countries to truly take charge of their own development programs, have surfaced.

Busan emphasized new approaches to aid effectiveness. It started a movement to view aid as a catalyst, not as an instrument to solve all development problems by itself. Busan launched a fresh emphasis by the development community on scaling up, another major theme of the Wolfensohn Center. It addressed the long-standing issue of lack of transparency in aid, a vital element of an improved accountability system. The International Aid Transparency Initiative had been launched at the Third High-Level Forum in Accra, but it was in Busan that development partners committed to a common, open standard for electronic publication of development assistance.

Since the close of the Center in 2010, work on aid effectiveness has continued as a core part of the Brookings Global Economy and Development (GED) program. Program scholars played a substantive role in the organization of the Busan agenda. We also encouraged Secretary Clinton to participate in the event, a strong signal of the importance that the United States attached to this priority. We worked on the follow-up design of the Global Partnership for Effective Development Cooperation. We helped set up the president's Global Development Council to provide advice from the business community to the U.S. president on development. We contributed to the Sustainable Development Goals, organizing and writing the report for the UN's High-Level Panel on the post-2015 Agenda, and taking an active role in the Addis Ababa Financing for Development conference, the Sustainable Development Goals Summit, and the Paris Climate summit in 2015. More recently, we have participated in a panel on the reform of the DAC and advised the Business Commission on their report on "Better Business."

GED's development effectiveness work has expanded beyond the scope of the Wolfensohn Center, but the core intellectual foundation and partnerships with outside agencies are rooted in the initial work done at the Center. And though many of the larger challenges and dysfunctions of the overall aid system—including fragmentation, volatility, and unnecessary overlap and duplication—have certainly not been solved, the Center's pioneering empirical and conceptual research on these issues has made it easier for aid agencies and outside advocates to pursue incremental reforms.

Measuring the Quality of Aid

QuODA Second Edition

NANCY BIRDSALL, HOMI KHARAS, *and* RITA PERAKIS

*Nancy Birdsall is the president of the
Center for Global Development.*

*Homi Kharas is senior fellow and deputy director for the Global
Economy and Development program at the Brookings Institution.*

Rita Perakis is program coordinator to the president at CGD.

*The Center for Global Development and the Brookings
Institution are grateful to their funders for support of this work.*

A s demonstrated by the Paris Declaration on Aid Effectiveness and Accra Agenda for Action, the development community has reached a broad consensus on what constitutes good practice for the delivery of development assistance. But since these high-level agreements were made, there has been almost no independent quantitative analysis of whether donors are meeting the standards they have set for themselves.

This brief provides a summary of the forthcoming second edition of the Quality of Official Development Assistance (QuODA) Assessment sponsored by the Brookings Institution and the Center for Global Development.[1] QuODA aims to help fill the analysis gap with emphasis on objective and quantifiable indicators. We hope this preliminary summary of the forthcoming second edition

Editors' Note: This policy brief was originally published in advance of the Fourth High-Level Forum on Aid Effectiveness, held in Busan, Korea, November 2011.

83

of QuODA will help to inform discussions at the Fourth High-Level Forum on Aid Effectiveness in Busan.

WHAT IS QUODA?

QuODA uses the findings of the *Survey on Monitoring the Paris Declaration* and additional sources to create 31 indicators that measure donors' performance in 2009–10 (box 1).[2] The indicators are grouped into four dimensions that can be interpreted as objectives of good aid: *maximizing efficiency, fostering institutions, reducing burden,* and *transparency and learning.* We assess a total of 31 donors—the 23 countries that are members of the OECD Development Assistance Committee (the DAC) plus 8 major multilateral agencies.[3]

BOX 1   The Four Dimensions of QuODA and Their Indicators

MAXIMIZING EFFICIENCY
Share of allocation to poor countries‡
Share of allocation to well-governed countries ‡
Low administrative unit costs‡
High country programmable aid share‡
Focus/specialization by recipient country*‡
Focus/specialization by sector*
Support of select global public good facilities‡
Share of untied aid*†

FOSTERING INSTITUTIONS
Share of aid to recipients' top development priorities*‡
Avoidance of Project Implementation Units*†
Share of aid recorded in recipient budgets*†
Share of aid to partners with good operational strategies‡
Use of recipient-country systems*†
Coordination of technical cooperation*†
Share of scheduled aid recorded as received by recipients*†
Coverage of forward spending plans/Aid predictability*‡

The scores on the individual indicators provide the basis for ranking donors on the four dimensions. We do not create overall rankings; having separate rankings for each dimension allows users to identify easily specific strengths and weaknesses of each donor.[4]

QUODA SECOND EDITION FINDINGS

This year's QuODA assessment is primarily based on aid disbursed in 2009. Total aid flows in 2009 from the bilateral and multilateral donors on which we report were just over $122 billion, spread across 152 recipient countries and about 18,000 development projects valued at $250,000 or more. Table 1 shows our latest rankings of 31 donors on the four dimensions. Some key findings:

REDUCING BURDEN
Significance of aid relationships‡
Fragmentation across donor agencies‡
Median project size*‡
Contribution to multilaterals‡
Coordinated missions*†
Coordinated analytical work*†
Use of programmatic aid*†

TRANSPARENCY AND LEARNING
Signatory of IATI‡
Implementation of IATI data reporting standards#
Recording of project title and descriptions
Detail of project descriptions
Reporting of aid delivery channel
Completeness of project-level commitment data*
Quality of main agency evaluation policy#
Aid to partners with good M&E frameworks‡

New indicator added for 2009 assessment. The 31 indicators are flagged by the type of source that advocates for use as a benchmark: * Recipient governments; † Paris Declaration; ‡ Academic literature.

FIGURE 1 The Three Largest Donors on the Four Dimensions of Aid Quality

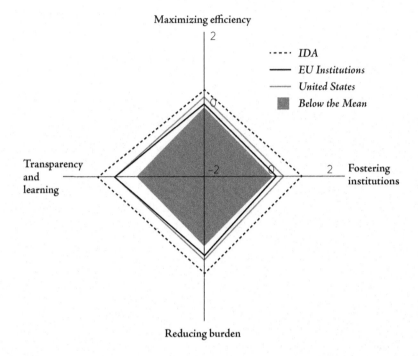

- Three of 31 donors are in the top ten in all four dimensions: IDA, Ireland, and the United Kingdom.

- Most donors score poorly on one or more of the dimensions; that suggests that most have plenty of room to improve.

- In three of the four dimensions, the best-in-class agency is a multilateral. On the other dimension, *fostering institutions*, smaller bilateral donors are at the top, namely Denmark and Ireland.

- Multilaterals appear to benefit from having greater independence from political considerations. Their aid is untied and much less fragmented, and their larger projects reduce the administrative burden on recipients.

- The largest donor, the United States, does badly. It is among the bottom six in three dimensions, but does make the top half in *transparency and learning*.

- The next largest donor, the European Union, is in the middle of the pack on three dimensions and third in *transparency and learning*. Its large size seems to create the means and the pressures that lead to greater transparency.

QUODA SECOND EDITION: MARKED IMPROVEMENTS

Donors improved on all dimensions except *maximizing efficiency*. But those gains, while statistically significant, are relatively modest.[5] They can be interpreted either as too slow to make a material difference, given the low baseline and the urgent need to improve to help meet the Millennium Development Goals, or as a possible sign of steady improvement that is making a difference. Only subsequent editions of QuODA will reveal if these changes are part of a trend.

Changes by Dimension

There has been little overall change in *maximizing efficiency* between 2008 and 2009. The allocation of aid to poor countries increased substantially because debt relief to Iraq, a relatively rich aid recipient, ended in 2008. But donors became far less selective, both by country and even more so by sector, and they channeled slightly less aid to well-governed countries. There is strong evidence that aid to well-governed countries is more effective in achieving development results, although aid to fragile states may be a good use of money. QuODA users should keep in mind individual donors' objectives when judging them on these indicators.

Scores on *fostering institutions* improved (figures 2 and 3). Five out of eight indicators in this dimension come from the *Survey on Monitoring the Paris Declaration*. Although most absolute targets were not met according to the survey report,[6] donors did improve modestly, especially in the share of aid going to partners with good operational strategies.

Change in *reducing burden* was mixed. More donors coordinated their analytical work and missions, there was more use of programmatic modalities (rather than projects), and a greater share of aid was channeled through multilateral agencies. But the average donor had a smaller project size in 2009, suggesting continued fragmentation of aid efforts.

FIGURE 2 Donor Scores on Fostering Institutions, 2009

The most positive change was in *transparency and learning.* Two additional agencies have signed onto the International Aid Transparency Initiative (IATI) since last year (the Global Fund and the African Development Fund) and, significantly, 11 donors and agencies have already started to publish aid information in accordance with the agreed-upon standards, or have submitted a plan to do so this year.

The record on learning through evaluation is much harder to assess because donors have failed to develop or agree on any common reporting standard regarding their evaluation policies and practices. We added our own new indica-

FIGURE 3 Change in Fostering Institutions, 2008–2009

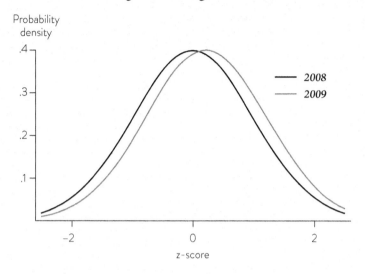

tor this year to reflect our assessment of donors' evaluation and learning policies, but we could not do so for actual practices.[7]

Changes by Key Donor

The United States continues to struggle to become a more effective donor. It slid back in 2009 on several important indicators of aid quality, including specialization by country and sector and untied aid, which declined from one-third to one-quarter.

The United States does have strengths. By our new measures, USAID may now have the best evaluation policy of any development agency in the world; it shows major improvement in providing aid to countries with good operational strategies.

The European Union, now one of the largest aid providers, improved in all dimensions except *reducing burden*. The EU has made good progress in untying aid (from 50 percent to 79 percent), has almost eliminated the use of project implementation units, which can undermine country capacity, and has significantly increased its use of country systems. The EU has also made a commit-

TABLE 1   Ranking of Donors by Aid Quality Dimension

Donor	Maximizing efficiency	Fostering institutions	Reducing burden	Transparency and learning
Australia	16	17	18	9
Austria	31	25	14	23
Belgium	21	23	28	31
Canada	17	11	19	14
Denmark	15	1	5	20
Finland	18	10	17	4
France	14	22	25	28
Germany	28	13	20	15
Greece	30	31	26	25
Ireland	8	2	2	7
Italy	23	19	24	29
Japan	7	7	23	13
Korea	20	15	30	18
Luxembourg	13	29	16	30
Netherlands	25	12	11	16
New Zealand	11	24	4	11
Norway	24	16	27	10
Portugal	9	18	8	27
Spain	26	21	22	21
Sweden	22	5	10	8
Switzerland	27	27	29	19
United Kingdom	10	8	9	5
USA	29	26	31	12
AfDF	1	4	15	6
AsDF	3	6	6	22
EC	12	14	12	3
GFATM	2	9	13	2
IDA	6	3	3	1
IDB Special	5	28	1	26
IFAD	4	20	7	24
UN (Select Agencies)	19	30	21	17

Source: Authors' calculations.

ment to transparency. It is an IATI signatory and has started to report its aid according to IATI standards.

The World Bank's International Development Association is one of the oldest and largest multilateral aid agencies. It consistently ranks among the best aid agencies in each dimension. Almost by definition, IDA has a strong focus on assisting the poorest countries, a focus it accentuated in 2009.

IDA, however, is increasingly active in countries where others are also active, reducing the significance of its aid relationships. Its projects tend to be large (second only to the Asian Development Fund in 2009), but it has not improved its coordination of missions or analytical work with others. IDA is a signatory to IATI and has started to report according to IATI standards. It has emerged as the top donor in our *transparency and learning* category.

An Agenda for the Busan High-Level Forum on Aid Effectiveness

HOMI KHARAS, KOJI MAKINO, and WOOJIN JUNG

Homi Kharas is senior fellow and deputy director for the Global Economy and Development program at the Brookings Institution.

Koji Makino is senior adviser to the Director-General, Operations Strategy Department, Japan International Cooperation Agency.

Woojin Jung is policy analyst, Korea International Cooperation Agency.

Today's world is shaped by growing economic integration alongside growing economic divergence. Over two dozen developing economies are expanding at rates that previously appeared miraculous, reducing poverty at unprecedented rates. Conversely, thirty-five developing countries with a combined population of 940 million can be classified as "fragile," or at risk of suffering debilitating internal conflict.[1] The potential for globalization to act as a positive force for development contrasts with the prospects for globalization to threaten, or be unable to protect, development through a failure to deal with the challenges of hunger, poverty, disease, and climate change. Many developing countries have neither the safety nets nor the macroeconomic institutions to manage global economic shocks. Developing countries today are quite differentiated in terms of the challenges they face and their capacity to respond.

Editors' Note: This is the introductory chapter from the book *Catalyzing Development: A New Vision for Aid,* edited by Homi Kharas, Koji Makino, and Woojin Jung, published by Brookings Institution Press in 2011.

International support for global development is now couched in terms of a broad strategic vision of long-term engagement to assist countries to sustain progress and evolve into partners that can help build a stable, inclusive global economy. This support is built on three pillars:

+ An understanding that the responsibility for sustained development lies principally with the governments and institutions of each developing country, with foreign assistance playing a supportive, catalytic role.

+ A recognition that a broad array of engagements between countries contribute to development, principally through trade, investment, finance, and aid.

+ A desire to fashion an improved operational model for development cooperation that reflects the differential challenges of sustainable development, the diversity of state and nonstate development partners, and the dynamics of sustained development.

Aid must be understood in this context. It can only play a catalytic role, not a leading role, in development. Development will not happen because of aid, but aid can make a difference. Developing countries are responsible for their own development. Aid is but one of many instruments of development, and the catalytic impact of aid is often seen when other forces like trade and private investment are unleashed because of better economic policies and institutions supported by aid programs.

There have been many visible improvements in the operational model for aid since the late 1990s—untying, greater alignment with global priorities such as the Millennium Development Goals, more decentralized operations, use of country systems and budgets, and better donor coordination. But other problems with the operational model have emerged:

+ The mandates for aid have expanded—growth, debt relief, humanitarian assistance, anticorruption and governance, delivery of public services, state building, and climate change adaptation, to name a few. With such broad mandates, there are no simple metrics of success by which to measure the impact of aid. Some suggest the need for a new architecture, in which aid is measured in a different way and oriented toward specific targets.[2]

+ Aid is terribly fragmented, with the number of official development assistance (ODA) projects surpassing 80,000 annually, delivered by at least 56 donor countries, with 197 bilateral agencies and 263 multilateral agencies.[3] The number of tiny aid relationships is daunting and, with more players, aid is becoming less predictable, less transparent, and more volatile. Despite an advisory from the Accra High-Level Forum on Aid Effectiveness to "think twice" before setting up new multilateral aid agencies, the number continues to grow. Only one multilateral development agency is known to have closed since World War II (the Nordic Development Bank). Alongside this, a new ecosystem of private development agencies has emerged—philanthropic foundations, international NGOs, church groups, corporations, and universities which command significant and growing resources. The actions of these groups are little understood, and they remain on the fringes of official development cooperation.

+ The governance of aid is seen as bureaucratized and centralized at a time when more attention is being focused on the quality of aid because of pressures on some large donors to cut back on (or slow growth in) aid volumes. The result is overlap, confusion, and a lack of leadership in some areas.

Against this background, a major international forum on aid effectiveness will convene in November 2011 in Busan, Korea, under the auspices of the Development Assistance Committee of the OECD (OECD/DAC). The Busan meeting comes at an important juncture. Because aid is clearly not sufficient to achieve development, it is sometimes misconstrued as being unnecessary, despite the growing evidence that aid is working at both micro and macro levels.[4] The simple conclusion that aid does not work, while true in selected cases, is crowding out the more complex story of how aid helps in numerous different—but often unmeasurable—ways. Aid, as a government-to-government form of development cooperation, can also be perceived as an inferior alternative to private sector, market-determined processes and hence less relevant for development in today's world. Against this antiofficial aid movement, the Busan meeting must recapture the idea that ODA is a major instrument of development cooperation and can be made more effective if the right lessons are learned and if operational models are improved.

The goals of the Busan meeting are ambitious. They are nothing less than an attempt to generate a better understanding of how to improve the human condition—a twenty-first-century charter for global development cooperation by generating sustainable growth, achieving the Millennium Development

Goals, and investing in a range of global public goods, like climate mitigation. Ultimately, that means cooperating to achieve sustainable results at scale. That can be done by nation-states organizing and leading development cooperation by generating the right enabling environment for development, by promoting productive businesses in a competitive setting, and by, through an inclusive process, tapping into the energies of billions of citizens worldwide engaged with development. Figure 1 illustrates this proposition for better contextualizing the role of effective aid in supporting development.

ASIAN EXPERIENCES WITH AID AND DEVELOPMENT

In many ways, the vision for aid expressed in figure 1 has already been implemented in much of Asia (although Asian countries have not had to confront climate change until recently). In a number of Asian countries, the development experience shows a limited, yet pivotal, role played by aid. The host country for the Busan High-Level Forum (HLF4), the Republic of Korea, perhaps best exemplifies the contributions that aid can make when targeted in the right

FIGURE 1 A New Vision for Aid: Catalyzing Development

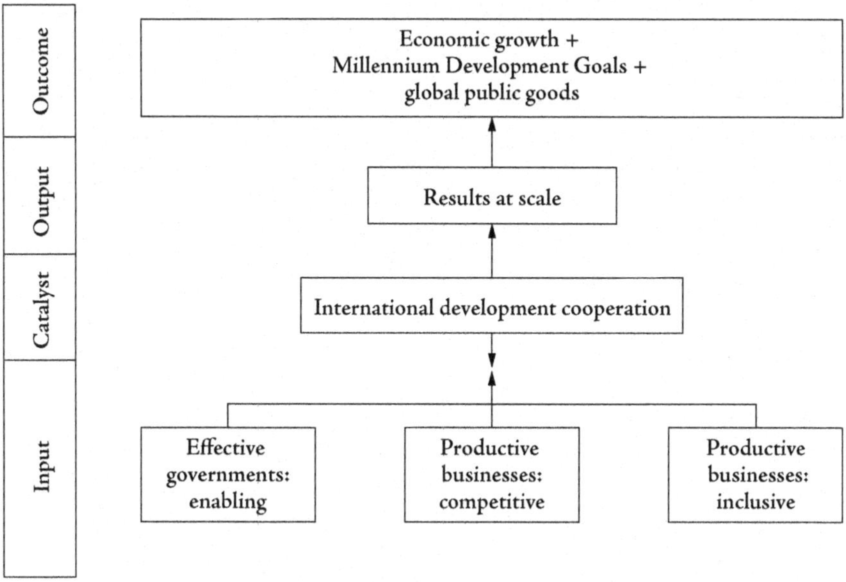

way and tailored to country circumstances. Korea brings a unique perspective in moving through the entire spectrum of aid, from being a major recipient to being a major donor within a span of fifty years (see the case study for Korea in box 1).

Other Asian experiences also provide a reminder that the lessons drawn from Korea's experiences with aid are applicable to other countries; a sustainable development trajectory must encompass self-reliance, the building of local capacity, and the evolution of development assistance to fit changing development priorities. Brief case studies of Cambodia (emerging from a fragile state), Indonesia (a large country trying to scale up development), and Vietnam (development partner with a strong national strategy) show aid working successfully in very different environments (see boxes 2 to 4 below). These studies reveal common themes and lessons that illustrate three important principles of the successful use of aid to catalyze development, despite vastly different circumstances and economic policy approaches by recipient governments.

First, *diverse aid* providers can bring complementarities, resources, and expertise, and Asian countries benefited from the broad array of development partners. At times they were able to secure assistance from one partner even when another was unconvinced of the development approach. Such "competition" among development partners goes back to U.S.-Japanese differences in approaches in Korea, World Bank–IMF differences in approaches in Vietnam, and the division of labor among donors in Indonesia. In each Asian case study, aid has been leveraged with private corporate sector investments and an emphasis on trade as a key development strategy.

Second, *differentiated* aid approaches are needed to take into account recipients' characteristics, histories, and priorities. This is the essence of country ownership. For the most part, Asian countries have been able to receive aid in a form appropriate to their situation. This has been driven by strong expressions of country needs, expressed by government leadership of the development agenda and over aid resources.

Third, *dynamic* approaches are needed to adjust assistance over time as development conditions evolve. Graduation strategies and hard timetables can provide a sense of urgency and the need for speed in development programs. As the examples below show, aid in Asia has constantly adapted its approach to the evolving needs of countries, whether it be the move from grants to loans in Korea as the purpose of aid shifted, or the evolution of aid instruments toward budget support in Vietnam, or the sequenced approaches to capacity development in Cambodia, or the scaled-up approach to hydrological management in Indonesia.

The conclusion: aid works, when done right. That requires starting from an assessment of development needs and only then developing an aid strategy. Too often today the process is reversed, with donor-defined aid strategies driving development outcomes.

Our case studies suggest that in Asia aid has been effective in countries that have stable long-term donors who are invested in the success of their projects and in the development of their partner. The Asian examples point to the need for aid to be sustained over time but with graduated modalities to capture fully all development benefits. Strong local leadership is critical to align aid with evolving national development priorities. This does not always mean full agreement with donors on all aspects of development, but it does imply finding the right avenues for mutual cooperation. And capacity development beyond improvement of specific technical talent emerges as a key success factor in all the Asian cases.

THE AID EFFECTIVENESS AGENDA TODAY

Since 1960 rich countries have given $3.2 trillion in aid to poor countries, mostly through a handful of bilateral and multilateral institutions.[5] Despite misgivings as to its effectiveness, aid continues to enjoy strong political and public support in rich countries. Emerging economies also have substantial development cooperation programs. And a variety of private international NGOs (INGOs), foundations, corporations, and individuals are actively engaged. Aid has become a $200 billion industry: $122 billion from the OECD/DAC donors, $53 billion to $75 billion from private donors, and $14 billion from emerging economy donors.[6] The last two components are growing rapidly. China, India, Brazil, Venezuela, Turkey, and the Republic of Korea, to name just a few, have developed aid programs that could soon each surpass $1 billion annually.

For most of the past decade the aid agenda has focused on increasing the volume of aid flows—with considerable success. Net ODA disbursements from members of the OECD/DAC rose from $54 billion in 2000 to $122 billion in 2008.[7] This is a substantial increase even if it is not as high as hoped for when

BOX 1   Republic of Korea

Aid to Korea has been adapted to changing country circumstances. Before and immediately after the Korean War (1950–53) aid to Korea was focused on military support and humanitarian relief, which was crucial for the survival of the country. As Korean institutions became more stable and capable after the 1960s, development interventions were scaled up, first by graduating from grants to concessional credits, then to nonconcessional financing, and finally to private finance (appendix table 1). Korea was fortunate to have two stable long-term donors—the United States and Japan—providing financial and technical cooperation. Recently, Korea has joined the group of OECD/DAC donor nations.

One reason for the success of Korea's experience with ODA was its strong country ownership and leadership. Korea knew what it wanted and was not intimidated into accepting donors' policy preferences. The United States put a greater emphasis on stability, which implied relatively short-lived, non-project aid, and it was sometimes conditional, with expectations on how aid dollars would be spent. For example, using relief aid for investment was prohibited by the United States. However, the Rhee regime expressed a desire for more investments, the separation of economic aid from military aid, and long-term predictable aid in accordance with the national development plan.

Under the Park administration, the Korean government formed an Economic Planning Board to prepare five-year economic development plans. (Launched in 1961, the Economic Planning Board was responsible for development planning, annual budget preparation, and coordination of foreign aid and foreign investment.) Aid was linked to the country's planning and budget process. The Park administration maintained a policy focusing on large-scale enterprises despite the recommendations of U.S. advisers to focus more on small and medium-sized enterprises. Most of the assistance in Korea was allocated to finance the government's industrial and financial policies implemented by *Jaebeol* (a Korean form of business conglomerate), particularly in import-substituting or export-oriented, private enterprises such as the POSCO steel mill, funded mainly by Japanese repatriation payments.[a] Many of these cases were remarkably successful. The emphasis on focusing aid on investment in large economic infrastructure and services contrasted with a low aid-allocation priority for health and education, as these were financed by Korean society itself.[b] Korea and its U.S. advisers also had different approaches toward fighting corruption. Instead of penalizing corrupt businessmen, Park expropriated their bank stocks and assigned them to invest in key import-substitution industries such as fertilizers.

Country-led development was made easier by a unique organizational structure that reflected Korea's special needs. When the U.S. operation mission system (in which the American ambassador holds jurisdiction over the disbursement of aid) was deemed inappropriate for Korea, it gave rise to the creation of the Office of the Economic Coordinator (OEC). In 1956 the OEC absorbed the functions of the Korea Civil Assistance Command and the UN Korea Reconstruction Agency and became the only aid coordinating agency in Korea. Unlike an earlier period when Japanese engineers and UN personnel in Tokyo were responsible for Korean aid, the OEC was placed in Seoul and Busan, hiring almost 900 Koreans along with 300 foreigners.[c] A decentralized structure enabled the OEC to formulate harmonized and home-grown assistance policies among key donors (appendix figure 1).

Throughout the aid process, Korea worked on capacity building. Between 1962 and 1971 more than 7,000 Koreans received training abroad, and additionally over 1,500 experts were sent to Korea by donor nations. A high proportion of the senior personnel in government, business, and academia received foreign training. While Korea sought to improve the quality of development projects by hiring leading foreign institutes, the planning and implementation responsibilities were largely in the hands of local people. For example, for the Geongbu Expressway, general project supervision was contracted out to a foreign expert on construction technologies but implementation and feasibility studies were handled by domestic engineers. When establishing the Korea Institute of Science and Technology with U.S. assistance, Korean project managers decided the orientation of the institute and picked the most qualified advisers, instead of waiting for experts to be sent. Investment of significant local resources and time in project implementation signaled strong Korean project ownership and was in line with local efforts to learn "how to fish."

a. KEXIM (2008); Chung (2007).

b. CBO (1997).

c. Lee (2009).

significant pledges were made at Gleneagles. The experience of the last decade is that ambitious targets for increasing aid volumes can work if there is strong leadership. Gratifyingly, prospects for aid volumes in 2010 are not as bleak as feared, despite the gravity of the public finance situation in many donor countries.[8] With the growth in aid from private and non-DAC donors, as well as resources from hybrid financing, issues about the quantity of aid revolve around questions of ensuring a better division of labor and better coordination of activities so as to avoid overlap and waste.

As scrutiny over public funding has grown, more attention has shifted to the quality of aid. Much of this agenda revolves around assisting partner countries to achieve self-reliant development. The prevailing framework for action on aid effectiveness has been articulated in high-level conferences at Rome (2003), Paris (2005), and Accra (2008). The Paris Declaration on Aid Effectiveness, endorsed on March 2, 2005, committed over one hundred countries and organizations to enhance aid effectiveness by 2010 by respecting five principles: ownership by recipient countries, alignment of development partners with country-led poverty strategies, harmonization of activities among development partners to avoid duplication and waste, results in terms of development outcomes, and mutual accountability for performance.

While there has been significant progress under the Paris-Accra agendas, a number of challenges have emerged. The growth of aid resources and aid donors has been accompanied by a fragmentation into ever smaller projects, with the mean project size falling from $2.01 million to $1.46 million between 2000 and 2008 (in real terms). Small can be good if it is innovative and later results in scaling up, but each project also has fixed costs of design, negotiation, and implementation, which reduces dollars available for final beneficiaries.

Recipient countries each received an average of 263 donor missions in 2007. Their senior finance officials spend one-third to one-half of their time meeting with donors; in the case of Kenya, Ghana, and others, governments have resorted to "mission-free" periods to allow officials time to handle their domestic obligations. The efficiency losses from this set of transaction costs are estimated at $5 billion by the OECD, prompting calls for more serious attention to be paid to issues of division of labor among donors.[9] Better division of labor would result in larger aid flows between a given donor and recipient and would reduce the number of donor-recipient aid relationships, as some donors would exit from some countries. In fact, the OECD/DAC estimates that if half of the smallest donor-recipient relationships were abandoned, only 5 percent of country programmable aid would have to be rechanneled. In some countries with strong leadership, like Vietnam, donor coordination has made good progress, leading to more effective use of aid, but this model cannot be readily applied to all countries, especially not to fragile states (box 2).

In the old aid architecture, coordination at the country level was done through UN Roundtables or Consultative Group meetings. The ten largest donors could be gathered in a single room and would collectively represent 90 percent of all aid to that country. Today, the share of the largest ten donors typically covers around 60 percent of aid. It is not easy for recipient countries to host a forum that is representative and inclusive of the experiences of all development partners while at the same time being effective in coordinating, harmonizing, and prioritizing activities.

In fact, excessive coordination can alienate small donors. Large recipient countries, like India and Indonesia, have already expressed their unwillingness to debate national policy issues with small donors, and several donors have reduced their support to these countries. But small developing countries cannot afford the luxury of alienating any potential donors. They need to find ways to ensure that small donors are not marginalized by building a relationship of development cooperation that is about more than just provision of money.

If aid is to be seen as a mechanism of development cooperation, an instrument for achieving results on the ground, it follows that aid must be governed and managed through processes within each recipient country, not just at the global level. Two types of aid relationships have matured: government to government and civil society to civil society. In each case, there is more to be done to reinforce these relationships, especially in situations where governments are weak and lack either capacity or legitimacy. But what urgently needs strengthening is links across these relationships: civil society donors to government recipients and government donors to civil society recipients. These links are weak and sometimes confrontational but cannot be ignored.

The 2008 *Survey on Monitoring the Paris Declaration* stresses that the pace of improvement had to accelerate in order to meet the targets set for 2010.[10] In particular, the report calls for strengthening and use of country systems, stronger accountability, and lowering of transaction costs for partner countries and donors in the delivery of aid. The discussions at the Busan High-Level Forum on Aid Effectiveness in 2011 will be based in part on the evidence from the

BOX 2 Vietnam

Vietnam has grown fast, dramatically reducing poverty from 58.1 percent in 1993 to 12.3 percent in 2009. Vietnam's development is especially remarkable since over the last thirty years it has had to recover from war (1955–75), adapt to the loss of financial support from the old Soviet bloc, and overcome the rigidities of a centrally planned economy. While problems such as inequalities persist—for example, poverty in Vietnam is concentrated among ethnic minorities in remote mountainous areas—the country is a worthwhile case study on how to develop rapidly based on economic integration, market liberalization, and the strategic use of aid.

Vietnam is one of the largest recipients of ODA, with aid volumes approaching $4 billion (compared with $1.5 billion in 1995). Although Vietnam receives a lot of aid, it is not an aid-dependent nation. ODA was only 4 percent of its GDP in 2009.

Vietnam shows strong country ownership of its aid receipts, led by the Ministry of Planning and Investment. Coordination is based on an internally drafted five-year socioeconomic development plan and a local version of the Paris Declaration called the Hanoi Core Statement. The government, rather than donor groups, has driven the poverty reduction agenda, sometimes defining priorities that are different from donors' priorities. After the 1997–98 East Asian crisis, Vietnam focused on stabilizing its economy, and reforms progressed very slowly until 2001, leading to a halt in structural adjustment lending from the World Bank. Only when the leadership felt comfortable did reforms start up again. Vietnam also allowed its program with the International Monetary Fund to lapse over disagreements with the pace of financial sector reform and audits of the central bank. It has resisted donor pressures for greater freedom of journalism and civil society development.

These examples are not meant to indicate that the decisions made by the government of Vietnam were always best from a development perspective but rather to demonstrate that a successful development partnership must be based on serious dialogue even if disagreements between development partners occur. The critical issue is to find ways of fostering cooperation in areas where agreement and progress can be made.

A result of strong country ownership is that donor aid in Vietnam has been well aligned with country priorities. With specific sectoral programs and projects working well, Vietnam has been able to organize an umbrella instrument to channel aid in support of these activities through the budget.

Initially, only a few donors agreed to general budget support for Vietnam, but once it showed a track record of success, more joined in. In recent years ten or eleven co-financiers provide budget support, accounting for 25 percent of ODA.[a] All ODA provided through budget support is automatically subjected to reasonably transparent financial reporting systems. It also has been disbursed on schedule, in contrast to project disbursements.[b] In particular, poverty reduction support credits are an exemplary practice on policy dialogue in a mature development partnership. Given the leadership and capacity demonstrated by the government, the instrument provides a soft financial incentive in place of conditionality.

One challenge that Vietnam faces is that its aid is becoming more fragmented as donors are attracted by its success. Vietnam has become a donor darling, with around twenty-eight bilateral donors and twenty-three multilateral agencies. The Paris Monitoring Survey of 2008 reports that Vietnam hosted 752 donor missions in 2007—more than three missions per working day. The number of missions conducted by some donors appears extremely disproportionate to the amount of aid they provide. For example, UN agencies provide less than 1 percent of ODA, but the number of these agencies operating in Vietnam increased from four in 2006 to twelve in 2007. While such aid is costly, Vietnam has been able to manage donors well. Large donors, such as the Six Bank Group, finance large infrastructure, while smaller donors, such as the Like-Minded Donor Group, the European Commission, and the UN, typically work in areas not served by the larger donors, addressing problems like social inequality and exclusion. Probably having more donors is a net positive for Vietnam, although waste and overlap may be occurring.

Vietnam's relative success in using aid is based on two pillars. First, Vietnam has a strong relationship with its major donors; 60 percent of its aid comes from its top three donors: Japan, the World Bank, and the Asian Development Bank. Second, infrastructure development has been identified as the key focus of aid money. Specifically, road transportation, power generation, water supply, and sanitation systems have been prioritized and developed.

a. OECD (2008).

b. Ibid.

third survey on achievement of the Paris Declaration targets for 2010. It is safe to say that at least some of the indicators will not be met and that a significant agenda will remain to advance the Paris principles. This agenda will need further articulation in Busan.

But equally, there must be a discussion around two other broad questions. How should other development actors, the so-called new players, who by and large were absent when the Paris principles were drafted, be incorporated in a new global aid architecture? And is there a need to adapt the Paris indicators to deal with new challenges of development, in particular to the emerging discussion on climate change financing, the practical problems experienced in applying the Paris principles to aid in fragile states, and the mixed results with capacity building?

We refer to this as the Paris++ agenda for Busan. Considerable work remains to achieve the Paris Declaration targets, and a focus on this should be maintained, but at the same time other agendas are pressing. Lessons from experience need to be absorbed. For example, Cambodia could have some lessons on phasing and sequencing of aid that are more broadly applicable to countries emerging from conflict. Its future prospects are still not assured, but considerable progress is already evident, thanks in part to the generous provision of development assistance (box 3).

This volume offers specific suggestions for framing an agenda for Busan through ten essays on game changers for aid—actions that we believe will transform the development landscape. We do not go into the details of how to pursue the Paris Declaration targets beyond 2010, even though this is an essential part of the agenda. Those discussions are well in-train through an extensive work program under the auspices of the Working Party on Aid Effectiveness of the OECD/DAC. Instead, this volume focuses on the "plus-plus" part of the agenda.

It is already evident that the Paris Declaration is most relevant to the portion of aid that is shrinking. To start with, the Paris and Accra Accords only cover ODA from DAC countries, covering perhaps 60 percent of total aid, a share that appears likely to shrink further as non-DAC donors and private development assistance are expanding aid faster than DAC donors. The other concerns are that the Paris-Accra processes have not been fine-tuned to reflect the specific challenges of fragile states, capacity development, and climate change, each of which accounts for a large portion of today's aid.

Table 1 shows how most of the increase in aid since the 1990s has gone into fragile states, where ideas like reliance on recipient country ownership and alignment of donors with country preferences and practices are difficult to implement and require unorthodox approaches. Fragile states received about $15 billion a year ($21 per capita) in aid in 1995–98 and $46 billion ($50 per capita) in 2005–08.[11] Even when the exceptional cases of Iraq and Afghanistan are excluded, ODA to fragile states grew considerably. In contrast, aid to non-fragile states hardly grew at all in aggregate and fell in per capita terms over this period, from $10.3 per capita to $10.0 per capita (the same broad pattern holds excluding the dynamic large economies of China and India). The reality is that only $20 billion a year goes to nonfragile states in a fashion that is programmable by recipient countries, or about 10 percent of total aid.[12] Thus the Paris-Accra discussions are relevant to only a small portion of total aid.

Figure 2 highlights the changing nature of the composition of total aid. Using approximations for the volume of aid from private assistance and emerging donors, DAC development assistance was over 80 percent of total aid in 1995–98. While allocations for fragile states (19 percent) and for technical co-operation (21 percent) were significant, the bulk of DAC aid (40 percent) went for other purposes.[13] By 2005–08, the aid environment had changed signifi-

TABLE 1 Aid to Fragile and Nonfragile States, 1995–98 and 2005–08[a]
U.S. dollars

	1995–98		2005–08	
Aid	*Billion*	*Per capita*	*Billion*	*Per capita*
ODA from DAC donors	73.3	...	119.0	...
Aid to fragile states				
Net ODA	15.3	21.4	45.7	50.4
Less ODA to Iraq and Afghanistan	14.7	21.8	28.3	33.1
Aid to nonfragile states				
Net ODA	39.3	10.3	43.5	10.0
Less ODA to India and China	33.9	20.6	40.1	20.9

Source: OECD/DAC, aggregate aid statistics online; World Bank, World Development Indicators online.

a. The sum of aid going to fragile and nonfragile states does not add to total net ODA because some aid is regional, not allocable by country, or used for non-country-specific purposes.

BOX 3 Cambodia

The polity and society of Cambodia are not yet free of fragility. The Khmer Rouge government, 1975–79, participated in genocide, which led to the deaths of 21 percent of the entire population. The overthrow of that regime did not end the violence, and peace efforts did not completely succeed until much later. In 1991 a cease-fire was finally agreed to by all sides. Although Cambodia attained political stability by the late 1990s, weak accountability and corruption of the government hamper the consolidation of a genuinely legitimate state. Cambodia is among the lowest countries in Transparency International's (TI) ranking of corruption. Between 2005 and 2009 Cambodia's TI ranking dropped from 130th (among 159 countries) to 158th (among 180 countries). Furthermore, due to the history of conflict, Cambodia presents a unique development challenge. In 2008 the population cohort of ages thirty through thirty-four was smaller than any other age group and had the lowest male literacy rate. The lack of middle-aged, highly skilled people is a serious problem for the management of state institutions.

Despite these drawbacks, Cambodia has achieved rapid growth, enjoying five years of double-digit growth in the decade before the 2009 global recession. It received $5.5 billion in aid from thirty-five official donors and also benefited from the activities of hundreds of civil society organizations. Foreign aid played a pivotal role in rehabilitating infrastructure and improving basic services, thereby providing the Cambodian people with peace dividends in an early stage of the peace-building process. Improved infrastructure served as a basis for the economic development in the later stage.

Because of Cambodia's poor human capital, donors have focused on state

cantly. Non-DAC official donors (5 percent) and private philanthropy (32 percent) became large players and are expected to grow even more. Climate change adaptation (as measured by Rio markers) emerged as a major component of total aid and is also certain to become even larger. The portion of aid going toward fragile states rose from 19 percent to 26 percent. The portion of core DAC aid shrank to just 19 percent of total aid.

In 2005, the year the Paris Declaration was signed, more than half the world's poor lived in stable, low-income countries (table 2). In 2010 only 10 percent of the world's poor live in such countries, while the majority live in middle-income and fragile states. The traditional aid model must respond to these capacity building but have addressed it through funding foreign experts. Technical cooperation has been about half of ODA in Cambodia but has been criticized domestically as being mostly supply driven, poorly coordinated, and a substitution for domestic capacity rather than an addition to it.

The Royal Government of Cambodia has tried to take ownership of the aid agenda through establishment of technical working groups in nineteen sectors and thematic areas. Through this mechanism, it has aligned aid with the National Strategic Development Plan but still finds that donors are uncomfortable with program-based approaches and budget support due to poor governance in the system. New donors like Thailand and China are important but have a development cooperation process outside this structure.

In Cambodia tangible impacts of aid can be most clearly seen at the level of specific programs. One example is the case of National Maternal and Child Health Center (NMCHC), which currently functions as the country's largest obstetrics hospital as well as the national training center for improvement of public health service. In the first phase of the project (1995–2000), priority was given to building the capacity of the NMCHC staff in both organizational management and specific health care skills. Building on the achievement of the first phase, the second phase (2000–05) expanded the training program for midwives and physicians across the country. This example shows how capacity can be developed in specific areas when foreign experts and local staff engage in a process of mutual learning.

changed circumstances. Aid was originally envisaged as an instrument to help low-income countries develop until such time as they could sufficiently provide for the material needs of their citizens. The complication for aid policymakers is that aid is often deemed unnecessary in middle-income countries and ineffective in fragile states—precisely where today's poor people can be found. Development cooperation in these settings requires differentiated strategies, usually tailored to each specific country case.

The Paris Declaration principles and targets have been most successfully implemented, and have achieved the greatest development impact, in stable countries where donors have reliable partners and have confidence in their abil-

FIGURE 2 Aid Composition, 1995–98 and 2005–08

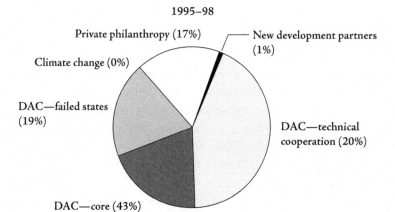

1995–98

Private philanthropy (17%)

New development partners (1%)

Climate change (0%)

DAC—failed states (19%)

DAC—technical cooperation (20%)

DAC—core (43%)

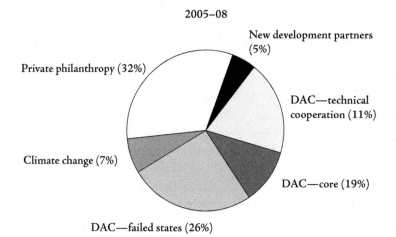

2005–08

New development partners (5%)

Private philanthropy (32%)

DAC—technical cooperation (11%)

Climate change (7%)

DAC—core (19%)

DAC—failed states (26%)

TABLE 2 Where Do the World's Poor Live?

Percent

State	2005		2010	
	Low income	Middle income	Low income	Middle income
Stable	53.9	25.6	10.4	48.8
Fragile	19.6	0.9	23.7	17.2

Source: Based on Chandy and Gertz (2011).

ity to deliver the right sorts of interventions and reforms. But as the demography of global poverty has evolved, donors will have to adjust to different environments.

PLAN OF THE BOOK AND SUMMARY FINDINGS

The new environment for aid depicted in figure 2 shows where important conversations are needed at Busan to enhance aid effectiveness and improve aid architecture. This volume is an effort to inform these conversations through research on each of the three key topic areas: new players, new challenges, and new approaches.[14]

Chapters 1 through 5 discuss the new aid ecosystem from the perspective of the new players, including non-DAC donors (chapter 2), international NGOs, philanthropists, and a vocal public engaged in thousands of civil society organizations (chapter 3), and multinational corporations (chapter 4). The existing global aid architecture, built around a few major official donors, is straining to accommodate this diversity of views and must become better networked (chapter 5). With so many interacting stakeholders, it may not be possible to have a single architecture, as in the past, but rather a set of guidelines, responsibilities, and accountabilities to shape how each group should act and interact—what might be called a new aid ecosystem.

Chapters 6, 7, and 8 describe the new challenges that must be considered today. The details of implementation, sequencing, and phasing of aid in fragile states, for capacity development and for climate change, are being vigorously debated, with no clear understanding of the best way forward.

Some thirty-seven fragile states, with one-third of the world's billion extreme poor, have development needs that are quite different from those of other countries. Already there has been a diversion of aid resources toward fragile states, where development outcomes are far harder to achieve and sustain, raising issues of scale of activities, phasing, and sequencing (chapter 6). The same risks pertain to climate change financing. Despite all the talk of additionality, there is concern that more resources for climate mitigation will mean fewer resources for development and that development funds will be channeled prematurely toward climate adaptation activities. At a minimum, because climate change financing has aspects of a public good and universal implementation, it is not easy to integrate delivery modalities with development financing practices that focus on selectivity (chapter 7). In both these cases, and to achieve development more broadly, partner countries need to upgrade their technical and administrative capacity to absorb and utilize to maximum benefit the bewildering array of new resources. Yet capacity development is one of the least well understood aspects of aid, and several donors are radically rethinking their approaches in order to mainstream capacity development (chapter 8).

Chapters 9, 10, and 11 discuss several new approaches that appear promising in delivering better results. Aid must move beyond small successes, with projects to demonstrate that it can achieve results at scale. Donors can have a far-reaching impact even in large countries, as the experience of Indonesia shows (box 4). More donor agencies are focusing on the need for interventions that have the potential to be scaled-up in terms of impact (chapter 9). Technological change also opens up the possibility for far-reaching improvement in the transparency and quality of aid data, with benefits that could amount to $11 billion by some estimates, especially if new sources of information, like beneficiary feedback and local evaluation, are collected (chapter 10). And more recipient countries are finding that the practical experiences of their peers with implementing development programs are of enormous value. South-South cooperation has been enthusiastically welcomed (chapter 11).

Taken together, the ten chapters that follow this overview provide specific recommendations for game changers that could radically improve the development results from aid. They provide an action agenda for the Busan HLF4. Gaining consensus and developing an implementation plan will be not easy, but there is a compelling need for new thinking on aid. The Busan HLF4 provides an opportunity to mobilize the political support needed to move the agenda forward.

NEW PLAYERS

Chapters 2, 3, 4, and 5 look at the new players in the aid architecture.

New Development Partners

Kang-ho Park (chapter 2) highlights the rise of new development partners, countries that are not part of the OECD and that may not have subscribed to the Paris Declaration but that are now providing significant resources for development. He estimates that these cooperation programs were tiny in 1995, accounting for only $1 billion, or 1.7 percent of ODA, but that they may now account for $15 billion; by 2015 new development partners could disburse one-fifth of ODA if their growth continues to outstrip that of developed country partners.

As much as money, new development partners bring valuable know-how and technology to their development cooperation. They are valued by recipients for their practical experiences in overcoming development challenges and in implementing successful strategies in an environment that is close to that faced by today's developing countries. Many of the new donors present a challenge to the norms and standards of development aid. Their guiding principles are Southern solidarity, mutual benefit, and cooperation. Many are simultaneously recipients and providers of development funds. Some even reject the term *aid* as not fitting their concept of mutual benefit and cooperation. In this view, the blending of aid with other instruments to achieve economic, commercial, and political benefits for both development partners is simply how mutually beneficial cooperation functions. It is a different approach from that of traditional aid donors, which demand conditionality in return for assistance.

New development partners do not fit within the frame of the existing aid architecture. Some of the Paris concepts, such as untying of aid and provision of resources through programmatic means, go against the perceived advantages of new development partners, namely the provision of their own development experiences in a speedy way with emphasis on the how-to aspects of implementing development projects and programs. The Paris emphasis on harmonization is also seen as diminishing the new development partners' contribution, since harmonization limits the scope for alternative approaches and is dominated by larger, more powerful donors. There are no incentives for new development partners to participate in such efforts.

BOX 4 Indonesia

Indonesia is the largest country in the ASEAN, and its political stability and economic development is crucial to the development of the rest of the region. As one of the East Asian miracle countries, it reduced the number of people living in poverty from roughly 50 million (about 40 percent of the population) in 1976 to approximately 20 million (about 11 percent of the population) in 1996. Development in Indonesia has been pursued along three parallel axes: growth, poverty reduction, and security. In the second half of the 1980s Indonesia implemented policy reforms in such areas as trade, foreign direct investment, and tax revenues to reduce reliance on primary commodities. These reforms were highly successful, resulting in average annual growth rates of 7 percent through the mid-1990s.

Indonesia has a strong relationship with its primary donor, Japan. Around 30 percent of the electricity used in Indonesia comes from the power plants developed or enhanced with Japan's ODA, 30 percent of dam capacity was developed with Japan's ODA, and a quarter of the rice that Indonesian people eat every day comes from paddy lands developed with Japan's ODA.

Other donors were also important but in different areas. There is evidence of a successful division of labor. The United States focused its aid mainly on education, governance, and health, while the Asian Development Bank (ADB) extended loans for infrastructure projects. The Indonesian government has taken ownership of its aid and actively coordinates its development partners. In 2009 the Jakarta Commitment was signed by the government and twenty-two donors as a local version of the Paris Declaration.

There is some common ground. All development partners agree on the principle of country ownership, although there may be differences in how this is interpreted. All development partners have also agreed on the Millennium Development Goals as a valuable framework for establishing country development objectives. The issue is with implementation.

Park proposes an elegant solution, based on the long-standing international principle of common but differential responsibility. Applying this solution to development assistance, he suggests that development partners be tiered into three groupings: DAC donors that have subscribed to the Paris principles but that have still to implement many of the aid effectiveness targets; non-DAC OECD or EU countries that are committed to the shared values of the OECD

One striking feature of Indonesia's experience is the long-term engagement exhibited in some programs. For example, the Brantas River Basin development project in East Java was set up to manage a watershed of forty rivers. It was created in 1961 and continues to this day; the Japanese government has been providing assistance to the project continuously for fifty years. Every decade the plan is reviewed to see if goals are being met and updated. The gradual institutional evolution of this project, in the relationships between central and provincial authorities and other stakeholders, is at the core of the efficient water resource management seen today throughout Indonesia.

The long-term horizon taken to resolve a major development issue like water resource management encouraged supporting institutions to be developed along with the infrastructure of dams and irrigation canals. Local capacity was built; 7,000 engineers and technicians were trained through the Brantas project, for example, many of whom have gone on to work in other projects across Indonesia. Their skills were honed through a series of joint works with foreign experts on river basin development. This project showcases the synergies between hard aid (development of the actual dam) and soft aid (capacity development) and the extent of development externalities that can accompany successful projects when they operate at scale. At the same time, the Brantas project operated with strict budget constraints; social obligations were funded out of project revenues, not additional grants. Impacts, not resources, were scaled up.

and hence are prepared to take the Paris principles as a reference guide; and other countries that are both recipients and providers of aid and that would abide by a more flexible, but defined, set of principles.

In Park's view the missing element in the aid architecture is any effort to develop such a tiered approach. The current dialogue tries to persuade new development partners to join the club of traditional aid donors. But there are few incentives for this, nor can the exchange of views reduce the inherent tensions of different approaches. Instead, he advocates that the Busan HLF4 be a platform for new development partners to base their own standards and responsibilities for aid effectiveness that will maximize their potential development contribution.

Private Development Aid

Sam Worthington and Tony Pipa (chapter 3) discuss international aid that flows from private philanthropic sources in developed to developing countries.[15] This private development assistance (PDA) includes international NGOs, foundations, individual philanthropists, corporations, universities, diaspora groups, and religious congregations and networks. The key distinction of this type of private funding is that it is philanthropic in origin, as opposed to direct foreign investment or remittances, which may also have important development impact but have quite different motivations.

The scale of PDA is significant. It is estimated that private philanthropic aid from fourteen developed countries totaled $52.6 billion in 2008. Extrapolating this to all developed countries and making adjustments for underreporting, the actual figure for PDA could be in the range of $65 billion to $75 billion.[16] Although many individuals contribute to PDA, it is increasingly organized, project-oriented, and consistent with international norms on delivery. PDA can no longer be caricatured as small-scale, humanitarian assistance. In a 2006 survey of InterAction's members, 73 percent of respondents identified long-term sustainable development as a primary program area.[17] The largest global INGO, World Vision International, counts 46,000 staff, manages a $2.5 billion global budget, and is larger than several official DAC donors.

International NGOs are both local and global. They regularly establish a long-term presence in poor communities, generating community trust and the expertise necessary to be effective. A 2008 five-country analysis of a hundred INGOs and local civil society organizations found that 90 percent of INGOs had been working in country for at least five years, 77 percent for more than ten years.[18] Between 90 and 99 percent of INGOs' in-country staff are local citizens.[19] Globally, networks of NGOs form a conduit for sharing development knowledge and innovations based on an increasingly extensive body of evidence. Many INGOs have entire divisions dedicated to evaluation; the 2008 survey found that 92 percent of the INGOs had measurement and evaluation systems. The foundation sector is in the midst of a metrics revolution, pursuing new and better methodologies for impact assessment.[20] Unfortunately, much of this is unpublished, so the aggregate contribution of PDA to development results cannot yet be measured.

PDA is complementary to ODA, although because they have different approaches and areas of focus they are sometimes opposed to each other. PDA strives to be innovative, people-centered, long term, and grounded in local adaptation.[21] It works with communities and local civil society in the delivery of public services. In contrast, ODA grows out of, and is influenced by, the strategic political considerations of donor countries.[22] Its primary point of entry is at the national level, supporting national governments and plans, state capacity, physical infrastructure, and social programs.

Taken together, PDA and ODA offer a more robust definition of "country ownership" than that suggested by the Paris Declaration. Worthington and Pipa call this taking a whole-of-society approach. They call for a greater voice for local civil society in the articulation and assessment of development programs and a formal role for NGO representatives at DAC ministerial meetings. In return, the organized PDA sector would take responsibility for developing norms of behavior and transparency to permit a more constructive dialogue with ODA agencies and recipient governments. In many ways, this proposal is similar in spirit to that of Park: recognize and seek to maximize the development contribution of new players while encouraging them to organize themselves in an agenda-setting process that provides a "grand bargain" of inviting their participation in return for specific responsibilities.

Private Corporations

The private sector has long been seen as the key to sustained growth and development, but private corporations have traditionally been viewed as motivated solely by profit, so traditionally the relationship between the private sector and aid has been largely passive. The logic was that if aid could improve the enabling environment for business, the private sector would produce the investment and jobs that would create economic growth and alleviate poverty. Because private sector resources are so large, this logic meant that aid could be leveraged many times if properly focused on a private sector development agenda.

Jane Nelson (chapter 4) suggests that focusing on creating an enabling environment for business is essential but not sufficient. She argues that this is a simplistic picture of the private sector's evolving contribution to development. Among other approaches, she documents the growing concept of "impact investing" as "actively placing capital in businesses and funds that generate social and/or environmental good and at least return nominal principal to the investor."[23] Nelson cites studies suggesting that impact investments could grow to $500 billion in the next ten years. With this scale, impact investors and the networks that support them are creating effective leadership platforms featuring new development models that blend economic viability and market-based approaches with social and environmental objectives.

The private sector has not always been regarded as a champion of development, and the first priority is to ensure minimum standards that avoid exploitative types of development that have been seen in the past. One way of doing this is through the business leadership coalitions that are being formed at the country level to focus on development and on poverty alleviation. Some of these coalitions are freestanding and some are dedicated units of well-established chambers of commerce. These convene multistakeholder initiatives and mobilize private sector engagement in development at national and global levels. The contributions of the private sector are several: delivering base-of-the-pyramid products and services; building accessible, affordable, and reliable physical and communications infrastructure for remote and low-income groups; leveraging science and technology; building skills; and spreading international norms and standards. The private sector renders these contributions by making core business practices more development friendly (by establishing value chains with low-income producers for example); through corporate philanthropy; and through policy dialogue, advocacy, and institutional development.

Nelson's view is that, while there are many examples of projects in which private and official aid sectors collaborate, these are often small in scale and impact. She advocates an approach in which groups of companies and other stakeholders join forces in collective action to solve development problems.

Nelson singles out two areas for action. First, private corporations can help donor countries take an approach toward development that addresses trade, investment, and commercial ties as well as aid. Second, business leaders in recipient countries can be mobilized to champion strategies and public campaigns for inclusive and green growth. Nelson suggests targeting selected sectors—such as agriculture, forestry, health, water, infrastructure—in national multistakeholder pilots. The private sector in each pilot country would take on agreed roles and responsibilities. The innovative feature of Nelson's idea is that cooperation with the private sector be organized on a sectoral basis rather than on a donor-recipient basis. There are only a few examples of such vertical funds in the current aid architecture; expanding this to include inclusive and green growth would be a worthwhile way of showcasing the development potential of public-private partnerships.

Aid Coordination

Ngaire Woods (chapter 5) tells powerful stories about the lack of coordination of aid and the problems caused by the asymmetrical relationship between small developing countries and powerful donors. She distinguishes between coordination and cooperation. The latter refers to joint activities, usually harmonized, to achieve common goals. But Woods suggests that cooperation is a far-off goal (as reflected in the declining share of aid channeled through multilateral agencies, one of the major instruments for cooperation). She suggests that, while cooperation may be desirable, it is unlikely to be pervasive given the rivalries and differences in approach and experiences among development partners.[24]

Woods argues that coordination is a more realistic goal because all parties stand to benefit. Coordination seeks to avoid waste and damage when the actions of any one development partner affect the outcomes of another's activities. As she says, "Coordination is not ambitious; principally it serves to prevent inadvertent damage caused when donors are ignorant of each other's actions." In Woods's view the key ingredient of coordination is information sharing. But how?

Woods describes two levels of coordination: standard setting for all donors at the international level and country-level coordination of international agencies active in any specific country. While she reports on some progress on both fronts, the pace is slow. Woods documents the problems that have emerged with trying to use meetings for coordination: far too many stakeholders (because donors have not yet developed an adequate division of labor); some of them ill informed, with only limited experience of the country; many of them with too little technical expertise and too little institutional memory. The result: limited impact, leading in a vicious cycle to less attention being given to proper planning and to attendance at meetings.

Woods proposes that aid recipients should manage the coordination process but warns that this will not be easy. Quoting the World Bank, she notes that "to date, the move to genuine country-led partnerships that effectively combine ownership and partnership is being made in only a few IDA countries, typically in one or two sectors." She lists various arguments in favor of a country-led approach, including the incentive to coordinate effectively, as citizens reap the benefits in terms of development effectiveness, and the information to make sure that coordinated approaches meet country needs. But she cautions that donor incentives work in the opposite direction and that therefore much stronger political will is required to implement a country-led coordination model. Not only must donors provide resources to strengthen the capacity of countries to manage aid by themselves, but they must also make sure that well-meaning donor officials on the ground give governments enough space to manage by themselves—even if that means allowing them to make mistakes. Woods concludes that trust is the missing ingredient that needs to be created through high-profile political events such as the Busan HLF4.

NEW CHALLENGES

Chapters 6, 7, and 8 present important new challenges facing development aid.

Fragile States

Foreign aid to support economic development in fragile states is fraught with contradictions. State building is inherently an indigenous process, and foreigners must find ways to be part of the solution, not part of the problem. The gap between need and ability to implement successful development projects is greatest in fragile states. Many fragile states suffer the effects or aftereffects of conflict, with destroyed infrastructure coexisting with destroyed institutions and service-delivery mechanisms. The need for justice and security in postconflict environments means that achievement of a durable peace is the overriding objective rather than economic development per se.

Shinichi Takeuchi, Ryutaro Murotani, and Keiichi Tsunekawa (chapter 6) divide fragile states into two groups, those in a "capacity trap" and those in a "legitimacy trap." The former cannot deliver basic security and services to the population. The latter cannot satisfy people's expectation of enhancement of social inclusion, economic equality, and political participation. Countries that fail in either regard risk suffering a reversal into conflict—in fact a country reaching the end of a civil war has a 43.6 percent chance of returning to conflict within five years.[25]

Takeuchi and colleagues stress two points. First, they caution that the interdependence of traps in fragile states implies that solutions must be broad based and long term. Quick results should not be expected; sustainability is hard to achieve. But without significant assistance dealing with a range of development challenges, the risk of a development collapse is high. Better metrics for measuring state building are needed. Second, in cases in which the central government has difficulty in capacity building, a bottom-up approach may offer opportunities to construct a legitimate state. When development projects are designed and implemented with well-structured participatory approaches that protect the socially weak, as in the case of community development councils (CDCs) in Afghanistan, they generate trust in elected community leaders, providing the foundations for legitimacy while also delivering priority services for the public who have a positive view of the results.[26]

But there is a warning here as well: because state building must be based on an indigenous political process, the donor community may find it hard to accelerate the pace of change simply by increasing the volume of aid resources. Finding the balance between excessive aid that is wasted and too little aid to make a systemic difference is the heart of the problem. Regional mechanisms can provide insight into the appropriate balance.

Climate Change

Climate change poses a challenge to development aid on three counts. First, the significant resources needed to fight climate change have the potential to divert money from other forms of development assistance. Kemal Derviş and Sarah Puritz Milsom (chapter 7) point out that large new bilateral funds have sprung up recently, most notably Japan's Hatoyama Initiative, which has pledged $11 billion (of which $7.2 billion is ODA) over three years (2010–12) for mitigation and adaptation efforts. Under the Copenhagen Accord, rich countries promised to provide "fast-start financing" to developing countries for 2010–12 of approximately $30 billion and to try to mobilize $100 billion a year by 2020, almost as much as total ODA today.[27]

It is evident that all climate financing cannot be in the form of ODA, considering the costs to address climate change are unprecedented: the UN Framework Convention on Climate Change (UNFCCC) estimates costs for adaptation alone to be between $40 billion and $170 billion a year.[28] Rather, the scale of climate financing needs requires a hybrid approach, where aid is leveraged with nonconcessional resources as in the Global Environment Facility model.

The second challenge is that climate change adds to development needs, and developing countries worry that climate concerns could slow their growth and poverty reduction trajectories. This is especially true in the large emerging economies—India and China—that depend heavily on coal to power their development. Both adaptation and mitigation activities are costly for development.

Third, climate change requires verification and accountability or, more broadly, strong governance. The mutual accountability processes developed in the aid architecture are "soft." They revolve around debate, an exchange of views, inclusive participation of many stakeholders, and sharing of experiences. Accountability in the aid world is more about relational approaches than about substantialist, regulatory, or legal processes. In fact, the latter (also termed *conditionality*) have been largely discredited as a tool of effective development cooperation.

But climate change requires verification. If parties cheat on climate emissions (and the incentives to cheat are significant because of the trade-off seen between long-term, sustainable growth and faster, short-term, "dirty" growth), the whole world suffers. It is imperative that climate funding be combined with a verification strategy. Conversely, the incrementality of climate funding also needs to be verified, something that is conceptually hard to do given the intrinsic link between adaptation and poverty reduction and practically hard to do with the rudimentary state of transparency and "statistical markers" of aid.

Derviş and Puritz Milsom wrestle with these issues, complicated by ethical overtones. Climate mitigation funding is considered by some as a "compensation," paid to developing countries by rich countries for their past pollution transgressions, and by others as an incentive to participate in the provision of a global public good for the mutual benefit of the world. Their proposed solution is a two-track approach. Track one would be global, with efforts to identify the cheapest way of reducing worldwide carbon emissions by sector and country and to evaluate progress made. This should be kept separate from development assistance. Track two would be sectoral, seeking limited agreement on specific proposals rather than a single undertaking. For example, moving toward an agreement on forest conservation may be more palatable in terms of the impact on economic development. This track needs to be implemented at the country level through National Adaptation Programmes of Action (NAPAs) and Nationally Appropriate Mitigation Actions (NAMAs).

Derviş and Puritz Milsom argue forcefully that climate mitigation is not aid but rather a payment for a global service and should be accounted separately from development assistance. Help for adaptation, on the other hand, is more like other development assistance and can be accounted as such.

Capacity Development

Akio Hosono, Shunichiro Honda, Mine Sato, and Mai Ono (chapter 8) describe the evolution of thinking on capacity development (CD). Although CD was highlighted in the Paris Declaration as a key crosscutting theme for development effectiveness, it has not been easy to construct a consensus on good practices on the basis of existing experience. At times CD has been conceived of as a means to facilitate new aid approaches of general budget support and sectorwide programs. This led to one focus on strengthening of public financial management systems; use of these systems became part of the Paris Declaration targets.

But this focus of capacity has now been recognized as too narrow. The Accra Agenda for Action highlights the need to broaden CD to actors beyond the national government (local governments, civil society organizations, media, parliaments, and the private sector) and to areas beyond financial management. This trend of broadening the scope of CD is also in line with the most widely cited definition, from the DAC, viewing capacity as a holistic and endogenous process of people, organizations, and society as a whole.

With this broader scope, new analytical frames have been applied to capacity. The key insights are that capacity cannot be viewed as a simple technical gap but rather as an evolutionary process of systemic change. The former requires clear specification of the gap; the latter allows more room for flexibility, learning by doing, and adaptation to a constantly changing external environment. Time and space are needed, and must be consciously created, for mutual knowledge and learning creation.

Based on selected case studies of successful CD, the authors discuss a set of success factors: the enabling environment and context (such as decentralization and autonomy of local institutions); ownership, awareness, and determination as the fundamental drivers of an endogenous CD process (like the demand for better schools in Niger); specific triggers and drivers that give impetus to capacity (like an innovative mechanism to remove bottlenecks hampering local collective action); mutual learning and trust building for cocreation of innovative solutions; scaling up good-practice CD pathways; and the role of external actors in supporting CD.

The conclusion: CD is too important to be left as something to happen spontaneously. External assistance can yield significant results, even in difficult environments, but these must be based on an appropriate analytical understanding and on well-articulated, yet flexible, pathways. Reading between the lines, there is a tension between the slow pace and flexibility needed for successful CD and the increasingly short-term, metric-focused orientation of a results focus for aid.

The Busan HLF4 can help with the formalization, institutionalization, and mainstreaming of CD. There are several global networks on CD, such as the CD Alliance and the Learning Network on CD (LenCD), as well as country-level initiatives and sector-specific initiatives (for example, education). This learning should be supported and extended through further rigorous case studies, development and refinement of CD analytical tools (including national CD strategies, assessments, guidelines, and indicators), and expansion of mutual learning opportunities through dialogue and field-based experimentation.

NEW APPROACHES

The final chapters, 9, 10, and 11, offer new approaches to delivering aid.

Scaling Up

The past decade has seen a tremendous spurt of innovation in piloting new approaches to development, exemplified by processes like the World Bank's Development Marketplace. This has been accompanied by a renewed emphasis on evaluation in an academically rigorous way through randomized trials and case studies. But the search for effective development interventions has not yet resulted in an institutionalized approach to scaling up to maximize the development impact. That, argues Johannes Linn (chapter 9), is because scaling up is typically an afterthought in development projects. He suggests that evaluating the scaling-up potential in partner countries should be a major focus of attention for aid donors.

Linn defines scaling up as "expanding, replicating, adapting, and sustaining successful policies, programs, or projects in geographic space and over time to reach a greater number of people." Linn separates two common failures in scaling up. A type 1 error is when a successful innovation or activity is not scaled up, and a type 2 error is when scaling up is done but is inappropriate or done wrong.[29] The novelty of his argument is that the large development banks (and some countries) often try to go to scale but on the basis of insufficient piloting, testing, and learning as well as on inappropriate phasing, resulting in problems with effective operation.

Like capacity development, scaling up can be formalized in analytical frameworks that identify key drivers, spaces, pathways, and intermediate indicators. But Linn notes that few agencies have undertaken systematic scaling-up reviews to assess how their internal incentives and procedures facilitate or hinder scaling up, although some recognize the need to scale up to translate experiences and lessons into broader policy and institutional change.[30] Sometimes termed the micro-macro linkages, scaling-up pathways have received little attention in the follow-up to small pilots.

Scaling up is easier when outcomes are narrowly measured and projects are simple. That is the experience with vertical funds. But what is a strength to the program can be a challenge in other areas. Vertical fund evaluations comment on the substitution of resources from other priority areas (and complications with ensuring long-term fiscal sustainability), on the limited attention to capacity development and to broader policy formulation and implementation, and on the difficulties in partnering with others once the model to be scaled up is determined.

Linn argues that the scaling-up agenda cannot move forward unless there is greater political support. If development partners would agree to introduce the objectives of scaling up explicitly into their mission statements and operational policies, as well as into evaluations, then there is a better chance that the range of development pilots now being undertaken can be leveraged into sustainable development progress.

Transparency

At Accra transparency and accountability were emphasized as essential elements for development results. The International Aid Transparency Initiative (IATI) was launched to provide improved information on what donors were doing. But Homi Kharas (chapter 10) points out that the consensus on the importance of transparency has not translated into an urgency for action. Despite the new ecosystem of aid players, transparency is restricted to a small group of traditional donors and has largely bypassed new development partners or PDA. Kharas warns that the development community is losing the war in communicating a compelling story of successful aid interventions and that lack of transparency, especially at the partner country level, is an obstacle to better development impact.

Transparency is a vital tool for mutual accountability. It is most useful when rule enforcement is difficult, as is the case between development partners. In such cases, information is not provided to implement traditional command-and-control rules (the conditionality approach) but to allow a variety of accountability structures, like parliamentary and civil society oversight, to develop norms and standards that result in improved outcomes.

Kharas emphasizes the importance of building up the demand for information. Too often transparency has been approached from the supply side, with agencies supplying information that is never used or databases being established without a clear understanding of what is required. Overreporting is costly and has led in many cases to reporting fatigue. Nevertheless, significant information gaps still exist, because the current process of providing data is not demand driven.

At the global level, too few donors provide adequate information. The IATI is a useful start, but only half of the aid provided by DAC donors is covered by IATI signatories, and only the Hewlett Foundation subscribes to the IATI among PDA and new development donors. Coverage is therefore around one-third of total ODA. A critical objective is to improve this, either through more signatories to IATI or through donors developing their own similar functionality. Aid data at the global level need to be understood as a public good. All donors would benefit in terms of better strategies if they properly understood the three Ws of transparency: Who is doing what where.

But it is at the local level where gaps are most acute and the benefits likely to be largest. There are now several aid databases at the recipient country level, but data quality is poor and access often limited. Donors have little incentive to provide information and occasionally are unable or unwilling to respond to country requests. Resource predictability, links with budgets, prioritization to minimize gaps between resources and needs, and better analysis of development impact through beneficiary assessments are among the benefits to be had from greater local transparency of aid.

Kharas emphasizes the opportunity provided by new IT tools and systems. Open-source data exchanges can allow local databases to be seamlessly linked to global databases and can permit aggregation of unique agency databases, without the need for a single, comprehensive database, which is viewed as impractical. Geo-referencing can overlay aid resources with survey data showing development needs. Mobile telephony can provide real-time beneficiary feedback in a way that yields extraordinary development impact improvements in some controlled experiments and gives a voice to those demanding better information.

Many of these tools are already being piloted by official and private donors alike, but there is no systematic process for constructing an information spine to support development. Kharas suggests that the benefits of such an effort would be considerable, citing estimates of the gains from transparency that are upward of $10 billion annually, compared to one-off costs of only tens of millions of dollars.

South-South Knowledge Exchange

South-South cooperation (SSC) was introduced as a global topic involving debate among developed and developing countries during the Accra HLF. Hyunjoo Rhee (chapter 11) defines it as developing countries working together to foster sustainable development and growth. She also relates it to triangular cooperation: OECD-DAC donors or multilateral institutions providing development assistance to Southern governments with the aim of assisting other developing countries.

Rhee shows that significant benefits can be gained from SSC, often related to broader programs of regional integration and to knowledge sharing and advice based on practical experiences with implementing projects or resolving development issues. The regional dimension is critical to maximizing the development impact because it permits nonaid instruments to be used. Rhee gives the example of the Greater Mekong subregion, where transport corridors have been built to connect countries in Southeast Asia. The impact has been raised by knowledge sharing on the soft infrastructure of customs procedures, trade facilitation, visa processing, cross-border trucking agreements, and the like, subjects that are inherently South-South in nature simply because of the geography of the region.

Rhee emphasizes appropriate knowledge exchanges through SSC. Recipient needs may be better understood by other Southern countries that have experienced similar situations. Language and cultural familiarity make knowledge transfers more effective. Costs are lower, so "value for money" is perceived as higher. But against this, SSC results in greater donor fragmentation and is often a top-down process driven by political considerations rather than development needs. There is limited monitoring and evaluation, although informal feedback appears positive.

The most significant constraint is the lack of information about the potential for SSC. Recipients are not aware of experiences that others have been through, and development partners may not have extensive cooperation agreements with all countries. There is no process for matching supply and demand. Rhee proposes formalizing SSC at the Busan HLF4, starting with universally agreed definitions. She proposes using regional organizations to match supply and demand.

There already exist a number of global platforms for South-South exchange, including the World Bank Institute, the UNDP, and sector funds.[31] Rhee argues that we should build on these and on her proposed new regional platforms, linking them into a global network for South-South cooperation, with four pillars: an information and networking pillar, a technical pillar for matching supply and demand, a financial pillar to match resources and needs, and an advisory pillar to help formulate better SSC projects and evaluate the experiences.

NEXT STEPS FOR BUSAN: AN ACTIONABLE AGENDA

Aid effectiveness may be considered a narrow topic, but there are few issues in the world today where there is a near consensus on goals (sustainable growth plus the MDGs, broadly defined, plus global public goods) shared between multinational corporations, civil society, and rich and poor country governments. The consensus on goals among diverse players in the new aid ecosystem is the greatest strength of the global aid architecture.

The chapters in this volume focus on game changers that could significantly improve aid and development effectiveness. Each chapter considers case studies in order to make practical recommendations for improving aid effectiveness. Taken together, the recommendations would make a material difference in the lives of millions of people. Table 3 illustrates the main elements of the proposed Paris++ agenda for Busan. It suggests the shape of an effective division of labor between aid actors, shown in the columns, along with how these actors could be organized in networks to coordinate their activities. The table also suggests, in each row, how each actor might take a differentiated response to key issues. Taken together with suggestions for better ways to implement new approaches in terms of transparency and scale, the result should be a significant improvement in aid effectiveness.

But in implementing this agenda, the chapters in this volume also contain notes of caution. Aid can only be a catalyst, not a driver of development. Aid can work, and has achieved notable successes in even the most disadvantageous country settings. But it is not a panacea. In particular, there are six warnings that recur:

+ Do not expect fast results. In many places, the impact of aid is felt in the long term and results are not achieved in a linear fashion. Patience, along with sequenced interventions, is needed. Long-term interventions must be the norm. More resources cannot always accelerate the pace of change; indeed, sometimes too much external funding can inadvertently damage weak domestic institutions.

+ Successful pilot projects are not enough of a game changer. Aid must change development processes, whether through capacity building, transparency, or scaling up.

TABLE 3 Paris ++ Agenda for Busan

Issue	DAC donors	New development partners	Private aid	Corporations	Organizing networks
			New players		
Core development activities	Meet Paris Declaration targets	Provide low-cost infrastructure	Support social development	Improve investment climate	Country-based, country-led
New challenges Fragile states	Focus on capacity and legitimacy	Focus on capacity and legitimacy	Protection of vulnerable populations	Implement OECD/ UN guidelines	Country-based, donor-assisted
Capacity development	Holistic approach	Organize South-South knowledge exchange	Build local civil society capabilities	Skills training supply chains	Global, regional, and national platforms
Climate change	Separate mitigation from aid; support NAPA and NAMA	Separate mitigation from aid; support NAPA and NAMA	Advocacy; community resilience	Support Green Growth Institute; new funds and technologies	Global and sectoral organization; national plans
New approaches Transparency	Provide up-to-date complete data linked to budgets	Meet minimum agreed data standards	Publish aid volumes and evaluation lessons	Endorse transparency standards	Establish standards and databases, globally and nationally
Results at scale	Include scaling up in mission statements	Provide hybrid financing partnered to investments	Mobilize Southern civil society	Support base of pyramid and inclusive business modes	MDGs (UN-led), growth (G-20-led), climate change (UNFCCC-led)

+ Country ownership cannot be equated with government ownership. Broader concepts of "whole of society" are needed, as well as judgments on responsible governments, and these inevitably involve political calculations. Aid cannot be treated as an apolitical activity.

+ Harmonization has its limits: the diversity of challenges and development partners and approaches should be celebrated, not excoriated.

+ Verification of development results, especially in climate change, will inevitably return. This should not be interpreted as new conditionality but as part of a broader process of dialogue toward shared development objectives.

+ Aid, as a concept, is becoming blurred, and hybrid financing systems are being developed. The aid architecture must link with other resources for development.

Ten Actionable Game-Changer Proposals for Seoul

The Busan HLF4 can be a significant milestone in aid effectiveness. As a dialogue forum, it can bring together a number of new players on an equal footing to debate development issues. That would already represent a break from the past. But it would be disappointing if the Busan HLF4 concluded without actions. The chapters in this volume put forward concrete proposals to help focus international negotiations and to promote internal thinking within development agencies. The proposals need to be debated and tested, consensus needs to be built, and implementation issues considered. They must be costed and subjected to value-for-money analysis. The proposals are as follows:

1. Establish a three-tiered approach to aid effectiveness principles with minimum standards (including on ownership/alignment, capacity development, information sharing, and an ODA-GNI target) to be developed by new development partners.

2. Add Northern and Southern civil society representation to the OECD/DAC ministerial from groups committed to establishing and implementing PDA norms and responsibilities.

3. Add private sector representation to the OECD/DAC ministerial from business groups that are partnering with donors and governments to

drive inclusive and sustainable growth. Select pilot countries and sectors to implement and evaluate such collaborative platforms.

4. Promote aid coordination led by aid recipient governments.

5. Provide broad-based, long-term support to fragile states, focusing on the formation of a legitimate state. Regional approaches could be promising.

6. Further mainstream the capacity development perspective in policies of partner countries, donor organizations, and other new development actors and promote it through flexible, long-term, and sequenced approaches that specify capacity "for what."

7. Link aid and climate change financing in a "resources for development" framework. Develop a two-track approach to climate change financing: a global approach to minimize the cost of carbon reduction by selection of least-cost country and sector interventions; and a narrow approach to sector-specific agreements, starting with forest conservation and country-based adaptation and mitigation plans.

8. Encourage aid agencies to introduce scaling up into mission statements, operational guidelines, internal incentives, and evaluations.

9. Develop regional approaches to South-South cooperation that can then be linked into a global network for South-South cooperation, with two pillars: a technical pillar to match supply and demand and a financial pillar to match resources with needs.

10. Commit all aid providers to promote transparency, development evaluation, and beneficiary feedback at the recipient country level by systematic use of new IT tools and open, web-based provision of information.

APPENDIX FIGURE 1 Flow Chart, Office of the Economic Coordinator

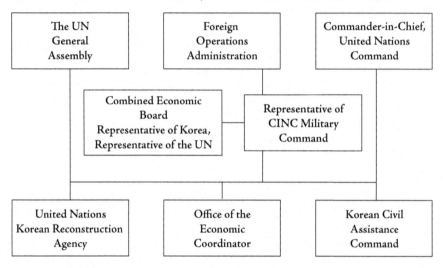

Appendix Table 1-1. Role of Aid in Korea's Development

Period	Purpose and needs	Form and modalities	Sector and composition[a]	Reliance on aid	Major donors[b]
1942–52 Korean War	Short-run relief	Grants (100%), relief goods	Education, land reform, consumer goods	Only foreign savings[c]	U.S.
1953–61 Rhee	Defense, stability, rehabilitation	Grants (98.5%), commodities, technical cooperation	Agriculture, nonproject aid, military aid, consumer and intermediary goods	Heavily dependent on aid[d]	U.S., UN
1962–75 Park	Transition, long-term growth	Concessional loans (70%), technical cooperation, volunteers[e]	Social-overhead capital, import-substituting and export-oriented large industries, project aid, intermediary and capital goods	Diminution of the absolute and relative importance of aid[f]	U.S., Japan
1976–96 Chun, Roh T. W.	Balance between stability and growth	Nonconcessional financing	Sector loans	Removal from the IDA lending list	Japan, Germany, international financial institutions
1997–2000 Kim Y. S.	Financial crisis	IMF bailout packages	Structural adjustment program	Graduation from ODA	IMF, IBRD

Source: OECD statistics; Chung (2007); KDI (1991); Mason and others (1980).

a. Food, beverages, and manufactured items are classified as consumer goods; crude materials, fuels, and chemicals are intermediate goods or raw materials; and machinery and transport equipment are classified as capital goods. The majority (77 percent) of project aid was allocated to public overhead capital reconstruction and modern industrial sectors such as manufacturing, mining, transportation, and communication. Nonproject aid consists of surplus agricultural commodities provided under Public Law 480 and development loans that were used to purchase agricultural commodities.

b. From 1953 to 1961, 83 percent of all assistance and 99 percent of bilateral aid came from the United States. During the period 1962–75, the share of U.S. assistance was reduced to 61 percent, while Japan became the second-largest donor, accounting for 29 percent of total aid. During 1976–90 Japan provided 63 percent of total aid. Significant increases in aid were also recorded by Germany over this period.

c. The average annual per capita aid for 1945–53 was $5.50 (10 percent of per capita income). Total aid over this period was $853 million, averaging $105 million a year.

d. Korea relied heavily on aid for day-to-day needs, defense, and reconstruction. Aid as a share of GDP averaged 14 percent, making up almost 100 percent of foreign savings and 72 percent of imports. More than half of tax revenue (54.1 percent) in 1957 came from a counterpart fund derived from the sales of foreign aid supply.

e. The Peace Corps started to serve in Korea in 1966 to promote social reform, empowerment, and local capacity building.

f. Overall assistance declined over this period, after peaking in 1957 at $383 million. By 1962 it had fallen to $232.3 million. Average annual economic aid during 1962–67 was $155 million, or $3.60 per capita. In the 1970s the Korean government maintained cordial relationships with the IFIs but did not count on them for substantial financing, even during the 1973 oil crisis. Given growth rates of 10 percent, the long delays generally experienced in approving and implementing foreign assistance projects were seen as more of a drag than a help to Korea's development.

REFERENCES

Ainsworth, Martha, Denise Vaillancourt, and Judith Hahn Gaubatz. 2005. *Committing to Results: Improving the Effectiveness of HIV/AIDS Assistance.* Washington: World Bank.

Alesina, Alberto, and David Dollar. 1998. "Who Gives Foreign Aid to Whom and Why?" Working Paper 6612. Cambridge, Mass.: National Bureau of Economic Research (June).

Arndt, Channing, Sam Jones, and Finn Tarp. 2010. "Aid, Growth, and Development: Have We Come Full Circle?" UNU-WIDER Working Paper 96. Helsinki: United Nations University World Institute for Development Economics Research.

CBO (Congressional Budget Office). 1997. "The Role of Foreign Aid in Development: South Korea and the Philippines." September (www.cbo.gov/doc.cfm?index=4306&type=0).

Chandy, Laurence, and Geoffrey Gertz. 2011. "Poverty in Numbers: The Changing State of Global Poverty from 2005 to 2015." Brookings.

Chung, Young-Iob. 2007. *South Korea in the Fast Lane: Economic Development and Capital Formation.* Oxford University Press.

Collier, Paul, and others. 2003. *Breaking the Conflict Trap: Civil War and Development Policy.* Oxford University Press.

Grantmakers. 2009. "Grantmakers for Effective Organizations. Evaluation in Philanthropy." Washington.

Hudson Institute. 2010. *Index of Global Philanthropy and Remittances: 2010.* Santa Barbara, Calif.

InterAction. 2009. "The Other Partner: NGOs and Private Sector Funding for International Development and Relief." Washington.

IPCC. 2007. *Climate Change 2007: Synthesis Report.* (Contribution of Working Groups I, II, and III to the Fourth Assessment Report of the Intergovernmental Panel on Climate Change.)

KDI (Korea Development Institute). 1991. *Forty Years of Korean Finance.* Vol. 4.

KEXIM (Korea Export and Import Bank). 2008. "International ODA Trend."

Lee, Heonjin. 2009. Research Paper P-3, "Economic Aid Policies of the United States for the Republic of Korea 1948-1960." Seoul: Hye An.

Long, Carolyn. 2008. "Foreign Assistance Reform Monitoring Initiative: Final Report." InterAction.

Mason, E. S., and others. 1980. *The Economic and Social Modernization of the Republic of Korea.* Harvard University Press.

McKinsey and Co. 2010. "Learning for Social Impact: What Foundations Can Do." April.

Monitor Institute. 2009. "Investing for Social and Environmental Impact: A Design for Catalyzing an Emerging Industry."

OECD. 2008. *Survey on Monitoring the Paris Declaration: Making Aid More Effective by 2010* (www.oecd.org/dataoecd/55/34/42056862.pdf).

OECD/DAC (Organization of Economic Cooperation and Development, Development Assistance Committee). 2010. "Getting Closer to the Core" (www.oecd.org/dataoecd/32/51/ 45564 447.pdf).

———. 2006. *The Challenge of Capacity Development: Working toward Good Practice.* Paris.

———. Various years. "Aggregate Aid Statistics" (www.oecd.org/dataoecd/50/17/5037 721.htm).

Rennie, Ruth, Sudhindra Sharma, and Pawan Sen. 2009. "Afghanistan in 2009: A Survey of the Afghan People." Asia Foundation (www.unodc.org/documents/afghanistan).

Rogerson, Andrew. 2010. "2010 DAC Report on Multilateral Aid" (www.oecd.org/dataoecd/ 23/17/45828572.pdf).

Severino, Jean-Michel, and Olivier Ray. 2009. "The End of ODA: Death and Rebirth of a Global Public Policy." Working Paper 167. Center for Global Development, March.

Tuan, Melinda. 2008. "Measuring and/or Estimating Social Value Creation: Insights into Eight Integrated Cost Approaches." Seattle: Gates Foundation.

World Bank (Resource Mobilization Department). 2008. "Aid Architecture: An Overview of the Main Trends in Official Development Assistance Flows."

———. Various years. World Development Indicators.

5

Youth Inclusion in the Middle East

RAJ M. DESAI

Youth "bulge," demographic "tsunami," "youthquake" . . . these expressions now seem commonplace when applied to the Middle East. But starting in 2006, while the world was preoccupied with security concerns in that region, the Wolfensohn Center highlighted problems that had been long neglected. Among the development challenges facing the Middle East and North Africa, one of the most critical has been the failure of governments in the region to provide economic opportunity for its young people. In a region where two-thirds of the population is under the age of thirty, the youth unemployment rate has hovered around 30 percent—the highest in the world, roughly double the global average, and approximately four times as high as for older workers.[1] In April 2005 James Wolfensohn was appointed special envoy for Gaza disengagement by the Quartet on the Middle East, a group of major powers and the United Nations promoting the Israeli-Palestinian peace process. During his year as Gaza envoy, at a time when analysts were principally concerned with the Iraq and Arab-Israeli conflicts, terrorism, oil, and democracy-promotion,[2] James Wolfensohn recognized that the majority of Middle Eastern youth were involved in a different fight—for better education, jobs, and affordable housing.

Against this backdrop, the Middle East Youth Initiative was launched in

2006 as a collaborative project between the Wolfensohn Center for Development and the former Dubai School of Government (now the Mohammed bin Rashid School of Government). Soon thereafter, the initiative was joined by Silatech, a nonprofit social enterprise based in Doha. This partnership aimed at promoting a greater understanding of the challenges of economic and social inclusion for youth across the Arab world. Between 2006 and 2012, the initiative helped shine a light on the socioeconomic constraints facing young people in the region and identified ways in which policy and programs could best respond to the needs of youth as they transitioned to adulthood. Moreover, the initiative was able to translate research into action through relationships with policymakers, youth-serving nongovernmental organizations, and the private sector.

With its focus on the consequences of youth exclusion, this initiative of the Wolfensohn Center anticipated many of the catalysts associated with the Arab Spring uprisings that began in late December 2010 and early 2011. General economic and political discontent combined with demographic shifts whereby first-time job seekers were facing long periods of unemployment, stagnating real wages, and higher costs of living—even as the economies in which they lived were expanding—precipitated an enthusiasm for revolution that the region had not seen since the 1950s.

The Middle East Youth Initiative highlighted a central problem that had been plaguing the region for several years. When Middle Eastern economies rebounded in the early 2000s after a decade of slow growth, young people expected to see improvements in their living standards. Instead, education systems continued to fail in preparing young workers for competitive labor markets; youth unemployment levels remained the highest among developing regions; new job seekers faced a deteriorating quality of employment; and too many young people were forced to delay marriage and family formation. The global downturn after 2008 intensified this generational struggle for greater economic inclusion.

The original focus of the initiative was to elaborate a research strategy focused on microeconomic analyses of labor markets and youth behavior. As a result, the initiative developed a series of country-focused analyses built within a common framework that explored the impact of institutions and norms (formal and informal) on youth perceptions and attitudes toward their own livelihoods. These findings emphasized: (i) the influence of labor market regulations and the public sector on youth investments in education, (ii) the role of institutions in education and how they discouraged tangible skill development; and (iii) the effects of youth expectations regarding employment preferences, marriage incentives, and career development.

The initiative also recognized the need for evidence-based assessments of impact. There was little information being collected across the region as to whether skill development, career guidance, job search support, and entrepreneurship promotion programs had a positive impact on the economic lives of young people—or how to expand successful programs and implement them at the scale needed to resolve the economic challenges facing the region's youth. The Middle East–North Africa region was possibly the most under-evaluated in the world with respect to youth-oriented interventions; just as youth-focused programs were increasing in salience, this lacuna undermined the ability of decisionmakers to judge the quality of programs. Consequently—and through its partners such as Silatech—the initiative participated in efforts to expand the range of evidence gathering on youth programs in the region, including methodologically rigorous impact evaluations.[3]

Under the umbrella of the initiative, experts in various fields—labor and public economics, sociology, political science, and public policy—began to produce papers on the problems of youth-to-adult transitions, unemployment and under-employment, and problems of self-employment in the region.[4] Several of these papers were compiled into the anthology *Generation in Waiting*, examining the problem of youth employability in the region and documenting the economic cost to Arab economies in stark terms (the book's introduction is reprinted here).[5] In the pages of the *New York Times*, columnist Thomas Friedman said of this book:

> It contends that the great game that is unfolding in the Arab world today is not related to political Islam but is a "generational game" in which more than 100 million young Arabs are pressing against stifling economic and political structures that have stripped all their freedoms and given them in return one of the poorest education systems in the world, highest unemployment rates and biggest income gaps.[6]

After the Middle East Youth Initiative began disseminating its research, moreover, the international development community, research institutes, and nongovernmental organizations all showed a marked shift toward efforts to support entrepreneurship and greater economic opportunity for Arab youth. Some, such as the RAND Corporation, had developed similar initiatives in parallel.[7] Others that launched their own Middle East youth initiatives included the Open Society Foundation (in 2011),[8] Mercy Corps (in 2011),[9] the Center for Mediterranean Integration (in 2013),[10] and the Clinton Global Initiative (in 2011).[11] In addition, several governments in the region also expanded their range of programs supporting youth entrepreneurship, job placement, and other active labor market programs.[12] And in his landmark Cairo speech calling for "a new beginning" in relations between the United States and the Muslim world, President Barack Obama argued that "education and innovation will be the currency of the 21st century," and that no development strategy could "be sustained while young people are out of work."[13]

Policy analyses produced by the initiative also had an impact on dialogues regarding regulatory and educational reforms in some countries. Several analyses identified the strong predilection among youth for public sector jobs—above private and nonprofit sector jobs, or self-employment. For example, a policy brief on the subject of Syrian youth—also reprinted in this volume—noted that despite the Syrian government's effort to shift away from government interventions toward private sector solutions, incentives in the public sector, including higher wages, generous benefits, pension coverage, and job security, merely reinforced preferences for public sector employment.[14] Similar findings were substantiated in Egypt, Yemen, West Bank/Gaza, and Morocco. Other briefs focused on skill shortages and the poor job prospects of university graduates. In 2010 Syrian foundations, along with NGOs and international organizations (including the Middle East Youth Initiative), held a forum on prioritizing vocational training in the twenty-first century.[15] Tax and regulatory reforms aimed at incentivizing private sector expansion were implemented in Egypt.[16]

The Middle East Youth Initiative also pointed to the important role that social entrepreneurship could play in capitalizing on the youth "bulge" by spreading a better sense of social commitment, by easing constraints on small businesses, and by providing opportunities for the region's expanding circle of philanthropists. A flagship report recommended the development of institutional alliances to boost economic opportunities for youth and to integrate the Middle East into a rapidly changing global economy.[17] In her closing remarks at the U.S. Presidential Summit on Entrepreneurship in April 2010, Secretary of State Hillary Clinton, holding a copy of the report, opened her speech by remarking "This [report] is hot off the presses produced by the Wolfensohn Center for Development at the Brookings Institution . . . this is an issue whose time has come."[18] In subsequent years, foundations in Qatar, the United Arab Emirates, and Bahrain launched initiatives aimed at supporting social entrepreneurs.[19]

In many ways, findings from the work of the Wolfensohn Center also presaged the role of the political economy in the conflicts that emerged out of the turmoil of the Arab Spring—in Libya, Yemen, and especially in Syria. In Syria, for example, as in other Arab economies that were not dependent on oil exports, the private sector had become so coopted by the ruling regime that it could not come close to generating the number of jobs needed to absorb new labor market entrants. Since the civil war began in Syria, the patronage networks that characterized the Assad regime have persisted into a wartime economy, with most Syrian businessmen remaining entrenched in their networks of privilege.[20]

The work of the initiative ultimately influenced some other notable initiatives and efforts. By the time the Arab Spring was under way, the Middle East Youth Initiative was being absorbed into the Arab Economies Initiative within Brookings's Global Economy and Development program. In 2012 the Arab Economies Initiative published a book, *After the Spring*, that was substantively influenced by the Wolfensohn Center's activities and research, especially in its focus on the economic imperatives of addressing demographic challenges in Arab economies. In 2016, moreover, a new volume on youth in the Middle East, *Young Generation Awakening* (analyses of youth on the eve of the Arab Spring), promoted the thesis—now much less controversial following the work of the Middle East Youth Initiative—that socioeconomic conditions (as opposed to political repression, religious extremism, and violence) were central to the development of the Arab Spring events.[21] Finally, published early in 2017, a special issue of the journal *The Muslim World*—with articles contributed by several participants in the Middle East Youth Initiative—offered a more recent survey of the state of youth in the Arab World, identifying the areas of unfinished business, and in some sense, a continuation of the agenda heavily influenced by the Wolfensohn Center.

The marginalization of Arab youth is now widely seen as a critical source of the appeal of extremism and one of the primary drivers of recruitment of youth by terrorist groups in the Middle East and North Africa, thanks, in no small part, to the work of the Wolfensohn Center. Moreover, the pathologies associated with long-term youth exclusion in the Middle East have recently been felt in aging Western nations, where youth who face slower starts in the job market, declining real wages, and the prospect of lower lifetime earnings have suffered from social isolation, despair, health problems, and, in the United States, higher mortality.[22]

Indeed, the claim that long-term prosperity and stability hinges on the opportunities afforded to youth as they make transitions from school to work and from youth to adulthood are as relevant today as they were a decade ago. Ultimately it will be on the back of the generation of young people that the Middle East and North Africa —and other regions—will build a future middle class that acts as a catalyst for more open and democratic societies.

Generation in Waiting

The Unfulfilled Promise of Young People in the Middle East

NAVTEJ DHILLON *and* **TARIK YOUSEF**

*Navtej Dhillon is the director of the Middle East
Youth Initiative and a fellow at the Wolfensohn Center
for Development at the Brookings Institution.*

*Tarik Yousef is dean of the Dubai School of Government
and a nonresident senior fellow at the Wolfensohn Center
for Development at the Brookings Institution.*

The Middle East has been characterized as being in the grip of two great games.[1] In the first game, the interests of Middle Eastern nations and western powers intersect to shape geopolitics. The second game—less visible in our daily headlines—involves people and governments trying to advance economic development. But today, a third game, even less well understood, is being played out in the Middle East. This is the *generational game* in which the largest youth cohort in the Middle East's modern history is striving for prosperity and thereby shaping politics.

In recent years, the Middle East has come to be defined by a series of dichotomies: democracy versus authoritarianism; Islam versus secularism; and economically successful versus stagnant. No matter what the fault lines, they all

Editors' Note: This is the introductory chapter from the book *Generation in Waiting: The Unfulfilled Promise of Young People in the Middle East,* edited by Navtej Dhillon and Tarik Yousef, published by Brookings Institution Press in 2009.

share a generational dimension. It is the young who are pressing against existing economic, political, and religious institutions and norms and forging new ones. This generational game is unfolding in a competitive global economy where young people in the Middle East seek the affluence and openness enjoyed by their peers in other parts of the world.

Over the past two decades, the demographic transition in the region has resulted in a young working-age population that is now the most important resource for Middle Eastern economies. Generally, a large working-age population, and proportionally fewer dependent children and retirees, can free up resources and increase savings, creating better economic and social outcomes. In this regard, there has been tremendous progress: the high mortality and illiteracy rates of past generations have given way to a generation that is healthier and more educated. There have been large gains in more equitable distribution of education between women and men.

However, development in the Middle East is proving uneven, bypassing the majority of young people. Previous generations benefited from free education, public sector job guarantees, and strong state support in the form of subsidies and entitlements. But for those born in the 1980s and later, these institutions, which once ensured intergenerational equity and social justice, are no longer working. The severity of demographic pressures has strained public sector employment and subsidized education systems. Even if these institutions could accommodate the youth bulge, they are not well suited in a world where innovation and entrepreneurship are the drivers of economic growth. As a result, young people in the Middle East are falling further behind their peers in other parts of the world, such as East Asia.

Today in the Middle East, education systems are failing to provide relevant skills, and labor market prospects for young workers are deteriorating. Young women are gaining more education but face widespread exclusion from the labor market. Delayed marriage is becoming a common phenomenon in some countries as young people face obstacles to family formation posed by unemployment, high costs of marriage, and lack of access to affordable housing. Together, these deficits are weakening economic mobility for current and future generations.

With this book, it is our objective to promote a better understanding of the material struggles of young people, which are bound up in larger questions about the Middle East's economic development and politics. This volume brings together perspectives from eight countries to analyze how young people are transitioning to adulthood and to elucidate how institutions are shaping these transitions. Our hope is that this volume will be viewed not within the narrow context of demography or security but rather within a larger agenda of inclusive development in the Middle East. The ultimate goal is to convince policymakers that reforms that tackle the disadvantages of younger age groups can potentially reduce the inequities that exist across income and gender.

CHOOSING A FRAMEWORK TO STUDY YOUNG LIVES

A number of theoretical frameworks have been used to analyze the lives of young people in different countries and regions. The most common are the neo-classical economic framework of human capital formation and the sociodemographic framework of life course.[2] The former stresses the importance of education and skills of young workers and their contribution to productivity and growth. The latter considers individual transitions and trajectories and their relationship to institutions and historical periods.[3] In addition, the concept of *social exclusion* has been adopted to understand the factors that prevent certain groups from fully participating in the normatively prescribed activities of the society in which they live.[4]

More recently, international organizations have put forth policy frameworks. The World Bank's *World Development Report* of 2007 highlights the opportunities for accelerated economic growth and poverty reduction that can occur when policies and institutions that influence the human capital development of youth are strengthened.[5] A report by the National Research Council in the United States focuses on the extent to which rapidly changing global forces affect youth transitions in developing countries, specifically the transitions to five key adult roles: adult worker, citizen and community participant, spouse, parent, and household head.[6]

In this volume, we build on these frameworks, taking the most relevant aspects of each and applying them to the Middle East. Three major features of our framework are as follows. First, we depart from the traditional approach of studying facets of young people's lives, such as education or employment, separately. Instead, we assess three major interdependent transitions: education, employment, and family formation. Here we pay special attention to marriage where possible, given the availability of data, because social norms in the Middle East make the transition to family formation critical to full social inclusion.

Second, we recognize that individual transitions and trajectories are part of a life course, which is often shaped by the history, economy, politics, and culture of Middle Eastern countries. Events, time, and geography, as well as the agency of individuals, modify and influence transitions. This realization leads us to recognize how life courses have varied across historical periods and national contexts.

Finally, throughout this volume, we stress the importance of institutions and the incentives they generate in influencing young people's transitions. We define institutions as rules and regulations that govern the education system; markets for labor, credit, and housing; and nonmarket institutions such as social norms.

Through this framework, it is our hope that policymakers and future researchers will see the lives of young people in a more interconnected way and recognize that young lives are institutionally patterned. In using this framework, this book marshals the best available data and evidence to elucidate the lives of young people. While it contributes to a better understanding, it also exposes the limitations of our knowledge given the lack of high-quality and available data in the Middle East.

GENERATION IN WAITING: STRUCTURE OF THE VOLUME

This volume contributes to the growing interest in young people as it relates to development policy and practice. The chapters that follow attempt to provide a comprehensive assessment of the three major transitions of young people in eight Middle East countries.

In chapter one, Navtej Dhillon, Paul Dyer, and Tarik Yousef place the transitions of young people in a larger historical context, arguing that the challenges facing young people today in the Middle East did not exist a generation ago. They argue that previous generations faced a *traditional life course*, prevalent in mostly rural Middle Eastern societies, where the transition to adulthood was mediated by family and the community. An expanded role of state institutions between the 1950s and the 1980s paved the way for the *welfare life course*, where governments provided education, employment, and protection for citizens. Young people born since the beginning of the 1980s have faced a weakening welfare life course while at the same time a new life course has not yet fully emerged.

The authors provide a synthesis of how young people's transitions have become more complex and uncertain. While high demographic pressures and volatile economic growth have undermined the prospects of young people, Dhillon, Dyer, and Yousef emphasize the central role that existing institutions have also played in hindering economic development for the young.

In chapter two, Djavad Salehi-Isfahani and Daniel Egel posit that the discontent of young Iranians is receiving much attention from outsiders but that the understanding of the economic and social environment shaping their lives is limited. They present a detailed picture of Iran's fertility boom and bust from the 1970s to the 1980s that has paved the way for a youth bulge. In 1995 Iran had 13 million residents aged 15 to 29; this population is set to peak in 2010 at 20 million. Iran's reduction in fertility now presents the country with a "demographic gift" that can drive economic growth.

A foundation for human capital development is already in place in Iran. Salehi-Isfahani and Egel show that average years of schooling have doubled in a generation. However, young Iranians confront a highly competitive and exclusionary education system, where students compete to win the "university lottery." Once out of school, young Iranians confront unemployment and long waiting times for a first job. Transitions to employment are hampered by a rigid labor market that is ill prepared to absorb a labor force expanding by 3 to 4 percent a year. Faced with bleak employment prospects and high costs of marriage, young Iranians are forced to delay marriage and remain dependent on their families.

Salehi-Isfahani and Egel argue that the postrevolution "social contract" must be reformed and that the most severe necessity for this reform emanates from the large youth population and its continued exclusion. Some steps in this direction have been taken: the size of public sector employment has declined; public sector payroll freezes have been implemented; and recent changes in the 1990 labor law exempted small and medium-size firms from restrictions on hiring and firing. But there is still a way to go before Iran's education, labor, and marriage institutions can change to take advantage of the country's demographic gift.

In chapter three, Ragui Assaad and Ghada Barsoum show that the transitions of young Egyptians are being shaped by the recent changes in Egypt's economic and social environment. Starting in 2004, an economic revival led to a drop in unemployment rates. However, poverty levels remain unchanged because of the rapid growth of low productivity and nonwage employment. Young workers have been most affected by these changes, enduring the lowest earnings and the slowest increase in real earnings.

Assaad and Barsoum identify access and quality as two major challenges facing the education system. Young girls in Upper Egypt and youth from low socioeconomic backgrounds are highly vulnerable to early school dropout and nonenrollment. They identify the Egyptian labor market as grappling with three trends: it is increasingly young, has more females entering the labor market, and is made up of highly educated job seekers. As the youth bulge peaks, the number of new entrants in the labor market increased from 400,000 per year in the late 1970s to around 850,000 per year in the early 2000s. Assaad and Barsoum conclude by assessing the effectiveness of recent education and labor market reforms.

In chapter four, Edward Sayre and Samia Al-Botmeh turn our attention to the acute rupture between demographics and development in the West Bank and Gaza: a rapidly growing youth population with diminishing economic prospects. Sayre and Al-Botmeh posit that in the past Palestinian workers had two main sources of employment. Israel once provided a third of all Palestinian jobs, but in recent years the Israeli labor market has been closed to Palestinian workers. In addition, Palestinians once migrated to the Gulf States for work, but those jobs are now dominated by South Asian migrant workers. As a result, young Palestinians face a protracted transition to employment. Highly educated Palestinians face diminishing prospects: the unemployment rate for 20- to 24-year-old university-educated men stands at 36 percent in the West Bank and 64 percent in Gaza.

Sayre and Al-Botmeh conclude that the public sector and international aid cannot create sufficient opportunities to absorb the burgeoning youth population. Fiscal strains will eventually force the Palestinian Authority to curb the expansion of its already large public sector, and no amount of aid can single-handedly stimulate growth and development. The authors underline the importance of lifting restrictions on the Palestinian economy and allowing freer movement of goods and labor into and out of the Palestinian Territories. In the absence of these preconditions being met and maintained, young Palestinians will be confined to a grim future.

In chapter five, Jad Chaaban focuses on Lebanon's post–civil war generation—a million strong between the ages of 15 and 29. He argues that Lebanon takes pride in its human capital, which is the only comparative advantage it has over its resource-rich neighbors. After the end of the civil war in 1990, Lebanon embarked on ambitious reconstruction efforts and record spending on education and health. However, these investments have not resulted in improved outcomes for the young. Educational inequities are large, with youth in poorer regions having lower enrollment rates than those in the cities; unemployment for young people is higher compared with adults; and emigration rates are alarming, with one-third of youth reporting a desire to emigrate.

Chaaban contends that political instability and the proliferation of conflicts, including the 2006 Hezbollah-Israel war, have created an unpredictable environment for young Lebanese. Persistent expectations of future conflict breeds apathy among the young, who see little point in setting long-term goals. Lack of opportunities has resulted in high levels of migration, perpetuating the vicious cycle of underdevelopment by draining the country of its human capital. In this context, Chaaban makes several recommendations for promoting greater economic and political inclusion of youth, such as improving access to education for students from poorer regions and encouraging public-private partnerships that employ young people.

In chapter six, Taher Kanaan and May Hanania provide a compelling analysis of the state of young people in Jordan. Kanaan and Hanania remind us that Jordan's recent history is characterized by sudden changes in territory, population, and economic shocks emanating from conflict in neighboring countries such as Iraq. They illustrate how the 1991 Gulf War, the second Palestinian intifada of 2000, and the U.S. invasion of Iraq in 2003 have led to an influx of migrants into Jordan. This coupled with an average population growth rate of around 2.7 percent among Jordanians has endowed the country with a major asset—its human capital. To tap into this asset, Jordan must create over 50,000 new jobs every year just to maintain current unemployment levels.

However, Kanaan and Hanania point out that Jordan is far from meeting this challenge. The recent period of positive GDP growth has not only failed to create enough jobs, but the jobs created have not been of sufficient quality to meet the expectations of an increasingly educated labor force. The majority of new jobs have been in the construction sector, and these have largely been taken by foreign workers. Women remain marginalized, experiencing high levels of unemployment. Bleak employment prospects are having an impact on prospects for family formation: the median age of marriage is increasing for both men and women, especially since access to independent housing has become more difficult during the recent real estate boom.

Kanaan and Hanania provide extensive analysis of recent reforms in the education and employment sectors. They argue that despite these reforms, Jordan's political, social, and economic institutions still must evolve considerably to meet the needs of its large youth population. An education system that continues to prepare youth for public sector employment must be fundamentally changed. Furthermore, to cope with high labor market pressures, the economy must invent new engines of job creation given that the public sector and migration are insufficient.

In chapter seven, Brahim Boudarbat and Aziz Ajbilou paint a portrait of a young generation in Morocco coming of age as their country grapples with three major challenges. First, the arrival of the youth bulge coincides with poor macroeconomic performance and sluggish economic growth, which has limited the opportunities for young citizens. Second, Morocco has undergone rapid urbanization during the last four decades, putting pressure on urban labor markets. Finally, persistent poverty continues to affect the young, especially in rural areas.

Through better education and access to decent employment, many young Moroccan men and women in this generation are more empowered to break the trap of poverty and social exclusion. Access to education has significantly improved, and the gender gap in primary education has narrowed. Even unemployment has been slashed in the past few years. But these improvements also mask new disparities. According to Boudarbat and Ajbilou, repetition rates in primary education are among the worst in the Middle East. Despite more investments in secondary education, Morocco's secondary enrollment rates remain low compared with countries with similar income levels. Transitions to work are defined by high unemployment and long durations of unemployment, especially among secondary and higher education graduates.

Boudarbat and Ajbilou argue that youth unemployment can no longer be seen as a business cycle phenomenon. While the spike in unemployment among educated youth results from the contraction of the public sector in the 1980s, it has mutated into a structural problem and a source of growing social tensions. The Moroccan government has responded with a proliferation of initiatives, such as the reform of the Moroccan labor code, to promote investment and the creation of special development zones. Still, according to Boudarbat and Ajbilou, the government's responses have been piecemeal and seldom evaluated to measure impact.

In chapter eight, Nader Kabbani and Noura Kamel focus on Syria's transition from a public sector–led economy toward a "social market" economy as the country becomes a net oil importer in the near future. Young people and their growing education, employment, and housing needs are an important impetus for these economic reforms. But because they prefer public sector jobs, they are also the source of resistance.

The challenge for Syria, argue Kabbani and Kamel, will be to build and sustain support for market reforms among members of the young generation who will be the benefactors of this change. What is first needed, the authors say, is reform in the education system. The mismatch between the skills of job seekers and the needs of employers is reflected in exceptionally low returns to education. In Syria, an additional year of schooling is associated with a mere 2 percent increase in wages compared with an average 10 to 15 percent increase globally. As part of the economic reforms, labor market outcomes for young workers will need to improve. Kabbani and Kamel show that youth unemployment has declined from 26 percent in 2002 to around 19 percent recently. Although many employed youth have found jobs in the private sector, the lure of public sector employment remains strong, especially among young women.

These employment preferences have an economic and social rationale: young women earn higher wages in the public sector; for men public sector jobs provide the stability and prestige necessary for marriage and family formation. While the Syrian government has reduced public sector employment and allowed private sector competition in many sectors, a number of recent initiatives may reinforce the appeal of government jobs. Public sector wages have increased repeatedly since 2000. Unless retrenchment policies accompany efforts to better align public sector wages and benefits with a thriving private sector, queuing for government jobs will continue and support for economic reforms will weaken.

In chapter nine, Ragui Assaad, Ghada Barsoum, Emily Cupito, and Daniel Egel concentrate on Yemen—the poorest country in the Middle East and one that faces deficits in both human development and natural resources. Given the continuing high fertility rate of over six children per woman of childbearing age, Yemen's population is one of the youngest in the Middle East: over 75 percent of the population is under the age of 25. The authors argue that with a dwindling supply of natural resources, low levels of human development, and high levels of poverty, Yemen risks losing a generation to poverty.

The authors show that Yemen has some of the poorest education indicators in the world with low enrollment and widespread illiteracy. Poor educational attainment, low retention, and poor standards in education quality are pervasive throughout the country, but they have a disproportionate effect on young women in rural areas. The Yemeni labor market is defined by limited employment opportunities in the formal sector. Youth employment is primarily confined to informal employment, which offers limited job security and few opportunities for career advancement. A high incidence of migration to urban areas within Yemen and internationally reflects the extent to which youth and families must travel in search of gainful employment.

In response to these challenges, the Yemeni government has undertaken a series of reforms designed to increase school enrollment and promote job creation in the private sector. Adoption of the National Children and Youth Strategy in 2006 reflects the government's commitment to improving the status of youth in Yemen. However, these efforts are constrained by a severe shortage of resources and limited institutional and administrative capacity. To begin to redress these shortcomings, the authors call on the international community, both in the West and among Yemen's richer neighbors, to increase aid and assistance to Yemen.

In the concluding chapter, Navtej Dhillon and Djavad Salehi-Isfahani focus on how Middle Eastern countries are responding to the problems of their young citizens and draw attention to major gaps in the current approach. They argue that more investments in schools, training programs, and subsidies targeting young people, while well-intentioned, do not address the underlying causes of social exclusion. They interpret the difficulties faced by young people as a consequence of failures in key market and nonmarket institutions. Transitions of young people are influenced by several interconnected markets such as education, labor, credit, housing, and marriage. For a new life course to emerge for Middle Eastern youth, institutions and key markets must be reformed.

Dhillon and Salehi-Isfahani outline ten institutional features of Middle

Eastern economies and societies that hold the potential for furthering prosperity and equity for the young generation. They argue that reforms can happen and that demographic pressures are already serving as a major impetus. They also propose principles for guiding future policies and programs. In this sense, the book ends with a meditation on not only the plights of young people, but also on ways in which public policy can improve their lives.

Why Young Syrians Prefer Public Sector Jobs

NADER KABBANI

*Nader Kabbani is the director of research at the Syria
Trust for Development, a non-profit governmental
organization headquartered in Damascus, Syria.*

After pursuing a public sector–led development model for five decades, Syria is moving towards establishing a social market economy. The Syrian government is introducing elements of a new social contract that relies less on government intervention and more on private sector solutions. The government has removed barriers to private sector entry for most industries, as well as schools, universities and banks, and it is reforming formal institutions, including labor laws, the public education system, and social protection programs. Economic reforms have revived the private sector and created opportunities for young people with the knowledge, skills, and motivation needed to better define their careers.

During this transition period, however, high youth unemployment rates have remained a major policy concern, driven in part by the youth bulge moving through the population. In 2007 the unemployment rate among young people in Syria was 19%—lower than estimates for the Middle East and North Africa

Editors' Note: This policy brief was originally published by the Middle East Youth Initiative in 2009. The material presented in this brief draws on work with Noura Kamel of the American University of Beirut and Leen Al-Habash of the Syria Trust for Development. Thanks are due to Navtej Dhillon, Djavad Salehi Isfahani, and others with the Middle East Youth Initiative for their valuable comments and suggestions.

(MENA) region (22% in 2005), but higher than the world average of 12% (International Labor Organization 2008). Young people in Syria represented 57% of the unemployed population, and first-time job seekers represented 78%. This indicates that, as in other MENA countries, unemployment in Syria is primarily a labor market insertion problem.

As part of its reform efforts, the government has considered reducing the number of public sector workers, but has yet to adopt any major policies in this regard. Economic incentives and institutions continue to induce young Syrians and their families to focus on securing government jobs. In terms of incentives, government jobs offer greater stability and benefit packages than jobs in the private sector. This is especially the case for young women, for whom the public sector provides more flexible working hours and better maternity leave policies. In terms of institutions, public schools focus on preparing young people for national exams, which lead to credentials that increase the odds of obtaining a public sector job, rather than developing key skills demanded by the private sector. After school, young people often find themselves unprepared for the realities of the labor market and typically rely on informal family connections in securing their first private sector jobs or queue up for government jobs (Kabbani and Kamel 2007).

From a public policy perspective, individuals' strategy of focusing on securing a public sector job does not correspond well with the government's attempts to transition to a social market economy or to better integrate the country into the world economy. A young adaptive workforce that is less focused on obtaining public sector jobs would be better able to take advantage of the demographic "window of opportunity" that could lead to higher economic growth rates. It would also lessen the burden of government wage bills and allow for a greater realization of the benefits of government reform efforts.

This brief examines how public sector employment policies affect the transition from school to work among young people in Syria, basing its findings on official data from Syrian Central Bureau of Statistics' labor force and household budget surveys.

YOUNG PEOPLE'S INTEREST IN PUBLIC SECTOR JOBS

Evidence suggests that young Syrians prefer public sector to private sector jobs. Findings from the 2003 Unemployment Survey indicate that over 80% of unemployed 15–29-year-olds were interested in public sector jobs and 60% sought jobs exclusively in the public sector. Among unemployed young women, 90% wanted public sector work and 71% were looking exclusively in the public sector (Huitfeldt and Kabbani 2007). Kabbani and Al-Habash (2008) confirm that preference for public sector jobs is higher among unemployed young women and find that it increases with age and educational attainment. They find that young men are motivated in their job search by family need and that social norms influence the employment choices of young women. The difference between predicted public and private sector wages for unemployed youth is also associated with public sector job preference, especially among women, meaning that job preference is associated with relative expected pay between the sectors.

The expressed preference of young people for public sector jobs must be compared alongside their actual behavior. One way to assess such preferences is to examine the association between higher educational attainment and public sector employment. Young people seek higher levels of educational attainment to increase their chances of securing a stable job with good wages and benefits. Indeed, there is a strong positive correlation between educational attainment and public sector work (figure 1). Among men, the share of workers with public sector jobs increases steadily from 5% among those with less than primary school education to peak at 61% among graduates of intermediate institutes (post-secondary vocational schools) and 59% among university graduates. Among women, the share of workers with public sector jobs increases from 2% among those with less than a primary education to reach 90% among intermediate institute graduates, before dropping to 68% among university graduates.

Preferences for public sector work on the supply side correspond with little change over time in regard to the overall share of workers in the public sector, which hovered around 25–28% between 2001 and 2007. This share is in line with a regional average of 25%, but is higher than a world average of 11% (Abrahart et al 2002). The share of employed young men working in the public sector held steady at just over 13% between 2001 and 2006, with a slight increase in 2007. Among young women, the trend was strongly upwards. The share of em-

FIGURE 1 Share of Employment in Public Sector
by Level of Education (Ages 15–29)

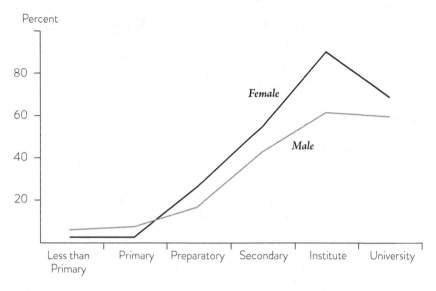

Source: Author's calculations.

ployed young women working in the public sector more than doubled over six years, from 15% in 2001 to 31% in 2007.

The trend among young women appears to have been driven by increases in their educational attainment (making more women eligible for public sector employment) as well as declines in their labor force participation rates during this period (driven partly by increased school attachment). The share of employed young women who completed post- secondary education nearly doubled from 24% in 2001 to 47% in 2007 (figure 2). This group can be divided into two sub-groups. The share of employed young women with post-secondary vocational (intermediate institute) credentials increased from 17% in 2001 to 30% in 2007 and the share of employed young women with university degrees doubled from 7.9% of the workforce in 2001 to 17% in 2007. As a result, by 2007, nearly half of all employed young women had post-secondary educational credentials.

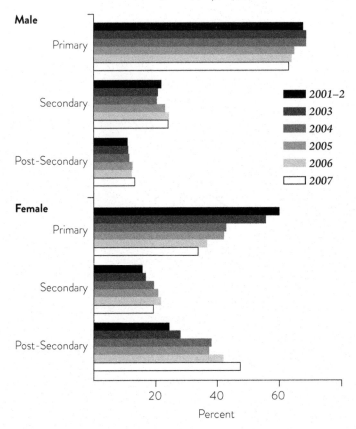

FIGURE 2   The Share of Employed Youth Working
in the Public Sector by Education

Source: Author's calculations.

Small gains in educational attainment were also recorded for young men. The share of employed young men who had completed post-secondary schooling increased from 11% in 2001 to 13% in 2007. However, for young men, increases in educational attainment translated only modestly into increases in public sector employment, keeping in mind that around 95% of young men in Syria are either in the labor force or in school, whereas only around 50% of young women are active in the labor force or in school.

PUBLIC SECTOR WAGES AND BENEFITS: A SIMPLE STORY

The previous section provided evidence that young Syrians prefer public sector jobs to private sector jobs. This section examines some of the incentives and trends behind this observation. We focus primarily on wages and pension benefits.

Public vs. Private Sector Wages

It is well-established that, like other countries in the MENA region, public sector benefits in Syria are higher than those in the private sector. The evidence on wages is less clear. In fact, in 2007 average monthly salaries in the Syrian public sector were 22% higher than salaries in the private sector. Comparing monthly salaries masks differences in educational attainment, hours worked, and levels of experience among workers across sectors. We limit these confounding factors by examining average hourly wages across levels of educational attainment for men and women between 20 and 29 years of age.

In 2007 hourly wages among young men in the private sector were higher than hourly wages in the public sector for those with low levels of educational attainment and those with university degrees (table 1). Hourly wages in the public sector were higher among intermediate institute (post-secondary vocational school) graduates. Young men with preparatory or secondary credentials had similar wages in both sectors.

Our finding of high relative public sector wages among intermediate institute completers is consistent with evidence from other studies. Huitfeldt and Kabbani (2007) find that the marginal rates of returns to education for men with an intermediate institute degree were virtually zero in the private sector, suggesting that the technical skills acquired there were of little use in the private sector. As noted above, intermediate institute graduates were the most likely group to work in the public sector among both men and women.

In 2007 average hourly wages among young women in the public sector were higher than in the private sector for all levels of educational attainment.* It is

---

*The sample size for young women with primary education or less working in the public sector was too small to include a point estimate. However, in line with other education levels, the estimate we obtained was higher than that for the private sector and increased to a greater degree between 2001 and 2007.

TABLE 1 Nominal Hourly Wage Rates and Trends by Sector (Ages 20–29)

	2006/2007				% Change (2001/02–2006/07)			
	Male		Female		Male		Female	
Educational Level	Pub.	Pvt.	Pub.	Pvt.	Pub.	Pvt	Pub.	Pvt
Primary or less	26.3	43.3	..	27.8	16%	51%	..	25%
Preparatory	40.6	41.6	42.7	25.2	65%	47%	64%	-1%
Secondary	43.5	43.4	46.9	34.7	70%	26%	62%	38%
Intermediate institute	54.3	45.8	65.0	37.2	70%	54%	79%	10%
University +	61.9	66.8	85.0	63.6	59%	56%	86%	76%
Total	42.1	43.5	65.0	34.2	59%	50%	91%	39%

Source: Central Bureau of Statistics; authors' calculations for change between 2001 and 2007.

interesting to note that hourly wages for young women were substantially lower than those for young men in the private sector, but significantly higher than young men's wages in the public sector. The latter finding is driven by lower average of hours of work for women in the public sector compared to men.

A key element in transitioning from a state-led to a social market economy is increasing the attractiveness of private sector jobs relative to government jobs, especially in terms of wages and benefits. Yet, despite a stated interest in public employment retrenchment policies, the Syrian government has increased public sector wages substantially since 2000. Between 2001 and 2007, the average nominal hourly wage of a public sector worker between 20 and 29 years of age increased by 70%, whereas the average hourly wage of a private sector worker increased by only 50%.

These wage differences may mask changes in the composition of the workforce. Thus, we break the analysis down by educational attainment, still focusing on 20–29 year olds. Between 2001 and 2007, public sector wages among young men increased more than private sector wages for all education levels with the exception of those with primary schooling or below. Among young women, public sector wages increased more than private sector wages for all education levels, making the differences between the hourly wages in the public and private sectors even more pronounced.

Our finding that public sector wages increased faster than private sector wages makes sense in light of announced government increases (Kabbani and Al- Habash 2008). In 2003, almost half the public spending increase came from an increase in the wage bill. In 2004, the government increased wages by 20% for 2 million workers and retirees at an estimated cost of 2.3% of GDP. In early 2008, the government increased public sector wages by 25% and required the private sector to raise wages by 15%, to counter rising food and energy prices (2008 wage increases are not reflected in table 1).* Despite evidence presented in table 1, wage increases have had progressive elements; the public sector minimum wage more than doubled over this period, from 2,115 Syrian pounds ($42) per month in 2001 to 4,805 Syrian pounds ($96) per month in 2006.

Thus, in terms of hourly wages, public sector jobs, which were already more attractive than private sector jobs for most groups, have become even more attractive over time. These findings do not bode well for getting young people to focus less on obtaining a "good" public sector job and more on looking for work in the private sector.

Pension Coverage

In addition to wages, workers care about benefits, work conditions, job security, and other factors. Job security is higher in the public sector, where it is virtually impossible to dismiss a worker. However, rigid labor laws and a cultural norm against laying off workers contribute to some degree of job security in the private sector. Work conditions are widely believed to be better in the public sector, especially for young women who worry about possible discrimination in the private sector. Benefits are also known to be higher in the public sector. Since Syria's education and health systems provide universal education and medical coverage, the main benefit to examine is pensions.†

Using data from the 2006–2007 Household Income and Expenditure Survey, we find that 89% of young public sector employees between the ages of

---

*Most wage increases were facilitated by higher oil revenues. This introduced elements of irreversibility in the budget accounts as oil proceeds are unlikely to remain high while higher wages will not easily be reversed (Kabbani and Tzannatos 2006).

†Universal education and medical benefits make public sector reforms that much easier and less costly for the government to consider. Also, there is one factor that we were not able to examine with available data: job advancement and wage progression opportunities. This aspect could well favor private sector workers, as is the case among university graduates in Morocco (Boudarbat 2008).

20 and 29 indicated that they were registered with the government's pension system. (Full-time government employees are covered, but workers on temporary contracts are often not.) By contrast, only 8.6% of young private sector workers indicated that they were registered in the pension system (figure 3). Pension coverage among young private sector wage workers increases with level of educational attainment, but never surpasses 50%.

This finding makes sense: Syria has one of the highest pension contribution rates in the region (15% of workers' salaries paid by the employer and 10% paid

FIGURE 3 Share of Young Wage Workers Covered
by Pension System (Ages 20–29)

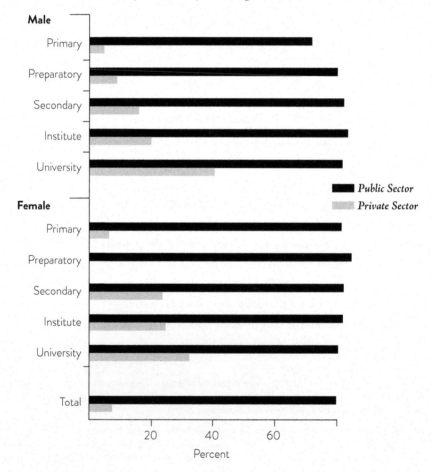

Source: Author's calculations.

by the employee), which creates an incentive for private sector employers to not register their workers. As a result, Syria also has one of the lowest coverage rates in the region, reaching less than 30% all working-age workers (wage and non-wage).*

In Syria, pension benefits equal 75% of the average salary for the last two years of work. Eligibility for benefits begins after 15 years of service, at age 55 for women and 60 for men. Early retirement eligibility starts 5 years earlier for those with 20 years of service or at any age after 25 years of service. We estimate the present value of wages plus pension benefits for public and private sector workers, assuming that wages increase at 5% per year for all workers, a discount rate of 5%, that retirement starts at age 55 for women and 60 for men, that average life expectancy is 75 years, and that those covered by the system in their 20s will continue to be covered and those not covered will continue not to be covered. We hold constant differences in effort by benchmarking hours worked at 40 hours per week.

Under these assumptions, our analysis suggests that lifetime earnings for young public sector workers exceed those for private sector workers among all groups except men with a primary education or below. The differences were greatest for young women across all education levels (figure 4). These findings help explain the attraction of public sector work for young job seekers, especially young women.

CONCLUSIONS AND RECOMMENDATIONS

In this brief, we argue that economic incentives and institutions (both formal and informal) have encouraged young Syrians to prefer public sector jobs over private sector jobs. Job preferences among young job seekers strongly favor the public sector. Also, educational attainment is highly correlated with employment in the public sector. The findings are consistent with the idea that higher educational attainment is one way of accessing "good" public sector jobs.

Despite stated government interest in public sector retrenchment policies,

*The 10% employee contribution covers 7% for the regular pension and 3% for occupational hazards. A second system provides casual workers with insurance against disability and death due to occupational hazards. This system is financed by a voluntary 5% of salaries paid by workers. We do not include it here.

FIGURE 4 Present Value of Lifetime Earnings
with Pension Benefits (Ages 20–29)

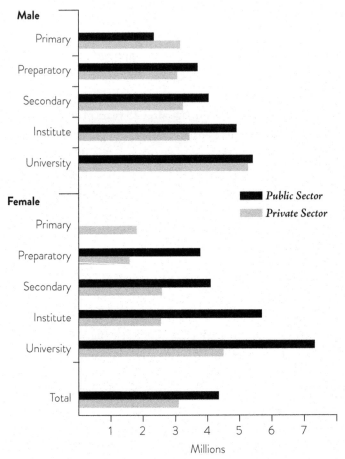

Source: Author's calculations.

the share of workers in the public sector has remained steady over the past seven years, at around 27%. Average hourly wages of young men are similar in both sectors, with only less educated workers and university graduates receiving higher wages in the private sector. Average hourly wages of young women are significantly higher in the public sector for all levels of educational attainment. When expected pension benefits are included, the earnings gap between public and private employees widens and the only remaining private sector wage advantage is for young men with an elementary education or below. Recent public sector wage increases have widened the wage gap further, making government jobs even more attractive.

The higher levels of wages and benefits offered through public sector jobs make it in the private interest of young people to follow traditional school-to-work trajectories in order to secure a government job. For young Syrians, this means focusing on their studies and doing well on national exams. However, given that Syria has initiated a series of economic reforms to move the country towards a social market economy, we argue that it would be socially optimal to align incentives so that young people are more focused on developing key skills and technical abilities necessary to succeed in a global economy.

The Syrian government, and other countries transitioning from command economies with strong traditional institutions to more open economies, should consider removing disincentives to seeking private sector jobs. In the case of Syria, this could entail:

+ Slowing the pace of future public sector pay increases, to bring public and private sector wages into alignment. To the extent that public benefits remain high, public sector wages could eventually be set below private sector wages.

+ Reforming the pension system, by lowering contribution rates and basing benefits on average work-life incomes rather than the last two years of work. This would make it easier for private sector employers to join the system. Pension reforms should be initiated soon to take advantage of the youth bulge entering the labor force, resulting in more people paying into the system compared to beneficiaries.

+ Reforming the public and private sector labor laws and removing regulations that ensure virtual life-long employment guarantees. This reform could involve the government introducing a new social contract in which public sector work is seen as a temporary public service rather than a life-long entitlement.

+ Taking steps to reduce wage and employment discrimination against women in the private sector by enforcing domestic laws and international agreements.

+ Introducing more flexible admissions policies to public post-secondary institutions, for example, by allowing extracurricular activities count towards admissions.

+ Developing labor market information systems that track career opportunities and identify occupations with good prospects, and making the information accessible.

REFERENCES

Abrahart, Alan Iqbal Kaur and Zafiris Tzannatos. 2002. "Government Employment and Active Labor Market Policies in MENA in a Comparative International Context," in *Employment Creation and Social Protection in the Middle East and North Africa*, edited by Heba Handoussa and Zafiris Tzannatos (Cairo: American University in Cairo Press).

Boudarbat, Brahim. 2008. "Job-Search Strategies and the Unemployment of University Graduates in Morocco." *International Research Journal of Finance and Economics*, Issue 14.

Huitfeldt, Henrik and Nader Kabbani. 2007. "Returns to Education and the Transition from School to Work in Syria," Institution of Financial Economics Working Paper No. 2007-1 (Beirut: American University of Beirut).

International Labor Organization. 2008. *Global Employment Trends for Youth.* (Geneva: International Labor Organization).

Kabbani, Nader and Leen Al-Habash. 2008. "Raising Awareness of Alternatives to Public Sector Employment among Syrian Youth," ERF Working Paper No. 387 (Cairo: Economic Research Forum).

Kabbani, Nader and Noura Kamel. 2007. "Youth Exclusion in Syria: Social, Economic and Institutional Dimensions," Middle East Initiative Working Paper No. 4 (Washington, DC and Dubai: Wolfensohn Center for Development and Dubai School of Government).

Kabbani, Nader and Zafiris Tzannatos. 2006. "Labor and Human Resource Development," in *Syria Country Profile* (Cairo: Economic Research Forum).

6

Investing in Early Child Development

JACQUES VAN DER GAAG

The Wolfensohn Center's research program on Early Child Development (ECD) was borne out of research and investments in the subject that Mr. Wolfensohn championed while at the World Bank. When Mr. Wolfensohn became president of the World Bank in 1995, the field of ECD was still in its infancy. The Bank had already committed large resources for separate projects and programs for child nutrition or education. But the need for a fully integrated approach to child development, covering health, nutrition, and stimulation during the early years (birth–five years of age) had only recently been seen as a valid area of development that institutions such as the World Bank should promote. When he left the World Bank in 2005, the Bank's commitment to ECD programs and projects exceeded US$2 billion.

Given the large number of other fields that competed for resources (such as infrastructure, agriculture, energy, and many others), this was quite an achievement. Other international organizations (for example, UNICEF) or nongovernmental organizations (for example, the Bernard van Leer Foundation) had focused on and funded projects that benefited mostly young children, but the driving motive was primarily a humanitarian one. However, in order to convince a minister of finance to take out a loan to fund ECD projects, economic development arguments were needed. Over time, the World Bank developed such arguments for investing in young children. The Bank started rigorous evaluations showing that ECD projects not only worked (that is, had the desired effects on the participating children) but also were highly cost-effective. The benefits of the long-term effects of such programs on the life-trajectory of the children far outweigh the initial investment in basic health care, nutritional support, and stimulation during the early years. These benefits include school readiness, progression to higher levels of schooling, better job prospects, higher earnings, fewer social problems as adults—in particular less criminal behavior—lower birth rates, better adult health, and, in the aggregate, a more prosperous society. Finally, scientific developments (in, for instance, neuroscience and epigenetics) continued to underscore the importance (if not the necessity) of providing young children with a safe environment, age-specific stimulation, good nutrition, and basic health care.

During Wolfensohn's presidency, the World Bank would become a strong proponent of ECD, linking the development of young children to the human development of a country.[1] Mr. Wolfensohn often joked that he was pushing for ECD because his wife told him so every night. Indeed, Mrs. Wolfensohn was a tireless ambassador for ECD, who literally traveled the world to explain the science, economics, and human necessity of investing in young children.[2] Their combined efforts have taken hold, both within the World Bank and in many other international agencies, such as the Inter-American Development Bank. ECD had become a corner stone of economic, or more precisely, human development.

Shortly after stepping down as World Bank president in 2005, Mr. Wolfensohn established the Wolfensohn Center at the Brookings Institution. Keeping with its broader focus on scaling up aid interventions (see chapter 3), the Center's work on ECD focused on how to achieve ECD results at scale. Over the years, collective knowledge of what works in ECD had greatly increased thanks to the rigorous impact evaluations that often were part of Bank-funded ECD projects. However, scaling up ECD projects to national levels and providing universal coverage of the birth–five population appeared to be very difficult. This was the particular challenge the Wolfensohn Center's initiative on Early Child Development took on.

The program began with an inventory of countries that had successfully scaled up programs that focused on young children. Most of these countries had started by focusing on only a part of the necessary integrated approach to preparing young children for a productive and successful life. Still, the Center's staff believed that valuable lessons could be learned from such partial approaches.

In May 2009 the Wolfensohn Center hosted a conference featuring case studies from five countries that had worked to scale up ECD programs in the developing world: Cuba, Madagascar, Macedonia, the Philippines, and South Africa. The conference provided a platform for the country authors to highlight key challenges and achievements in scaling up ECD in their countries, as well as an opportunity for the global ECD community to both gain from and provide valuable insight on how to effectively scale up early child development programs.

There were a number of prominent similarities among the five country case studies. First was the vital role of advocacy at the community level (parents and caregivers), the municipal level, the provincial level, and the national level. Such advocacy must be developed constantly to guarantee the long-term viability of the program. Second was the challenge of dealing with the multisectoral approach to ECD. Scaling up needs to progress at all participating ministries and other major players, which poses coordination challenges among often competing entities. One option discussed was to start with scaling up a partial (one-sectoral) program, such as child nutrition, and build the other components around this program at a later time. Finally, many participants noted as problematic the lack of program-specific data, such as region-specific indicators and local cost data, and the lack of local research capacity. Increasing region-specific academic training, both on the substance of ECD and on the research methodology, is critical.

The case study of South Africa—an excerpt of which is reprinted in this chapter—provides a good example of a successful partial approach. The country adopted a so-called Reception year for five-year-olds. Universal Grade R coverage became policy in 2001. The rollout of the Grade R program could subsequently inform the rollout of a national plan for integrated services for children age zero to four.

Researchers with the Wolfensohn Center, from the beginning, understood that scaling up successful projects would involve a lot a players, including all stakeholders and many champions, who could help with securing the necessary political support and resources, but also could provide knowledge and expertise to inform the scaling up process. In theory, the private sector would be an ideal partner for any government aiming for universal ECD coverage. As already stated above, ECD is relatively complex and involves many fields (health, nutrition, cognitive and non-cognitive development), and thus, at the government level, many ministries. Many governments are hard-pressed to pull off scaling up of such a complex program, especially since during the scaling up process, quality control is crucial. The resources, management expertise, and results orientation of the private sector could be a great complement to the government's efforts. Unfortunately, private sector involvement in ECD was still very scarce.[3]

To stimulate corporate involvement in ECD work, the Wolfensohn Center initiated in April 2008 a high-level conference in The Hague, the Netherlands, to promote support from the European business community for ECD. The goal of the conference was to bring the importance of early child development to the forefront of international economic debates and to develop strategies to increase private sector support for ECD in developing countries. In addition to the keynote speakers, Mr. and Mrs. Wolfensohn, participants heard from business leaders from a wide variety of companies, such as Unilever, TetraPak, LEGO, the Sesame Workshop, and Heineken. Her Majesty Queen Beatrix and Her Royal Highness Princess Laurentien honored the conference with their presence. The successful conference, the first of its kind in the European region, called for increased private investment in ECD and for stronger public-private partnerships.

A similar event, at the Wolfensohn Center at Brookings on December 4, 2009, focused on fostering support from North American business leaders.[4] The conference highlighted the positive impact of ECD on local communities, national economies, international markets, and long-term global poverty reduction. The conference called for the creation of a global business alliance for early child development that collectively could voice the importance of ECD as a critical development strategy. Mr. Wolfensohn underscored that ECD is no longer a fringe issue, but one that has a massive impact on how our world develops. Furthermore, to ensure future economic growth for an ever-increasing population, early child development must move to the forefront of international development.

Though the Wolfensohn Center's work on ECD ended in 2011, research on the subject at Brookings has continued and thrived in intervening years. In November 2013 Brookings and the China Development Research Foundation co-organized a conference on U.S.-China collaboration on early childhood development, which featured Deputy Prime Minister Liu Yan Dong and former secretary of state Hillary Clinton. Mr. Wolfensohn also participated in this event, where he urged Chinese policymakers to take the lead on ECD as a poverty reduction strategy as nations prepare for the post–Millennium Development agenda, and subsequently ECD was included in China's National Child Development Plan (for 2014-2020) for Poverty-Stricken Areas.

Much of Brookings's current work on ECD is now based within the new Center for Universal Education (CUE), whose research agenda is directly linked to the work initiated by the Wolfensohn Center. The first link is the work on scaling up. As already stated, lack of relevant data (especially at the regional or local level) is one of the factors hampering scale. In 2014 CUE initiated a research program on the costs of early childhood development (ECD) interventions. Initially this work consisted of mapping existing data and costing tools, but it quickly led to CUE establishing a multi-agency working group including members from the World Bank, the Inter-American Development Bank, the International Food Policy Research Institute, UNICEF, and the Abdul Latif Jameel Poverty Action Lab to help develop new data and tools. With the input from the working group as well as other ECD experts, CUE determined that a standardized costing tool for a broad range of integrated ECD interventions was needed by policymakers, funders, researchers, and practitioners. CUE entered into a collaboration with the World Bank's Strategic Impact Evaluation Fund (SIEF) to develop and pilot a costing tool designed to bring methodological consistency to estimating the cost of ECD programs.[5]

While the tool, based on an existing template used in South Africa, is intended primarily to appraise individual programs, it can be used to inform budget decisions and to compare costing across countries and interventions. The tool provides opportunities for cost-benefit and cost-effectiveness analysis, and for making better-informed investments. Piloting of the tool has taken place in Bangladesh, Mali, Mexico, Mozambique, and Malawi, across a range of interventions, from parenting interventions to micronutrient supplementation and pre-primary programs. In March 2017 the ECD Action Network (ECDAN), a partnership between the World Bank and UNICEF, endorsed this tool as a global benchmark to be used by ECD stakeholders across the developing world.

A new CUE activity on ECD in the developing world relates to the role of the private sector in ECD. Among the major barriers to achieving ECD at scale are inadequate and unreliable financing and the unwillingness of governments to commit resources. This can be explained in part by the fact that ECD programs require financing up front, while the benefits accrue over a lifetime. Myopic politicians need to be convinced that ECD services are a good investment. Furthermore, other than, say, basic education services, there are many different formats for ECD services, ranging from parental support, to community-based services, to large-scale institution-based programs. It is not always clear in advance which format works best in which environment. There is a need for experimentation, evaluation, and subsequent adaptation of the most successful approach.

Public-private partnerships (PPPs) as well as payment by results mechanisms, which can allow for more flexibility to achieve outcomes, may be promising solutions. One new mechanism, which combines PPPs with payment by results and impact investing, is the social impact bond (SIB). Through a SIB private investors provide upfront capital for a social service, and government pays investors based on the outcomes of the service. If the intervention does not achieve outcomes, the government does not pay investors at all. Development impact bonds (DIBs) are a variation of SIBs, where the outcome funder is a third party, such as a foundation or development assistance agency, rather than the government. The provision of upfront risk capital differentiates impact bonds from other payment by results contracts. CUE at Brookings has become a leader in studying and advocating for this new tool and has provided a comprehensive global assessment of this relatively new finance instrument for social interventions, as well as an examination of the use of impact bonds for ECD projects.[6]

In addition to bringing in the private sector management approach to achieve social service delivery, impact bonds (i) shift the risk of the initial investment to private investors, (ii) change the focus from input financing to outcome financing, (iii) allow for experimentation with new forms of service delivery, and (iv) develop strong and independent monitoring and evaluation capacity. Experience with impact bonds for social service delivery is still limited. However, if impact bonds are successful in bringing in new actors and stakeholders to expand ECD services, they may prove to be an effective instrument for scaling up some of the many effective programs that already exist around the world.

A final initiative at CUE, relevant for ECD, addresses quality, capacity, and gaps in knowledge of learning outcomes. The Measuring Early Learning Quality and Outcomes (MELQO) project was initiated in 2014 to efficiently generate locally relevant data on children's learning and development at the start of school, and in pre-primary learning environments, with specific relevance to inform national ECD policy and stimulate global monitoring. Through a consultative process designed to draw on the best experiences in measuring early childhood development to date, MELQO has developed modules that measure child development and learning, for children between four and six years. The project is co-convened by CUE, UNICEF, UNESCO, and the World Bank, with technical leadership from the University of Nebraska.

These modules are designed to be used as measures of child development and learning, identifying areas of strength and challenge, and then to integrate these tools into national systems to monitor progress toward goals over time. The modules are therefore intended to be adapted to national standards and can also be integrated into existing assessments—meaning that the modules could be used as a starting point for national assessments and also be used for global and regional monitoring.

Ultimately, the Wolfensohn Center's Early Child Development Initiative had two key objectives. First, as a research goal, it sought to build on the many successful and promising project-level evaluations to help create an evidence base for how to implement ECD programs at scale, providing universal coverage at national levels. Second, drawing on the Center's convening and influencing power, the Initiative sought to bring together key stakeholders to share lessons learned and gain greater political buy-in for investing in ECD. Today, while much remains to be achieved, we know more about scaling up ECD programs than we ever did before, and governments, the private sector, and NGOs around the world are increasingly looking to this evidence to help them implement sound ECD strategies.

Scaling Up Early Childhood Development in South Africa

Introducing a Reception Year (Grade R) for Children Aged Five Years as the First Year of Schooling

LINDA BIERSTEKER

Linda Biersteker is head of research at the Early Learning Resource Unit in Cape Town, South Africa, and is an instructor for the University of Victoria's Early Child Development Virtual University course on Africa.

THE DEVELOPMENT OF THE GRADE R INTERVENTION

In South Africa early childhood development (ECD) refers to "the processes by which children from birth to nine years grow and thrive, physically, mentally, emotionally, morally and socially" (Department of Education, 1995). This broad definition necessarily involves policies and programs from several departments. Similar to governance arrangements in many other countries, three departments, those of Education, Health, and Social Development (Welfare),

Editors' Note: This is an excerpt of Wolfensohn Center Working Paper 17, originally published in April 2010. Commissioned by the Wolfensohn Center for Development at Brookings, it is one in a series of case studies that examine issues of early child development at the country level. It has been edited for length and style; the full paper is available for download at the Brookings Institution website (www.brookings.edu/research/scaling-up-early-child-development-in-south-africa-introducing-a-reception-year-grade-r-for-children-aged-five-years-as-the-first-year-of-schooling/).

have the primary responsibility for ECD services. The Office of the Rights of the Child in the Presidency is guardian of the National Programme of Action for Children and has a monitoring brief for the NPA and reporting requirements on the Convention on the Rights of the Child.

South Africa has prioritized the ECD provisioning option of lowering the age for state-supported education programs to include a pre-primary or reception year. In 2001, through White Paper 5—"Early Childhood Development"—the Department of Education committed itself to the establishment of a national system of provision for children aged five years,[1] the largest ever South African public sector policy commitment to ECD. The goal is for all children to have access to a reception year program by 2010, and for 85 percent to attend Grade R at a public school. Accredited Grade R programs should be established at all public primary schools by 2010 (Department of Education, 2001b). Subsidization of the reception year is poverty targeted. Children falling within the poorest 40 percent of schools will receive the highest per capita level of grants in aid. The intention is that some community-based centers will form part of the public system of provision, but only if a public primary school option is not available or accessible to the child or for piloting purposes.

Three types of accredited Grade R are therefore provided for:

+ programs within the public primary school system,

+ programs at community-based ECD centers, and

+ independent (private) provisions.

All reception year programs are required to register with provincial education departments, accredited reception year educators should be registered with the South African Council of Educators (a professional body), and there should be approved training for all educators who do not yet have a specialized qualification to teach the reception year.

Curriculum for five-year-olds forms part of the National Curriculum Statement for the Foundation Phase (Grades R to 3 or approximate ages five to nine years). The focus is on Literacy, Numeracy, and Life Skills programs. South Africa follows an outcomes-based education (OBE) system, which clearly defines the outcomes to be achieved at the end of the learning process with grade-related assessment standards. Outcomes for each learning area are based on achieving a set of critical and developmental outcomes, which focus on producing learners with knowledge skills and values for productive engagement in the workforce and a democratic and caring society (Moll, 2007a).

While from a curriculum perspective Grade R is the first year of primary schooling, it is differently financed and staffed. Since 2001 the government has funded Grade R in two ways. First, provincial governments–funded grants to community-based ECD centers on a per-learner basis. Second, a direct grant in aid from provincial education departments (PEDs) to school governing bodies, which employ the teachers, finances Grade R in public primary schools. Subsidization of Grade R is poverty targeted but "lags substantially behind funding for other grades in the same school and in 2005 was approximately seven times less than for a Grade 1 learner" (Biersteker & Dawes, 2008:200).

In summary, the Grade R intervention is a government-designed, educationally motivated intervention[2] that has built on existing school infrastructure. Although it is rolling out to all children, it is not at this stage compulsory—but is intended to have universalized and compulsory coverage by 2010 (Republic of South Africa, 2008).

The Development of Grade R

Roots in the Pre-Democratic Period

Though the apartheid government had taken very limited responsibility for pre-primary education (except for limited provision for white children), pre-primary education came onto the agenda in the late 1980s. In 1981 the report of the De Lange Commission of Inquiry into Education in the Republic of South Africa (Human Sciences Research Council, 1981) cited "environmental deprivation" as the main reason that children were not "ready" for school, and recommended the "partial institutionalisation of pre-basic education" in the form of a bridging period to achieve school readiness for as many children as possible prior to formal education. The 1983 White Paper on the Provision of Education in South Africa took up the recommendation of a bridging period of one to two years aimed at promoting school readiness prior to entry into basic education and also recommended priority be given to financing this in the interests of improving efficiency in the education system.

In 1987, following a two-year inquiry into the introduction of a bridging period prior to basic education, a report from the Department of Education and Training (1987) stated:

> On account of the necessity for developing school readiness, the selective introduction of a programme for bridging period education, where practicable, does appear to be desirable. It should be regarded as an enriched form of the entire pre-primary phase immediately prior to basic education, and will be made available to 5- to 7-year-olds.[3]

The Bridging Period Programme (BPP) was launched in 1988 as a pilot (Taylor, 1992). This took place within the Grade 1 year, thus requiring no additional subsidization. After a three-week orientation program on school entry, children were streamed into two groups: one group that needed a ten-to-twelve-week orientation and another group needing longer school-readiness training. The second group transferred to Grade 1 work after the ten to twelve weeks, or transferred to the bridging class. In large schools these made up different classes, but in others they were taught within the same class. In practice many children had a full year of bridging (Padayachie et al., 1994). While there were numerous inadequacies in the implementation of the BPP and no formal evaluation, this school-based intervention involved substantial numbers of children both in DET and the education departments in certain "homelands" and may well have prepared the ground for introduction of a reception year.

Policy formulation for ECD in a democratic South Africa began in the early 1990s as a focus area for the influential National Education Policy Investigation (NEPI) that investigated policy options for education for the mass democratic movement. The NEPI Early Childhood Educare report (NEPI, 1992) presented options within the school system for five- to nine-year-olds, including a pre-primary class for all five-year-olds and a range of options for services for children from birth to six years. The ANC Policy Framework for Education and Training Discussion Document drafted in 1994 included the NEPI recommendation of a reception year for five-year-olds, as well as a commitment to a policy for child care and development in the community for younger children. The framework included the deployment of state resources and a commitment to career path support for all ECD carers and teachers.

A World Bank–funded study was commissioned the same year to provide recommendations for support for the implementation of the reception year (Padayachie et al., 1994). The recommendation that nongovernmental organizations (NGOs) be used to support ECD policy development was prominent. The research team also stressed the importance of provisioning for younger children as part of an ECD strategy and included recommendations for a range of options for younger children. To further emphasize the needs of younger children, when the World Bank (as part of an Africa Regional Integrated ECD Initiative) selected South Africa for a case study in 1996, members of the previous study team pushed for a study of birth to four-year-olds (Biersteker, 1997).

ECD in the Reconstruction of Democratic South Africa

Since 1994 ECD has been recognized as a key area in the process of reconstruction and human resource development. In 1995 a director of ECD, Schools and Junior Primary, was appointed to the Department of Education (DoE). The 1995 White Paper on Education and Training identified early childhood as the starting point for human resource development. It committed government to providing ten years of free and compulsory schooling per child, starting with a reception year for five-year-olds. In 1996 an Interim Policy for Early Childhood Development was launched (Department of Education, 1996). This covered children birth–nine years but had a particular focus on phasing in a reception year for five-year-olds to facilitate the transition to formal schooling.

In 1996 the Coordinating Committee for ECD (CCECD), which had been set up to advise the DoE, suggested that a preliminary audit to inform the forthcoming ECD pilot project would be useful. The DoE, with funding from UNESCO, commissioned the two national civil society organizations on the CCECD—the South African Congress for Early Childhood Development (SACECD) and the National Educare Forum (NEF)—to conduct an audit focused on:

1. Training institutions for ECD, sources, and levels of practitioners' training
2. ECD service delivery
3. Data access in government and NGOs
4. Employment of practitioners
5. Subsidies for ECD and their sources

FIGURE 1 Time Line of Key Developments in
the Establishment and Rollout of Grade R

PRE-DEMOCRACY DEVELOPMENTS

1981 De Lange Commission into Education in the Republic of South Africa

1983 White Paper on the Provision of Education in South Africa

1987 Dept of Education and Training (DET) Bridging Period Programme

1990–92 National Education Policy Initiative: Early Childhood Educare Report

POST-DEMOCRACY DEVELOPMENTS TOWARDS GRADE R

1994 The ANC Policy Framework for Education and Training
Discussion Document

World Bank/CEPD Report

1995 White Paper on Education and Training

1996 Interim ECD Policy

1997–99 National Pilot Project

2000 Nationwide Audit of ECD Provisioning

2001 White Paper 5 Early Childhood Development

2001–02 TO Conditional Grant
2003–04

2004–05 TO Expanded Public Works Programme ECD Component
2008–09

2005 Draft Norms and Standards for Grade R Funding

2008 Norms and Standards for Grade R Funding

National Treasury Technical Assistance Unit Study

6. The nature/extent of private sector involvement in ECD (Padayachie et al., 1997)

Questionnaires were sent to 150 institutions of which 28 percent responded; 250 trainers (a 48 percent response rate), 400 trainees (a 40 percent response rate), and 37 funders from the private sector (a 62 percent response rate). While the study was very limited, it highlighted, among other things, the need for training capacity in rural and informal settlement areas; the fact that the majority of funding for ECD was from private sources; the issue of career pathing for ECD practitioners; the need for research on how ECD could contribute to job creation; and the need for an in-depth audit study.

In 1998 the DoE created a separate Early Childhood Development Directorate responsible for developing an ECD policy framework and planning and mobilizing resources in support of large-scale provision of ECD.

The Piloting Phase

To assist with policy formulation, the DoE instituted a three-year national ECD pilot project in 1997. The pilot ushered in a new, formalized government-NGO partnership governed by service contracts. This was guided and monitored by the CCECD, comprised of national and provincial education department ECD personnel, appointed ECD specialists, and representatives of teacher unions and national representative structures (SACECD, its training arm the SA Training Institute for ECD, and NEF).

Components of the National ECD Pilot Project (NPP)

The NPP, following the recommendations of the World Bank/Centre for Education Policy Development study and the Interim Policy for ECD, utilized existing provision systems for piloting Grade R. These included community-based ECD sites with children aged five years, and pre-primary classes that already existed in some primary schools. Current practitioners implemented the program, and NGOs provided training on a tender basis.

The Pilot Project had the following components:

1. An Interim Accreditation Committee to develop interim guidelines for the accreditation of practitioners. Guidelines for developing learning programs for Grade R children were also prepared.

2. Subsidy funding for Grade R learners at R2 per child per day for 200 days a year for up to thirty children in a class was provided to a sample of community-based centers selected for the pilot on the basis of fixed criteria. These sites were spread across the provinces according to population, covering urban and rural areas and poverty targeted areas.

3. Training by NGOs (selected by public tender) for practitioners working with Grade R classes in selected community-based and public primary

schools. While provincial schools were required to participate, the incentive for community schools to become involved was high, firstly on account of the subsidy but secondly because there was a perception that this was a step towards state support of teachers and more sustainable jobs.

4. A research and monitoring team, contracted by public tender, to assess the impact of the pilot and advise on the development of sustainable models for provision of a publicly funded reception year.

5. Provincial pilot project coordinators located in the PEDs to oversee implementation in their provinces. Provinces were responsible for paying subsidies and contracting and monitoring the training of practitioners.

6. An ECD Information Campaign to publicize the program and inform the participating providers.

The evaluators' report on the project raises a concern that ECD is not regarded as a core activity in provincial departments. This has detrimental budgetary implications for ECD—as the national DoE found out when the Eastern Cape, Northern Province (Limpopo), North West, and Free State absorbed the National ECD Pilot Project funds rather than spending them on the intended project, and in spite of completing detailed business plans. It influences the budgetary allocation to ECD, and when other educational sectors have overspent their budgets, money is shifted from the ECD budget (Department of Education, 2001c).

Not all the provinces had completed training at the end of the 1999–2000 financial year. The inability to meet the pilot requirements in terms of allocation of funding and completion of training in the pilot period were problems that needed to be considered in planning for the further rollout of Grade R in the post–White Paper 5 period.

Evaluation of the National ECD Pilot Project

The aim of the evaluation of the National Pilot Project (Department of Education, 2001c) was to draw out implications for policy. The evaluation team was asked to compare community-based sites' quality, equity, and cost effectiveness with those of school-based Grade R classes and Grade 1 classes with a substantial number of underage learners;[4] to examine the appropriateness of the norms and standards, adequacy of the subsidies, and effectiveness of the accreditation system set up by the Interim Accreditation Committee, and finally to draw out policy implications on the basis of their findings and documentation of other related processes provided by the DoE.

The research team indicates in the report that given the focus of the pilot project, the policy implications for Grade R only would be discussed. They identify key concerns (Department of Education, 2001c: 5–6) as including the best way to:

1. Ensure that Grade R (and ultimately ECD) is a core activity of the DoE

2. Identify the most cost-effective means of providing Grade R

3. Ensure quality provision of Grade R classes and ultimately of classes addressing younger learners

4. Discourage the acceptance of underage learners into Grade 1

5. Shift the burden of providing Grade R from poverty stricken families to the State

6. Support long-term poverty alleviation and social development through the promotion of sustainable Grade R provision

Conclusions from evaluation of the piloting project were that:

+ Grade R should become compulsory, thus fulfilling the commitment in the 1995 White Paper to ten years of compulsory education.

+ The new school admission policy would not eliminate underage learners in Grade 1 classes.

+ The location of Grade R classes should be determined by PEDs' financial capacity and ability to monitor quality and build accountability—proposing a combination of community and public Grade R classes. Adaptation of the norms and standards for school funding to allow schools to include Grade R as a legitimate expense would transform incentives to enroll underage learners to incentives to set up separate Grade R classes. For community sites, the evaluators proposed that they link formally with a primary school which would provide the funding or that the South African Schools Act be amended to allow community-based sites offering Grade R to register as independent schools to encourage quality control and integrate them into the existing subsidy system for independent schools.

1. The government is able to fund Grade R (there are many underage learners already in the system, increased efficiency, etc.).

2. Grade R quality needs to be improved—both public and community-based sites were offering similar quality but of a low standard.

3. ECD needs to become core educational business (not peripheral) and this should include resources and authority being vested in provincial ECD directorates. Further, the CCECD was too loose a structure for effective decisionmaking and should be replaced. The IAC process should be continued and expanded.

4. Issues such as the ring fencing of ECD budgets, consideration of who the employer of ECD practitioners should be, as well as professional registration and career pathing for non-formal practitioners, should be examined.

Literacy and numeracy attainment was assessed for four children aged five or six years in each of a sample of sites, comprising 110 community-based sites and 99 Grade R and Grade 1 public school sites. Learners in community sites underperformed their counterparts in primary and reception sites as they had during the 1997 baseline. The 1999 results indicate that while community site scores were still lower than school-based sites, numeracy had increased by 1 percent while school sites declined by 5 percent. Literacy scores at community sites declined by –1 percent compared with –8 percent in reception sites at schools.

Policy Finalization for Rollout

In 2000 the Department of Education undertook a nationwide audit of ECD provisioning in which 23,482 ECD sites, providing services to just over 1 million learners in all nine provinces, were audited (Department of Education, 2001a). This audit, funded under a European Union technical support agreement, provided comprehensive quantitative information to inform ECD resource allocation and policy development. This remains the best data source on ECD center provision for children up to seven years, except for those in school-based provision.

Informed by the findings of the national ECD pilot project and the audit, the DoE launched White Paper 5, "Early Childhood Development," in May 2001 (Department of Education, 2001b).

Rationale for Selection of Grade R

White Paper 5 explains, "Arising from the lessons learnt on the provision of the reception year in the National ECD Pilot Project, the Government proposes to establish a national system for the provision of reception year programmes to children aged five . . . (section 4)." It should be noted that the commitment to providing ten years of compulsory school education was also a driver: ". . . our medium term policy goal is progressively to realise our constitutional obligation to provide all learners with ten years of compulsory school education, including one year of early childhood development called the reception year" (White Paper 5, 1.4.2).

This built upon the recognition in the Interim Policy for ECD that Grade R was part of the government's commitment to compulsory general education.

As Wildeman and Nomdo (2004) indicate, the government's rationale for locating 85 percent of provision in the schooling system was based on claims that there are improved systems for accountability and quality control at primary schools and that service delivery would be able to use existing infrastructure.

THE POLITICS AND FUNDING OF SCALING UP

This section provides an assessment of the factors that led to the adoption of Grade R as part of the formal education system in South Africa, as well as the contribution of government and civil society that lead to it. It also examines the funding mechanisms used for the start-up of this national program.

Drivers for Implementation of Grade R as a Planned Universal Program

The political climate engendered by the liberation struggle and transition to democracy in 1994 provided a generally enabling environment for the expansion and development of ECD services in South Africa. A strong child rights movement led by civil society, including ECD organizations, developed in response to the denial of children's most basic rights and increasing state violence against children on account of their political activism. In 1990 the National Committee on the Rights of the Child was formed and work towards a program of action began.

The ratification of the Convention on the Rights of the Child in 1996 and the African Charter on the Rights and Welfare of the Child in 2000, as well as inclusion of guaranteed child rights in Sections 28 and 29 of the South African Constitution of 1996, provide the framework for prioritizing children in service delivery. The drafters of the National Programme of Action for Children ensured that ECD became a priority area here too, basing it on an analysis of the provisions of the CRC. This has, however, been a rather separate stream with a focus on monitoring child programs. The education route has so far proved to be the most effective channel for expanding ECD services.

Nevertheless, this alone would not have been enough as ECD specifically was not on the agenda of any political group. In the "planning for democracy period," politically well-connected and astute ECD members of the African National Congress and United Democratic Movement were able to use their influence to ensure that what was then known as "early childhood educare" got onto the policy agenda.

Padayachie et al. (1994) described three lines of action to ensure ECD was on the political agenda:

1. ECD proponents saw a need to develop a coherent vision with regard to national policy. This was accomplished through ECD getting onto the National Education Crisis Committee in 1990 and the creation of a National Interim Working Committee (NIWC) on ECD with the mandate to build grassroots support to help formulate the vision.

2. At the same time an ECD commission became part of the National Education Policy Investigation (NEPI), which was critical in legitimizing ECD.[5] The need to mobilize a broader support base was achieved through the process of disbursement of Independent Development Trust funding. This was a once off allocation of R70 million to ECD in 1991 for the poorest of the poor. A representative process was followed and very large numbers of grassroots ECD service providers were drawn in to determine how the allocations should be disbursed. This led to the establishment of the National Educare Forum (NEF).

185

3. There was a need to develop a process and structure to take ECD forward in unity during the political transition. This was achieved through bringing together the South African Association for Early Childhood Educare and NIWC to form the South African Congress for Early Childhood Development (SACECD) in 1994. Having a more "progressive" organization as the voice of the ECD movement is considered by many to have been a key enabler of getting ECD firmly onto the policy agenda. (Ironically, in the process of gaining political credibility, the movement lost much of its strong early education expertise in the form of more conservative but specialist ECE teachers).

All of this, as well as advocacy at the ANC Education Conference, paved the way for the inclusion of ECD in the African National Congress Education Policy Framework for Education and Training (the "Yellow Book"). The World Bank/CEPD South African Study on Early Childhood Development, which provided recommendations for the reception year, took place simultaneously with the formulation of ANC policy, which was spearheaded by Roy Padayachie, ANC member and then-chair of NIWC.

While university-based researchers spearheaded most education policy development, a dearth of ECD expertise in the tertiary sector meant that NGOs were centrally involved in the development of ECD policy. Early policy affirms community-based service provision, NGO innovation and service delivery, and the need for a continuum of ECD services to reflect the need for public/private partnerships to deliver ECD services. In essence, the expectations for ECD servicing were far wider than the Grade R year prioritized in White Paper 5.

The NEPI Early Childhood Educare report proposed program options within the schooling system for five- to nine-year-olds including bridging within the first year of school or a pre-primary class for five-year-olds before school and a range of options for children birth to six years. However, it was the early schooling options that were selected in the framework report—locating them firmly within the basic education ambit. One can speculate that this was a financial trade-off, which has been confirmed by the report writers, but this could also be seen as the inevitable result of locating ECD within education policy. This undoubtedly informed the terms of reference for the World Bank/CEPD study, which were "to assess the feasibility of adding a year for five year olds to the formal school system" (Padayachie et al., 1994:3). This study, however, recommended that a pre-primary year alone would be too little too late for the majority of young children and it made a number of recommendations for programs for younger children, an integrated approach and partnerships with government, NGOs, parents, communities, and the private sector.

The Interim Policy for ECD (Department of Education, 1996) also took a broad integrative approach to ECD services following the 1995 White Paper on Education and Training, which clearly located ECD within a broader development framework, stating (para. 74):

RDP programmes which address the basic needs of families for shelter, water and sanitation, primary health care, nutrition, and employment, are therefore particularly vital, and their successful implementation will improve the life chances of young children, and enable families and communities to care for them more adequately. From this perspective, ECD depends on and contributes to community development, and the education of parents should go hand-in-hand with the education of children.

The National ECD Pilot Project (NPP) 1997–1999, while focused on the reception year, was implemented largely in the community-based sector with its community link and more holistic full-day care, which offers protection, nutrition, and education.

The Choice of Grade R and Its Location in Public Primary Schools
As described previously, White Paper 5 was the vehicle through which Grade R was prioritized above other forms of ECD and, in a departure from previous policy, located the majority of Grade R classes in public primary schools. It is clear that up to this point the favored approach was broader and community-based. Even in the pilot project, Gauteng had piloted a holistic integrated approach and community schools were used. So, what happened?

The progression from interim to final policy had been extremely slow. Seleti (2007) describes the departmental process. In 2000 the then-minister of education, Professor Kadar Asmal, gave instructions for the development of White Paper 5 and a time frame of three months for its production. Departmental officials looked to the pilot project for systems and models that had worked and could be adopted for Grade R and for Pre-Grade R as well as drawing on the Interim Policy. According to Seleti (2007), there was extensive internal consultation with the National Cabinet and the National Treasury on its imple-mentation. The DoE had to persuade the Treasury that White Paper 5 did not provide for an additional cohort of ECD educators that would inflate personnel costs. The model adopted was to be developed through a preliminary condi-tional grant over three years with the intention that thereafter Grade R would be included in normal provincial budget systems. The intention to introduce Grade R gradually was articulated at department level (including PEDs) but not communicated to the wider ECD sector.

The government's decision to focus on Grade R has been the subject of a strong critique from civil society in particular (e.g., Porteus, 2001, 2004; and several press reports). Porteus points out that neither international research cited in White Paper 5, nor the NPP itself (even though it was biased in the di-rection of provision of reception year programming), supported a narrow focus on a reception year. Rather, the support was for the need for a more integrated servicing strategy, which would also be more consonant with the human rights approach to policy development within which ECD had been located during the transition to democracy. Concerns for the implications for weakening the community-based sector of moving towards school-based provision were also raised by ECD specialists in the NGO sector, through the media around the launch of White Paper 5.

Finally, it could be argued that White Paper 5 is primarily education driven and in this way builds on earlier Bridging-to-School models aimed at address-ing school readiness and preventing grade retention.

In particular there was no commitment to training and employing Grade R practitioners, which the sector had hoped would be addressed. Training was mentioned but not jobs, as government was not ready to increase its financial commitment to teacher salaries.

In summary, the decision to roll out Grade R within the schooling system was made by the DoE in consultation with Treasury. While the introduction of Grade R is presented in terms of meeting the constitutional obligation to "pro-vide all learners with ten years of compulsory school education, including one year of early childhood development called the reception year" (para. 1.4.2), the identified target is universal coverage. PEDs were meant to fund it and primar-ily to use the school infrastructure with a small component of community-based provision for implementation. The argument for the policy was child rights, economic investment, and redress of the disparities of poverty and apartheid.

Advocacy to Increase Public Awareness and Support for ECD

ECD is a national priority but is competing with many other national priorities. Advocacy is essential to bring ECD to the forefront in provincial and local budgeting and servicing where competing priorities tend to marginalize it. For ECD, holistically defined, the emphasis has more been on access to Social Security and other more general child rights issues such as immunization drives and child protection campaigns than on ECD center services and Grade R. This has been both from the side of government and advocacy groups (e.g., ACESS which has driven the entitlement to Social Security through the media and on occasions the courts). Certainly as services for birth–four-year-olds scale up with more of a focus on households as the site of early childhood development, there is likely to be more messaging aimed at parents and local authorities. The implementation guidelines for the National Integrated Plan for ECD (Department of Education, Department of Health & Department of Social Development, 2007) speak of advocacy and communication strategies. One could speculate that while Grade R is not yet compulsory and is oversubscribed, advocacy to encourage enrollment has not been essential.

Requirements for Implementing at Scale

In this section the requirements for moving from a pilot project towards universal provision are discussed.

Policy, Norms, and Standards

White Paper 5 indicated a number of areas to be incorporated within national policy, national norms and standards, and national programs for establishing a high quality national system of reception year provision. Included were:

+ the curriculum for the reception year,

+ development of an adequate poverty targeted grant-in-aid system for primary schools and an adequate subsidy system for community-based sites,

+ provincial management and implementation capacity, and ECD expertise,

+ the system of accreditation of ECD providers,

+ norms and standards,

+ a qualifications framework and career paths for ECD practitioners, registration criteria for ECD practitioners with the South African Council of Educators,

+ representation of ECD practitioners within the Education Labour Relations Council, conditions of service for ECD practitioners who are employed by school governing bodies and publicly subsidized community-based ECD sites,

+ a governance model for the incorporation of publicly subsidized community-based ECD sites within the public system of reception year provision,

+ a strengthened policy advisory forum with key social partners, and

+ inter-governmental and inter-sectoral coherence and focus on ECD, with particular reference to the health and nutritional requirements of children aged five years (Department of Education, 2001b: 6.1.9).

According to key informants interviewed for this study, apart from the policy as set out in White Paper 5 and the Conditional Grant support at national and provincial levels, at the time of the paper there was no implementation plan or costing developed for rollout of Grade R. This seems to have been the case until quite recently. The absence of legislation was a particular weakness. Because Grade R is not included in the South African Schools Act No 84 of 1996, PEDs were not compelled to provide it or allocate resources even if they had been made available in the national budget process.

Funding for the Rollout of Grade R

It was extremely clear from the inequities in access to and quality of ECD provisioning in South Africa that rollout of Grade R as a universal service would have to be publicly funded. This meant that Treasury and Cabinet had to be convinced that it was an affordable option. An international expert in education policy and financing was consulted on the development of White Paper 5, and chapter 4.2.2 of the paper gives reasons for the fiscal affordability of the proposal and a cost-impact analysis.

The National Pilot Project had indicated that the provision of Grade R at community sites was substantially cheaper for the DoE than providing similar education at schools. This was because of low salaries for practitioners and parents covering food and other costs. The evaluators pointed out the unfairness of this disparity, both for practitioners and parents who were paying three times as much as they would in primary schools (Department of Education, 2001c). Nevertheless, in order to have an affordable option for the introduction of Grade R, the funding mechanism in White Paper 5 made use of the fact that community-based sites operate at a lower cost and proposed a funding system which would enable a combination of the lower cost of community-based centers while putting the school-based Grade R within easier administrative reach of PEDs for quality control and accountability. The mechanism for financing the cost was directly through school governing bodies.

Based on this model, the argument was that expansion would cost less than originally thought and that reception year programs could be expanded as a result of improvements in the flow-through efficiency of the system. Efforts to reduce bottlenecks in the early years of schooling through underage enrollment and grade repetition had started to be successful (e.g., tightening school entry age, introducing age grade norms) and the six–seven-year-old school age cohort was declining. Based on a cost index value of 1 for public primary school, reception year provision in schools has an index of 0.7 and in community-based centers of 0.4. The analysis also examined trade-offs of ECD expansion against other educational goals and concluded that "given the high priority of ECD as a social investment, we believe that a claim of about 15 percent of the budgetary space created by economic growth, demographic transition and efficiency gains is reasonable." (Department of Education, 2001b: 4.2.2.6.11)

Consequently, some of the staffing and salary anomalies today relate to the funding model introduced by White Paper 5. Similarly, the delays in finalizing norms and standards for Grade R funding, which would bring it closer to school norms, were undoubtedly a result of concerns for the affordability of the commitment. It is here that the policy commitment achieved early on for a year of pre-primary as part of basic education has been extremely significant as a lever for rollout.

Funding the Conditional Grant Phase of the Rollout
While financing of Grade R is a PED responsibility, in order to "kick-start" the development and implementation of the reception year at provincial level the National Treasury introduced a Conditional Grant for ECD.[6] This would

allow provinces a period in which to budget for the expansion of Grade R. The Conditional Grant targeted 4,500 sites with 135,000 learners and had the following components:

+ Funding to sites

+ Training of practitioners

+ Supplying basic equipment

+ Monitoring and support system

+ Providing advocacy and information

The national department oversaw the project and used its allocation to manage the supply of learning materials, provide district management training, and run an advocacy component. Provincial allocations were for learner subsidies to sites and the training of practitioners.

KNOWLEDGE TRANSFER, CAPACITY BUILDING, AND IMPLEMENTATION

In accordance with White Paper 5, South Africa is following a phased approach to introduce publicly funded Grade R classes across the whole public schooling system. Bringing a further 750,000 children into the system between 2001–02 and 2010–11 (recently revised to 2014) at an acceptable quality of service requires, in addition to funding, the development of curriculum, coordination systems, improvement of the educator skills base through training and support, additional physical infrastructure, increased provincial and district systems, and staff capacity for implementation and monitoring. In this section I consider some of the provisions that have been, or are being, put in place, as we move from small-scale pilot mode to full rollout. This section also highlights that once targets are reached and all reception year learners have access to a Grade R education, achieving quality of service may take considerably longer.

Pilot and Rollout

While the program elements remain similar, there are some changes in the way that Grade R is being implemented at scale compared with the piloting phase. Primarily, the focus shifted from services being largely community-based, to provisions in the schooling system. Secondly, the requirements for assessment and planning for the National Curriculum Statement are far more demanding than previous curriculum guidelines. Location in the school system was justified on the basis that requirements could be more easily met there, but there are challenges. It places practitioners at the "bottom of the pecking order" and subject to supervision by department heads who often have very little understanding of informal learning. The greatest challenge is that while school infrastructure and systems can be used, the scale-up requires the provisioning of classes, specific systems, and development of large numbers of teachers for the classes as well as additional district office and PED staff to support them.

An unfortunate consequence of the move to schools has been the weakening of the community-based sector. White Paper 5 made note of the loss to the community-based sector, which in 2000 provided for some 83 percent of children. It was anticipated that some better-off parents would continue to use community-based schools and that places would open up to younger children. This was proven to be only partly true. Because Grade R in the public schools is cheaper, many community-based sites have been seriously weakened by the move of children to public schools, as well as the higher costs of caring for younger children who require higher adult to child ratios. The issue of aftercare is also a critical one, as almost all community-based sites offered a full day program but Grade R is only part day, which can put young children at risk in the afternoons, particularly if parents are working. Only recently, since the 2005-06 financial year, has the drive to scale up the number of ECD sites registered by the Department of Social Development (DoSD) and subsidies for children under five years offered a life line to nonprofit community ECD provisions.

Capacity for Implementation

There are several aspects of implementation for which capacity needed to be developed once the project moved beyond the pilot stage. Significant investments were required for learner support material, teacher training, increased education department staff at national and provincial levels, and physical infrastructure.

Location of ECD in National and Provincial Education Departments
Initially Grade R fell under the ECD, Schooling and Junior Primary Directorate in the DoE (which focused on schooling from Grade 1 and the NPP). This was because of attempts to link lower primary and ECD more effectively. However, in 1998 an ECD directorate was formed. The move to an ECD directorate was very useful in taking forward the mandate of the Education and Training White Paper, which articulated a pre-Grade R system, as well as Grade R. However, the downside has been that although Grade R is meant to be part of the Foundation Phase, it is not automatically included in policy and systems. To facilitate a solid transition, the directorate has to ensure that Grade R stays on all departmental agendas and that it is part of the monitoring and evaluation system, the Education Management Information System, or EMIS, and systemic evaluation processes.[7]

In the provinces, the ECD directorate was not automatically replicated. ECD is often linked with other sections such as ABET, Special Projects, Psychological Services, and Institutional Planning, though some provinces do have their own directorates. The difficulty with this is that the staffing in the provincial units may not have ECD expertise and also that where staffing is stretched, other areas might be prioritized for administrative and support services. During the Conditional Grant period, it was necessary to appoint provincial coordinators to ensure that this project was kept on track. Staffing capacity in the DoE has increased considerably over the last few years to keep pace with both the rollout of Grade R and expanding services for children less than five years of age. However, there are many indications that provincial staffing capacity has been overstrained during the rollout period.

Wildeman (2004) explains that provinces unanimously indicated that a lack of personnel hampered successful implementation of policies as well as readiness to spend in the years of the Conditional Grant where underspending in several of the provinces was a severe problem. Grant conditions did not provide for necessary personnel. Wildeman and Nomdo (2004) note that the funding and expansion of ECD services are based upon the fiscal space brought about by declining enrollment trends and efficiency gains in the schooling system. White Paper 5 "indicates that freed-up fiscal space should not be consumed by the traditional schooling sector and more specifically by personnel expenditure" (Wildeman, 2004:12).

There are also concerns that while provincial and district office staff focus on policy implementation, many do not have the professional capacity to support teachers to implement the curriculum.

Aligning of Systems and Incentives

In addition to uneven implementation across the provinces (as can be seen in table 1 [p. 199]), the DoE has recognized systemic challenges in regard to Grade R rollout (Department of Education, 2008), including:

- Lack of systems to pay practitioners and upgrade qualifications
- Lack of accurate data (on salaries, qualifications)
- Different levels of funding across the provinces

A highly publicized example comes from Gauteng Province. In May 2008 Grade R teachers approached the press because their R2,000 salaries (approximately $240) are often seriously delayed, due to payment system problems. There are wide variations in salaries paid across the provinces, partly but not only due to different qualification levels. In 2008 Free State, Limpopo, and North West paid R5,000 a month to qualified teachers; Northern Cape paid R3,000; Mpumalanga paid R2,000 regardless of qualification, and in the Kwa-Zulu Natal teachers in primary schools received R1,750.

To address these and other issues, a Grade R implementation plan was approved by the Heads of Education Committee (HEDCOM) on March 17, 2008. Project management support has been provided at national and provincial level, an audit will be conducted of all practitioners to determine levels of qualification as well as salaries received, and most significantly the norms and standards for funding Grade R will be implemented.

The norms and standards for funding of Grade R, first gazetted for public comment in 2005, have been legislated (Republic of South Africa, 2008) and will be implemented from January 2009. They provide a legislative springboard for rollout of Grade R. While provisions largely speak to provisioning and funding, the norms and standards also provide for the development by the DoE of minimum inputs in terms of materials, staff qualifications, and so on. Key provisions include:

1. A pro-poor funding formula in which funding over the basic level is available to schools in the two poorest quintiles. This is intended to be used for inputs that compensate more disadvantaged learners through more materials and more favorable learner/educator ratios.

2. Provincial medium term expenditure framework MTEF budgets as the primary/exclusive source of funding for public and independent Grade R services in provinces.

3. Grade R learners are to be funded at 70 percent of the per-learner level of Grade 1 learners, but provinces have discretion in the setting of per learner expenditure allocations (down to 50 percent) as an interim measure to cover more schools in the early years of the rollout period, provided that national standards are met.

4. Provision for establishment posts for Grade R: Provinces may decide to convert a portion of the total allocation to a Grade R site(s) into a post or posts. This is determined annually. The only rider is that the allocation should cover both the personnel and non-personnel costs and should not exceed recommended personnel/non-personnel expenditure ratios. The personnel amount will be retained by the PED and practitioners paid by the PED. The other model is for funds for both personnel and non-personnel costs to be transferred to the school fund. This still excludes direct employment of teachers by departments and there is as yet no legislation requiring schools to implement Grade R, as they are required to provide Grades 1 upwards, which is a critical issue for the development of Grade R.

5. Community-based sites receiving public funding must be registered as independent schools and other schools may apply (according to criteria that have now been developed). In terms of the South African Schools Act, this allows these schools to be part of the funding formula. Wildeman and Nomdo (2006) query whether the funding formula will leave independent schools vulnerable to the termination of public support.

6. Information on Grade R will be included on the school funding norms and standards resource targeting list. This includes information on which schools are eligible for Grade R targeting, possess management readiness for implementation of Grade R (financial management, effectiveness of

the School Governing Body, quality of teaching and learning), and current and projected physical space available for Grade R.

7. Each PED must formulate a rollout plan for public school Grade R, using the information on Grade R eligibility, management readiness, physical space, budgets, per learner cost, learner coverage per school, and the pro-poor funding gradient.

8. Provision is made for monitoring of the appropriate utilization of public funds. This will include inputs such as class size, practitioner skills, and learner support materials, as well as learner performance.

Levels of per-learner funding differ widely across the country. For this reason, the norms and standards provide that the DoE and PEDs collaborate with a view to harmonizing these differences. Guidelines for costing a basic minimum package of inputs have been developed by the DoE, as well as a tool for planning the rollout, and a readiness assessment tool.

PEDs are in the process of amending current registration criteria, assessing readiness, and determining per learner costs and coverage per school. This has been the basis for PEDs MTEF budgets for Grade R, and schools will be provided with letters of allocations for the 2009 school year. The DoE has provided a training manual to the provincial departments to cascade to district level.

Accountability Mechanisms

At the Parliamentary Portfolio Committee for Education in June 2008, the DoE indicated that while additional provision in the MTEF has shown a true commitment to Grade R provision, it is a battle to ensure that provinces direct the money where it is intended. Accountability mechanisms include a statutory requirement for Annual Performance Plans by provincial departments. PEDs set Grade R targets as part of this process, and these indicate that PEDs are intent on rolling out Grade R. In addition, the norms and standards provide a lever. However, the need for more rigorous monitoring processes has been identified.

Meanwhile, in addition to the norms and standards process, rollout plans, and reporting, there will be additional contact with the provinces by the national government for monitoring purposes.

Provisioning

Infrastructure

The National Pilot Project evaluation report proposed that Grade R continued in community-based sites as well as in schools and recommended that community Grade Rs should be linked to schools as satellites for purposes of financial mechanisms of school sites (as had been piloted in KwaZulu Natal). However, the national government decided to utilize the schooling system, which is widespread in South Africa in rural as well as urban areas. Utilizing this for Grade R was intended to capitalize on its accountability mechanisms including:

1. Established school governing bodies,

2. Sustainable banking accounts and sound financial management, and

3. Existing infrastructure to facilitate service expansion for Grade R.

However, school management tends to be patchy among schools. Many are not in the position to manage their own finances, and there has been considerable investment in developing systems for the channeling of subsidies in the provinces.

The addition of Grade R classes to existing schools is not a simple matter. Primary school sites are not necessarily ideal in terms of infrastructure for Grade R provisioning. While there were under-utilized classrooms in some places, in a system where infrastructure backlogs are a widespread problem, the preference must be given to compulsory age learners (Grades 1–9) in terms of instructional space. Therefore, adding another grade (Grade R) may result in overcrowding or in infrastructural investment. Where classrooms do exist they are not necessarily ideal—for example, they can be far from toilets, which must be shared with the whole school, with no place for hand washing or to sleep if these are needed.[8] The existing infrastructure may be unsuitable for the type of experiential instruction integral to Grade R, which requires more space. In some schools there is no separate outside play area for young children. Furthermore, in 2006, 26 percent of primary schools were in overall very poor condition (Department of Education, 2007). All of this constrains the development of Grade R at public schools. Two key informants reflected that because of a backlog in classroom capacity for older levels, there was a break in the phasing out of community-based provision. In a presentation to the Parliamentary Portfolio Committee for Education in May 2003, the DoE indicated that its expansion plans for the next three years included maintaining the use of Grade R classes in community-based sites and also indicated that under-utilized and additional classrooms were being sourced.

The location of school- or community-based Grade R classes shows wide provincial variation. As can be seen in table 1, approximately 42 percent of coverage in 2004–05 was in community sites (Wildeman & Nomdo, 2004). The tendency has been for children to migrate to school-based sites from community sites, and the 2004 figure shows an increase of 2,629 classes since the Nationwide Audit (Department of Education, 2001a). By 2006, according to the NEIMS assessment, 57 percent (8,511 of 14,919) of primary schools offered Grade R (Department of Education, 2007).

In 2004–05 most Grade R classes in the Eastern Cape, Gauteng, and Limpopo were located at schools, but in the Free State, Western Cape, and probably North West use of community sites may well have persisted considering relatively low coverage in the schooling system in these provinces. In rural areas

TABLE 1 Publicly Supported Reception Year Sites at Primary
Schools and at Community-Based Sites by Province 2004–05

Province	School-based	Community-based	Total
Eastern Cape	1,357	675	2,032
Free State	78	393	471
Gauteng	469	91	560
KwaZulu-Natal	1,059	814	1,873
Limpopo	2,169	1,008	3,177
Mpumalanga	450	350	800
Northern Cape	149	177	326
North West	n.a.	775	n.a.
Western Cape	541	1,009	1,550
South Africa	6,272	4,517	10,789

Source: Personal communication with provincial education departments, Wildeman and Nomdo (2004:29)

n.a. = Not available

distances to primary schools may be extreme and involve river crossings, and community-based sites are often closer and safer. For this reason, the White Paper 5 guideline of 85 percent in public schools will be applied with consideration for the context. In some provinces community-based Grade R classes are being subsumed into the primary system, but in others this is not favored because of the job losses it will cause in the community sector and the low status of Grade R in many primary schools.

Currently, the DoE has put in an infrastructure request to Treasury for the building of approximately 1,300 disability friendly, customized Grade R units with their own toilets. These will be placed at schools in Quintiles 1 to 3 in areas where there is a real infrastructure shortage. Building is currently under way in some provinces. Western Cape, for example, has funds for 141 classes to the end of 2009 but needs 280 by 2010–11; in other provinces shortages are far higher.

The option of providing transport for children where numbers are low needs to be weighed against the benefits of building classrooms. Transport is provided, especially in rural areas to children for the compulsory schooling phase, which currently begins at Grade 1, and some provinces have extended this to Grade R learners.

Learner Support Material and Equipment

Grade R classrooms also require materials and furnishing. Provinces have therefore needed to supply these. Some only provide the per capita subsidy but others have supplied materials kits in addition. There is provision in provincial budgets for materials, and the DoE has developed a guideline for the basic minimum package. The guideline gives PEDs information on how to determine learner allocations (costs) in relation to the pro-poor gradients, then coverage per school, and lists for equipment. Some equipment is mandatory, but the guideline includes other equipment that could add value to the process. Provision is also made for personnel inputs and other operational costs that could be incurred at school level such as photocopying and cleaning.

Curriculum

The curriculum for Grade R forms part of the National Curriculum Statement Foundation Phase curriculum (Department of Education, 2002). For Grade R the focus is on three learning programs, numeracy, literacy, and life skills, and the intention is that these will be taught in an integrated, play-based, child-centered manner. There have been a number of challenges in this regard, which are discussed below.

Class Size

A practitioner-learner ratio of 1:30 is the recommendation in the minimum basic input guideline, attempting to resolve the issue where the primary school ratio is set at 1:40, and some provinces apply this to Grade R. Subsidy funding can be utilized for an assistant to reduce the ratio. A model for small schools still has to be finalized as in many rural areas and on farms there are far fewer children. In the Western Cape, Grade R classes of fewer than twelve children are subsidized, and in the Northern Cape the ratio may be as low as 1:7. Free State province has many farm schools on commercial farms, and the number of Grade R students is too few to make for viable classes, which is a major challenge to be addressed.

Capacity Building Strategy

Given a history in which formal qualifications were not available to most of those working as teachers of young children, finding suitably qualified personnel for an expanding Grade R sector has been a serious challenge. Add to this the problem that an ECD qualification does not at present lead to recognized employment, that there is no formal career path or clear articulation between the different levels of ECD qualification and the Bachelor of Education, and that the situation faces demand- as well as supply-side challenges.

Qualifications and Training

There is no comprehensive data source available on training levels in the ECD sector post the Nationwide Audit conducted in 2000 (Department of Education, 2001a), but at that time the vast majority of the 48,561 ECD practitioners working in ECD facilities were considered as underqualified. Only 12 percent were recognized as qualified educators by the DoE (a matriculation/secondary school leaving certificate plus at least a three-year diploma). In addition, some PEDs have redeployed excess primary school teachers to Grade R who need retraining. The DoE has identified the need to audit Grade R teacher qualifications in all sites and the EMIS has been adapted for this purpose.

White Paper 5: Early Childhood Development identified as challenges:

+ Inequities in the qualifications of ECD practitioners/educators

+ Absence of an accreditation system for trainers of ECD practitioners/educators (Department of Education, 2001b: 2.2.6).

To address these problems the DoE "undertakes to expand, over the medium term, its work on practitioner development and career pathing for reception year practitioners and pre-reception year practitioners" (5.3.4).

Historically, a lack of formal training opportunities for ECD practitioners led to the development of training programs offered by the nongovernment sector that were neither accredited nor recognized by education departments. With the establishment of the South African Qualifications Authority (SAQA) and the national qualifications framework (NQF), the possibility of upgrading to a recognized qualification became a reality. The National ECD Pilot Project's Interim Accreditation Committee became the ECD Standards Generating Body in 1999. By early 2003 qualifications and standards were registered by SAQA at Levels 1 (Basic Certificate in ECD) and 4 (National Certificate in ECD—secondary school leaving level) and Level 5 (Higher Certificate in ECD and Diploma in ECD). These developments have moved ECD training a long way towards standardization, allowing NGOs and private training providers to be accredited on the same basis as public providers.

In 2002 accreditation of ECD training providers began, mostly through the Education, Training and Development Practices Sector Education and Training Authority (ETDP SETA). The Council for Higher Education accredits some providers. In 2007, 156 training providers were accredited to offer ECD qualifications and standards (SAQA, 2007).

Capacity Building for PED and District Officials, School Staff, and Governing Bodies

While there has been a focus on management training for school governing bodies to handle their Grade R subsidies, and DoE support to PEDs on the requirements of the new system and rollout plans, there is a concern that PED staff themselves need professional training.

While it has been shown that a great deal of effort and planning is needed to achieve the access targets, far more of a concern to the DoE is providing access to a program of sufficient quality. To improve quality, DoE plans to develop support materials for practitioners, including posters and booklets with practical ideas. New draft standards for the Grade R program have been used in identification of model classes. The idea was to counter the largely negative impression of Grade R quality by having classes that are working well as examples. The minister of education therefore asked for 100 best practice schools. Each province identified at least ten and this year (2008–09) 200 will be spread across the provinces in relation to the distribution of Grade R classes. Most of these are in primary schools because it was there that the greatest problems were to be found (even though there are still challenges in the community schools). Best practice examples will be included in a booklet.

Partnerships, Civil Society, and Advocacy

The major role for civil society stakeholders in the rollout of Grade R has been to provide training services under tender to the national and provincial department. Initially NGOs undertook the bulk of training, training material development, and research support for the scaling up. Currently, more of the public Further Education and Training colleges have been drawn in as training providers. Initially, these colleges had not aligned the previous National Educare qualifications to the new ECD qualifications registered with SAQA. They have now been doing so, and a developing trend in some provinces is for the NGOs to work in consortia with the vocational Further Education and Training (FET) colleges.

The other role that civil society stakeholders are intended to play through the ECD Stakeholder Forum is as a communication channel from the DoE to service providers on the ground. This will be all the more important for developing services for younger children outside of the schooling system, as once Grade R becomes compulsory it will be subsumed in schooling stakeholder structures.

Private/public partnerships have not been a major feature of the rollout of Grade R, though the successful Takalani Sesame radio and television broadcasts, with support materials initiated in 2000, have been a partnership between the DoE, the South African Broadcasting Corporation, and the Children's Television Workshop, together with funding from a large financial institution.

The DoE is working towards an advocacy strategy for Grade R. Currently, DoE representatives make presentations at many public conferences and events organized by civil society to update the sector, in addition to holding regular meetings with PEDs. The vision for the advocacy strategy is that it will be aimed at all stakeholders—officials, principals, and parents.

PROGRAM ASSESSMENT

In this section, evaluations of progress towards universal Grade R provision at an acceptable level of quality are considered, as well as the probability that Grade R will be sustainable. So far, the National Pilot Project evaluation, discussed above, is the only study to have looked directly at the impact of the Grade R program on child outcomes and practitioner capacities, though this was a relatively minor part of the evaluation brief. Rather than evaluations of the model, the DoE focus has been on ongoing monitoring of how targets are being met. The Education Management Information System (EMIS) has been extended to collect information from community-based ECD sites as well as from schools for 2008. In 2007 the DoE appointed a task team to review White Paper 5 to make recommendations to the minister for further expansion and implementation. From August to November 2008, National Treasury conducted a research project on the state of readiness for achieving universal access to Grade R by 2010 on behalf of the DoE with a goal of identifying the best way to proceed with rollout.

In relation to outcomes, there is provision in the norms and standards for Grade R funding, for tracking learner performance as well as the input side, "for instance, that Grade R classes are of an appropriate size, that ECD practitioners possess adequate skills and that learners have access to appropriate learner support materials" (Republic of South Africa, 2008:250), indicating a move to results-based monitoring.

The second DoE systemic evaluation at the end of the Foundation Phase (Grade 3) in 2007 included some children who had participated in public Grade R in 2004, and this data set will be analyzed to see if there are any emerging trends.

In this section, the different assessments are described, the findings noted, and the likelihood of sustainability considered.

Scale Reached and Service Quality

Take Up of Grade R

Table 2 indicates the extent of the rollout for Grade R up to 2007 and what still needs to be achieved if the target for the financial year 2010–11 is to be met. Some critics maintain that universal coverage by January 2011 is an unrealistic target given the average expansion rate since 2004 of about 43,000 children per year, and that the likelihood that the system's capacity is reaching saturation point is a real threat. This has been borne out in the June 2009 announcement that there will be universal coverage by 2014.

Implementation rates across provinces suggest that some provinces will reach "universal access" by the due dates but that others may find this challenging. The PEDs have, however, indicated to DoE that they are on track, and Table 2 [p. 208] does not account for the number of children in community-based sites. The DoE estimates, based on the 2007 Community Survey, that there are another 200,000 children to be accounted for.[9] Lack of accurate data is a challenge to be addressed by the capturing of all Grade R classes, including those in stand-alone centers on the EMIS system.

Variation in coverage across the provinces to a great extent reflects provincial commitment to Grade R. For most services it is rural provinces that have poorest access, but the former homeland provinces of Eastern Cape, Limpopo, and KwaZulu Natal have the highest percentage of rollout in the public school system. This may be attributed to limited community-based provision and/or because the PEDs favor use of the school system.

Quality of Programming

"We shouldn't simply put a bad Grade R onto a primary school system, facing many challenges, because we have the money to roll it out."
—Education Policy Specialist

While it has been shown that a great deal of effort and planning is in place to achieve the 2010–11 access targets, far more of a concern expressed by DoE personnel is providing access to a program of sufficient quality. While it may be difficult to monitor and enforce ratios and provide infrastructure and equipment, curriculum implementation is even more challenging. Key informants for this case study noted a lack of staffing and transport at the district office level, which makes it difficult to provide for the monitoring, capacity building, and support needed to bring about quality in a rapidly expanding system.

A further difficulty for pre-primary classes in primary schools, as noted in several countries, is the strong tendency towards formality in the Grade R teaching practice (Biersteker, Ngaruiya, Sebatane, and Gudyanga, 2008). In South Africa, the reception year curriculum forms part of the National Curriculum Statement but is intended to be based on active learning experiences. In many primary schools, there is pressure for a formal approach, especially if heads of department and principals (and in some cases district officials) are not grounded in early childhood care and education methods. A strong focus on literacy and numeracy skills, plus teachers who themselves have not viewed play as educational and often have relatively low qualifications, has put play-based learning under enormous threat.

Two external studies of Grade R have examined inputs for Grade R in relation to what might be needed to achieve access and quality. The first, by Wildeman and Nomdo (2004) for IDASA Budget Information Services, looked at this from a budget perspective. The study examined where South Africa was in relation to universal access and also flagged the issue of whether quality of access would be adequate especially in poorer communities. This study noted PED informants' concerns about the consequences of low levels of per capita investments in ECD including:

+ Infrastructure and transport costs especially for training practitioners and site management committees

+ Low remuneration levels for practitioners drawing weak practitioners

+ Not enough funding to employ personnel to implement the policy, especially in regards to monitoring and quality assurance

+ Concerns that allocations for ECD do not allow for planned extension of the reception year

+ Lack of funds for learner support material.

Another study on the situation of Grade R policy and implementation in four provinces (Moll, 2007b) was contracted by a donor agency to inform possible priority interventions, and raised some key points of more general interest. Moll suggests that rollout at current rates would take another seven years (until 2014). In discussion with PED officials, the main challenges identified were:

+ Difficulty in retaining suitable Grade R teachers—this relates to the broad area of salaries, qualifications, and career paths (uneven set of principles according to which Grade R teachers are paid)

+ Stretched funding for Grade R because the subsidy is qualified subject to the availability of funding

+ Challenges in training Grade R teachers (capacity, cost, and funding and concerns in some provinces about the depth)

+ Limited provincial staffing capacity

Monitoring Impact

Systemic Evaluation

The DoE Systemic Evaluation provides a national framework for evaluating the education system at key transition stages, including: Grade 3, the end of the Foundation Phase; Grade 6, for the Intermediate Phase; and Grade 9, for the Senior Phase. It enables tracking not only of a learner's cognition, but also of progress towards the transformation goals of access, equity, and quality.

The first Foundation Phase systemic evaluation involved a survey of a 5 percent random sample of Grade 3 learners (52,000) in 2001. Achievement in literacy and numeracy averaged at 54 percent and 30 percent, respectively.[10] The second cycle of systemic evaluation of 54,000 Grade 3 learners in 2,400 primary schools took place in 2007. Key findings are an overall percentage score of 36 percent in literacy and improved 35 percent in numeracy.[11]

Some of the learners in this 2007 Grade 3 cohort will have attended Grade R classes, and the DoE has commissioned an analysis of the results in order to assess what impact preschool has had on children's performance in Grade 3. Given the early stage of the rollout of Grade R in 2004, the levels of poverty and disadvantage of many learners, and the challenges in the primary schooling system, it would be unlikely that there would be striking differences at this stage.

TABLE 2 National Enrollment in Grade R 1999–2007

Province	1999	2000	2001	2002	2003	2004	2005	2006	2007	Target	%
Eastern Cape	20,703	19,555	18,873	23,562	46,371	75,571	105,231	96,364	112,889	149,968	75
Free State	14,649	15,025	16,002	17,220	16,323	16,482	18,449	20,072	22,429	58,550	38
Gauteng	n.a.	21,368	23,920	28,189	31,666	34,690	41,073	47,314	49,931	168,664	30
KwaZulu-Natal	36,334	66,031	73,993	72,312	75,996	73,098	79,276	92,948	118,884	214,515	55
Limpopo	38,702	75,219	84,243	90,332	89,790	89,725	98,273	102,969	93,030	132,965	70
Mpumalanga	16,302	10,922	5,803	12,148	13,884	23,695	14,171	25,734	34,962	74,090	47
North West	3,444	3,193	3,176	3,142	4,325	5,625	9,737	15,311	16,143	81,137	20
Nortnern Cape	4,155	3,972	4,042	3,744	5,500	5,875	6,598	7,259	8,423	19,061	44
Western Cape	22,003	11,346	11,473	28,077	31,532	31,726	32,389	33,650	30,834	91,580	34
National	156,292	226,631	241,525	278,726	31,5387	356,487	405,197	441,621	487,525*	990,530	49

Source: Department of Education, EMIS Education Statistics, Briefing of Parliamentary Portfolio Committee on Education, June 3, 2008, for 2007. EMIS accessible at www.education.gov.za/emis/emisweb/statistics.htm ("Statistics at a Glance" Reports, 1999–2006). Parliamentary Portfolio Committee on Education, June 3, 2008, at www.pmg.org.za/report/20080603-early-childhood-development-briefing-department-education.

n.a. = Not available

* EMIS data exclude stand-alone ECD sites where the DoE estimates another 200,000 Grade R learners are enrolled.

A finding of the evaluation, which most likely holds for Grade R as well as Grade 3 classes, is that there were pockets of excellence within the system (where learners performed excellently), and they were not only found in the more affluent quintile 4 and 5 schools.

Monitoring Grade R Outcomes

The DoE intends, in accordance with the requirements of the Norms and Standards for Grade R funding, to introduce an assessment of Grade R outcomes, probably early in Grade 1. This needs to be carefully managed as school readiness testing was used in the past to bar children from Grade 1, which is counter to education policy.

Sustainability

Expansion of ECD in South Africa has been fortunate in that political will has continued to grow rather than decline, as increasing budgets signify. The threats to sustainability and rollout are primarily the lack of human resource capacity to implement, support, and monitor a system at the degree of quality that will make a difference. While there are valid concerns about the threat to the community sector and the formalization of Grade R through its principal placement in public primary schools, this location together with norms and standards for funding as an amendment to the Norms and Standards for School Funding makes it less vulnerable to political change. So, for example, even if there are no obvious impacts of the program on learner attainment in the Foundation Phase, it is more likely that there will be interventions to improve it than that it would be abandoned. Current plans seek to move towards a national harmonized strategy and to provide more intense systemic support.

Initial training, upgrading of qualifications, and ongoing professional development are significant challenges for building a Grade R that provides sustainable quality services. Employment of Grade R teachers will provide the incentive to invest in training both on the supply and demand side.

OVERALL ASSESSMENT AND CONCLUSIONS

In this section, the critical issues and lessons learned for the mass expansion of ECD services and programs in South Africa are considered. In addition to the way that Grade R rolled out, consideration is given to services for birth to four-year-olds, which are also set for mass expansion.

Critical Junctures in the Scale-Up of ECD Services in South Africa

There is little doubt that policy and legislation have been and will be very significant in enabling the scaling up process. Key points in the scale-up of ECD services both for five-year-olds and younger children have been the adoption of policy and legislation. Key challenges in the process have been in relation to the lack of a mandate to provide a particular service. In order for policy to be adopted there has had to be a great deal of political will, lobbying, and championing of the ECD cause. The extraordinary opportunities for public investment in new developmental policies at the time of transition to democracy provided the lever for the promotion of ECD. It is perhaps no surprise that it was education policy that drove ECD services, as education organizations had played a key role in the liberation struggle.

Overall Evaluation of the Scaling Up of Grade R

Despite some uncertainties about actual present coverage, which will be remedied by the inclusion of free-standing community sites in the EMIS and their registration as independent schools, there is enormous will and resource provision towards Grade R achieving universal coverage.

The intention is that Grade R becomes universal, compulsory, and accessible to all children, while the pro-poor funding formula provides for directing more resources to disadvantaged children, who (as evidence from around the world has shown) benefit most from early education interventions.

While there are many excellent Grade R classes, there are huge challenges with regard to the general quality of what is offered. There are concerns not only over the educational program but also over the health and safety of some facilities. Overcrowding is a problem in many areas, as is distance from the school in many communities. In some rural areas, numbers of children are too small to make the program viable, and transport needs to be provided. Currently this is done in the Western Cape and Gauteng. Underage enrollments continue, though on a smaller scale than in the past.

Impact has not yet been directly measured, but it would be surprising if it is large at this early stage. Quite apart from the challenges in Grade R itself and the Foundation Phase that follows, the compromised nutritional status of nearly a quarter of young children and the lack of early educational opportunities of the kind necessary for transition to schooling indicate that Grade R alone, while an important component, will not be a sufficient platform to address compromised early childhood development (e.g., Klop, 2005).

Given the challenge of introducing systems, monitoring, and evaluation, and the insufficient capacity of the community sector to absorb nearly one million five-year-olds, it has to be concluded that despite its inadequacies, the primary schooling system is the more realistic and convenient vehicle for Grade R.

REFERENCES

Biersteker, L. 1997, *An Assessment of Programmes and Strategies for 0–4 Year Olds. South Africa Case Study Report: Africa Regional Integrated Early Childhood Services Initiative*, Early Learning Resource Unit, Cape Town.

Biersteker, L. & Dawes, A. 2008, "Early Childhood Development," in *HRD Review 2008: Education, Employment and Skills*, A. Kraak & K. Press, eds., HSRC Press, Cape Town, pp. 185–205.

Biersteker, L., Ngaruiya, S., Sebatane, E., & Gudyanga, S. 2008, "Introducing Preprimary Classes in Africa: Opportunities and Challenges," in *Africa's Future, Africa's Challenge: Early Childhood Care and Development in sub-Saharan Africa*, M. Garcia, A. Pence, & Evans J., eds., World Bank, Washington DC, pp. 227-248.

Department of Education. 1995, White Paper on Education and Training. *Government Gazette*, Pretoria.

———. 1996, Interim Policy of Early Childhood Development, Pretoria.

———. 2001a, *The Nationwide Audit of ECD Provisioning in South Africa*, Pretoria.

———. 2001b, *White Paper 5: Early Childhood Development*, Pretoria.

———. 2001c, *Report on the National ECD Pilot Project*, Pretoria.

———. 2002, Revised National Curriculum Statement, Pretoria.

———. 2007, *National Assessment Report on Public Ordinary Schools in 2006*, National Education Infrastructure Monitoring System (NEIMS), Pretoria.

———. 2008, Presentation to the Parliamentary Portfolio Committee on Education, June 3.

Department of Education, Department of Health & Department of Social Development. 2007, *Guidelines for the Implementation of the National Integrated Plan for ECD*, Pretoria.

Department of Education and Training. 1987, *An Inquiry into the Introduction of a Bridging Period Prior to Basic Education*, Pretoria.

Department of Social Development. 2006, *Guidelines for ECD Services*, Pretoria.

Human Sciences Research Council. 1981, *Provision of education in the Republic of South Africa. Report of the Main Committee (the De Lange Commission)* Pretoria.

Klop, D. 2005, *The Stability of Language Disorders in a Group of Disadvantaged Grade 3 Children*, Stellenbosch: Speech, Language and Hearing Therapy, Faculty of Health Sciences, University of Stellenbosch, unpublished (Ref No 04/08/138)

Moll, I. 2007a, Early Childhood Development Curriculum in South Africa, in *Early Childhood Education—The Countries: An International Encyclopedia Volume 4* R. New & M. Cochran, eds., Westport, Connecticut: Praeger, pp. 1219–1224.

———. 2007b, *The State of Grade R Provision in South Africa and Recommendations for Priority Interventions within it*, A report prepared for the ZENEX Foundation, SAIDE, Braamfontein.

Naidoo, N. 2007, *Statistics on Education from the Community Survey and General Household Survey*, Presentation to the Department of Education, 11 December 2007, Statistics South Africa.

NEPI. 1992, *Early Childhood Educare: Report of the National Education Policy Investigation*, National Education Coordinating Committee/Oxford University Press, Cape Town.

Padayachie, R., Atmore, E., Biersteker, L., King, R., Matube, J., Muthayan, S., Naidoo, K., Plaatjies, D., & Evans J. 1994, *Report of the South African Study on Early Childhood Development*, Centre for Education Policy Development/World Bank, Johannesburg/Washington DC.

Padayachie, R., Moodly, J., Abrahams, F., Atmore, E., & Weitz, V. 1997, *Early Childhood Development: An Audit Study*, SACECD/National Educare Forum, Durban.

Porteus, K. 2001, "Fighting the Dragon: Globalisation and its attack on equity," *Quarterly Review of Education and Training in South Africa*, vol. 8, no. 2, pp. 8–17.

Porteus, K. 2004, "The State of Play in ECD," in *Changing Class: Education and Social Change in Post-apartheid South Africa*, L. Chisholm, ed., HSRC Press, Cape Town, pp. 339–365.

Republic of South Africa 2008, "Government Notice 26 SA Schools Act 1996 (Act No 84 of 1996): National Norms and Standards for Grade R Funding," *Government Gazette*, vol. 30679.

SAQA. 2007, *The Uptake and Impact of Qualifications and Unit Standards in the Subfield: Early Childhood Development*, Directorate Strategic Support: SAQA, Pretoria.

Seleti, J. 2007, *How Stakeholder Politics Shape the Trajectory of Early Childhood Education Policy: A South African Case*, Unpublished, Phd Thesis, University of Pretoria.

Streak, J., & Norushe, T. 2008, *Governance and Budgeting for Implementation of the National Integrated Plan with the Spotlight on the EPWP ECD Initiative. Scaling Up ECD (0 - 4 years) in South Africa*, Human Sciences Research Council.

Taylor, N. 1992, *The Bridging Period Programme: An Early Assessment. Report for the NEPI Research Group: Early Childhood Educare*, Unpublished.

Wildeman, R. 2004, *Reviewing Provincial Education Budgets 2004: Budget Brief No. 143*, IDASA, Cape Town.

Wildeman, R., & Nomdo, C. 2006, *A Response to the Proposed Funding Norms and Standards for the Reception Year (Grade R) Budget Brief No. 162*, IDASA, Cape Town.

———. 2004, *Implementation of Universal Access to the Reception Year (Grade R): How Far Are We?*, IDASA, Cape Town.

7

Global Governance for Development

JOHANNES F. LINN *and* COLIN I. BRADFORD JR.

A t the end of World War II, the creation of the United Nations (UN), the International Monetary Fund (IMF), and the World Bank under U.S. leadership established multilateral institutions with a global reach to help guide the postwar peace, recovery, and development process. This ushered in a new era of global governance. Since then, globalization has taken hold with an ever-closer integration of the world's economies, much reinforced by the fall of the Bamboo and Iron Curtains, with the opening up of China, and the break-up of the Soviet Union. At the same time the system of multilateral finance and development institutions grew with the creation of many new global and regional multilateral agencies, some as part of the UN system, others outside it. Among development finance institutions, the World Bank was joined by a growing number of regional development banks (RDBs) and "vertical funds"—multilateral funding agencies with special mandates, such as the Global Fund for HIV/AIDS, TB and Malaria. Moreover, in response to recurrent global financial crises, apex forums were established to bring together the leaders of key countries—most important, the G-7 summit of the leaders of the major Western economies (later the G-8, after Russia joined) and the G-20, set up initially as a group of finance ministers of major financial powers.

James Wolfensohn saw the need for effective global development institutions early on. During his ten years as president of the World Bank, he was involved in shaping key elements of the global governance architecture, fostering close cooperation among the global and regional development agencies, and participating in many global forums and leadership meetings designed to advance the global development agenda through multilateral action. He saw firsthand how the transformation of the world from a North-South/East-West divide into a "four-speed world" (see chapter 2) created the need for a change in the way the global governance system functioned, if it was to respond effectively to the rising global challenges (such as financial crises, epidemics, climate change, and other events) and to the shifting balances in the global economy, with the rapidly growing emerging market economies rightly demanding a greater voice in the way the global governance system was run.

After his retirement from the World Bank, the Wolfensohn Center for Development at Brookings provided a natural platform for James Wolfensohn to support an exploration of how the global governance system and key multilateral institutions needed to adjust if they were to help achieve the global development agenda of the twenty-first century. The Center's work on global governance focused on three interrelated sets of issues: first, the reform of the summit architecture, with an exploration of and advocacy for a move from the increasingly marginalized G-8 summit to a more inclusive, representative, and effective G-20 summit forum; second, reform of the IMF and World Bank governance structures to allow for greater voice and vote of emerging market economies and for a more transparent and competitive leadership selection process; and third, reform of the UN system to make it more effective in addressing global development and security challenges.

The main avenue for engagement on these issues was a series of seminars and conferences at Brookings organized from 2005 to 2012 jointly by the Wolfensohn Center (and after 2010 by the Brookings Global Economy and Development program) and by the Center for International Governance Innovation (CIGI) of Waterloo, Canada. These events brought together representatives from the G-20 executive directors of the IMF and World Bank and from G-20 embassies in the Washington area with experts from think tanks and academia for lively discussions on summit reform, IMF and World Bank governance reform, and reform of the UN. In addition, the two of us produced numerous policy briefs and op-eds on these issues, and James Wolfensohn and

Wolfensohn Center staff engaged with decisionmakers and experts in various G-20 capitals, as well as at the U.S. Treasury, to promote the global governance reform agenda.

In early 2007 Brookings Institution Press published a book we oversaw as an edited volume, *Global Governance Reform: Breaking the Stalemate*; the volume's conclusion is reprinted in this chapter. It covers a broad sweep of global governance issues including reform of the IMF, World Bank, United Nations, and international summits, as well as issues in global health and environmental governance. In his preface to this book, Brookings president Strobe Talbott aptly commented that "this volume by noted experts in their fields looks at both specific institutions and the international system as a whole. Its unique contribution lies precisely in that it examines the interaction between the individual institutions and the system and explores their interdependence" (p. vii).

In October 2007, based on the findings of this book and of our ongoing exploration of the available options, we reported in a Brookings policy brief that the reform agenda appeared to be gathering increased attention, but we also noted that "whether it will take a major crisis to bring about fundamental changes in the global order and in global governance remains to be seen. . . . We know from history and bitter experience that global crises cause devastation and suffering. The creation of a global governance system which reflects the new economic and demographic realities and responds effectively to new global challenges of the 21st century is urgently needed to help avoid crises and create a better future."[1] Tragically, a global financial crisis hit exactly a year later with devastating and lasting impact on the world's economy.

One of the few positive impacts of the financial crisis of 2008–09 was the realization by President Bush that a new global leadership forum was needed to tackle the crisis, one that brought the large emerging market economies to the table. The G-20 format, which the Wolfensohn Center had intensively advocated,[2] was a ready-made option, and the United States called for the first G-20 summit to organize a response to the crisis for November 15, 2008. On the eve of this first summit, James Wolfensohn published an op-ed (reprinted in this chapter) in which he welcomed the G-20 initiative, but also noted that Western powers needed to go beyond the summit formalities and adopt a new, more open attitude toward the rising powers. Moreover, he expressed his hope that "progress at this summit can restore governments' faith in the fruits of global cooperation and renew their interest in tackling global issues that remain unresolved. Our immediate charge is to deal with the crisis we can see. But it is my great hope that progress in addressing the financial crisis will open the door for progress on the world's other crises, which, though less visible, are no less important to securing our collective future."

In subsequent years, the Wolfensohn Center and then the Brookings Global Economy and Development program became intensively involved in supporting the new G-20 summit forum by engaging with the G-20 presidencies in the summit preparation process. This involved organizing informal preparatory meetings between G-20 sherpas and G-20 think tanks and their experts, preparing agenda proposals, and assessing progress with the G-20 summit process.

The first of these preparatory meetings was a full-day, off-the-record consultation with the United Kingdom's G-20 team for which CIGI and Brookings marshaled a diverse group of experts at Lancaster House in London on February 9, 2009, two months before the London G-20 summit. Prime Minister Gordon Brown opened the meeting. The UK G-20 team was primarily interested in reforming the existing international institutions and assessing the capacities and weaknesses of the international system as a whole to deliver international economic cooperation. Participants addressed IMF resources and reform, financial regulatory reform and the country composition of the then Financial Stability Forum, and other issues that became headlines as leaders met on April 2, 2009, in London at the nadir of the then raging global financial crisis.

Perhaps the most intensive of these engagements took place in connection with the 2010 G-20 Seoul summit, hosted by South Korea and leading the way as the first emerging market economy to serve as the G-20 presidency. At the request of Il Sakong, chair of the Korean Presidential Committee on the G-20 Summit, Colin Bradford and Wonhyuk Lim organized a major preparatory symposium of experts in Seoul and edited the proceedings for a book jointly published in 2010 by the Korea Development Institute and Brookings. Its title, *Toward the Consolidation of the G20: From Crisis Committee to Global Steering Committee*, echoes James Wolfensohn's call two years earlier for a broader and sustained role for the G-20.

Paul Martin, former finance minister and prime minister of Canada and widely regarded as the "father of the G-20," was an integral part of the planning for this symposium and contributed a paper on financial sector reform.[3] Former finance ministers of Turkey and Brazil, Kemal Derviş and Pedro Malan, as well as Pier Carlo Padoan, future finance minister of Italy, wrote papers on rebalancing the global economy. Another section in the Bradford and Wonhyuk volume, with chapters contributed by Thomas Bernes, Johannes F. Linn, and Paul Heinbecker, called on the G-20 summit to address the issues of IMF legitimacy and governance reform, to break the stalemate in the reform of the multilateral development system, and to work toward reform and synergy with the UN.

In the years since 2010, the global governance system has continued to evolve. The G-20 is now firmly established as a global leadership forum. Progress was made under the auspices of the G-20 in reforming the global finance and development system, with perhaps the greatest advances in strengthening international financial regulation under the auspices of the Financial Stability Board. There has been some limited progress in reforming the governance of the IMF and World Bank, with a difficult but inadequate rebalancing of representation, vote, and voice of developing countries and with some improvements in the transparency and openness of the leadership selection process of these two institutions. However, the dominance of the traditional Western powers in these institutions remained unchallenged. As a result, the emerging market economies pushed ahead in 2015 with strengthening or setting up alternative development finance institutions, including the Asian Infrastructure Investment Bank under Chinese leadership and the New Development Bank of the BRICS, reinforcing the fragmentation and regionalization of the global development system.

Between 2010 and 2017 the Brookings Global Economy and Development program remained actively involved in the global governance agenda: It continued to support the G-20 summit process every year, most recently by hosting a meeting of the Vision20 initiative, which aimed to set up some broad agenda options for the 2017 G-20 summit in Hamburg, Germany; it continued engagement on reform of the multilateral development system with policy briefs and blogs on IMF, World Bank, and UN reforms; and Homi Kharas, who had joined the Wolfensohn Center as senior fellow in 2007 and became the Global program's deputy director in 2010, served as the lead author and executive secretary supporting the High Level Panel advising the UN secretary general on the post-2015 development agenda (Agenda 2030).

However, despite—and perhaps in part because of—the success of globalization and the global governance system in supporting huge progress forward by integrating the world economy and dramatically improving the well-being of billions of people, the global multilateral development system now faces great challenges. In a 2009 Brookings Policy Brief, reprinted in this chapter, we were hopeful that with the lessons learned from the 2008–09 financial crisis, the creation of the G-20, and the election of President Barack Obama, the "old order" in global relations was giving way to a "new order." We postulated that under the old order "the nation state is the point of departure stressing the importance of sovereignty and national interest as key principles driving a unilateral and assertive foreign policy." In contrast, the new order has as its starting point "that we live in a global society where interdependency and recognition of common interests are the key principles to be pursued in reciprocal relations and with mutual respect across borders." While noting that the new order appeared to be gaining momentum, the brief ended with a warning: "If President Obama is believed to fail the test of competence at home or a major shock hits the United States, a reversal is possible in the U.S. In any case, significant changes in global governance will take time to transpire. We may well see a long period of transition with only gradual improvement in current institutions. In the meantime, pressures for increased regionalism, bilateral deals among the big players, geopolitical competition among power blocs and growing instability and threats from the 'excluded' will undermine international cooperation and the whole idea of a global order."[4]

In their 2016 Brookings paper "Toward a New Multilateralism," Bruce Jenks and Homi Kharas extended this notion of a "new order." They argued that a new approach to multilateralism and to the multilateral development system is emerging, "based on a number of underlying principles that can be summarized as follows: doing no harm to others, solidarity with developing countries, and sharing the burden of investing in global public goods. . . . With the adoption of Agenda 2030 and the Paris Climate Statement, we are seeing the emergence of a new conception of multilateralism that is increasingly basing itself on the establishment of international normative and reporting frameworks that encourage states to act responsibly and to mobilize their whole society—including business, civil society, academia, and science. This is at least in part a recognition of the reality that many of the collective responses required to meet today's challenges are no longer within the power of governments to deliver singlehandedly."

Despite these hopeful developments, recent changes in the world, at the geopolitical and the national political level, point toward not only a slowing of progress with global governance reform, but toward potentially dramatic reversals. Tensions among the great global powers have been rising; nationalism, populism, protectionism, and anti-democratic tendencies are spreading in many countries; and—especially in the United States under President Donald Trump—support for the multilateral institutions and their role in fostering global sustainable development may be seriously eroding. It appears that the "old order" is staging a strong comeback that risks reversing the progress the world has made since the infernos of two world wars in the first half of the twentieth century. In the coming months and years it will be critical to preserve and further advance the progress made in global governance as a way to "secure our collective future," as James Wolfensohn put it in his 2008 comment on the first G-20 summit.

Global Governance Reform

Conclusions and Implications

COLIN I. BRADFORD JR. *and* **JOHANNES F. LINN**

*Colin I. Bradford Jr. is a nonresident senior fellow in the
Brookings Institution's Global Economy and Development
program and at the Centre for International Governance
Innovation (CIGI) in Waterloo, Canada.*

*Johannes F. Linn is the executive director of the Wolfensohn
Center for Development and a senior fellow in the Brookings
Institution's Global Economy and Development program.*

The principal concern of this volume is that the international system comprising both international institutions and global summit-level steering
groups is inadequate to meet the challenges of the twenty-first century. Most of
today's international institutions were founded in the mid-twentieth century.
They were based on the global challenges and power configurations that existed following World War II, when colonialism still reigned, the United States
dominated the war-damaged industrial countries, and the cold war began to
create divides between East and West. Today, the world is more integrated, and
the divisions of colonialism and the cold war are matters of the past. Given their
dramatically increased shares of world trade and economic growth, the emerg-

Editors' Note: This is the concluding chapter from the book *Global Governance Reform: Breaking
the Stalemate,* edited by Colin Bradford and Johannes F. Linn, published by Brookings Institution Press in 2007.

ing market economies are rightly claiming a greater voice in decisions made by international institutions. No longer are the challenges facing the globe, unlike those of sixty years ago, the separate domains of specialized disciplines, professions, and institutions. They are interrelated, interactive, and intersectorial, and they demand more integrated and interinstitutional approaches.

But the conditions at the beginning of the twenty-first century do not seem ripe for any major systemic breakthroughs that would replace current structures and create new institutions. The vision and sense of urgency, the innovative spirit, and the leadership that brought the IMF and the World Bank into being at Bretton Woods in 1944 and created the United Nations in San Francisco in 1945 are not present today. Instead, the most feasible path to international reform seems to be to address global governance and substantive policy reforms within individual international institutions while simultaneously reforming global consultative and decisionmaking forums such as summits, in the hope of redirecting and reenergizing the dynamics of the international system through the synergistic and cumulative impact of the reforms undertaken.

THE NEXUS OF GLOBAL REFORMS

The main conclusion of this book and the discussions on which the chapters are based is precisely that individual institutional reforms in the IMF, the World Bank, and the United Nations—and in global health and environmental governance—are critical, but they are not sufficient to sustain themselves or to achieve the broader goal of increasing the effectiveness of the international system as a whole in dealing with today's challenges. Reform of the overarching global governance groups, especially the G-8 summit but also other regional and sectorial forums, is necessary if change is to be systemic, sufficient, and effective. It is this nexus of global reforms—the interaction and interdependence of individual institutional reforms and broader governance reforms—that defines the global governance reform agenda today.

The story is complicated by conflicting needs and global politics in the international community. On one hand, there is the need to recognize the substantial shifts in the relative economic, demographic, and political weight of nations in the global system—and hence the need to give greater voice and vote to the large emerging market economies in order to increase their influence, participation, and responsibility in managing world affairs. On the other hand, the smaller, poorer nations should not be left out or assigned a minor role in a system that favors the already powerful. Yet increasing the number of seats in the global groups or on the governing boards of institutions creates problems of efficiency and effectiveness. If anything, the global governance system needs to be streamlined to be effective. Legitimacy rests on the capacity to be both representative and effective, simultaneously.

Such conflicting requirements do not make the path to global reform an obvious or an easy one. No uniform solutions have appeared that can be applied throughout the system. Rather, the hope is that the combination of a variety of reforms and their cumulative effects across a broad range of institutions and groups will generate new channels for interests, ideas, and influence that will improve both the capacity of the system and its political governance, increasing in turn both its effectiveness and its representativeness. That is the imperative of the global governance reform agenda today.

The issue of conflicting challenges is well illustrated by reform in the IMF. The reform strategy decided on by the IMF board of governors in Singapore in September 2006 commits the board to reexamining the formula for determining voting power on the IMF executive board in order to give greater weight to selected large emerging market economies. In order to increase the weight of the smaller, poorer countries, IMF members also propose to achieve at least a doubling of the weight of "basic votes" (the equal number of votes given to all countries regardless of their size) in determining voting shares. This two-pronged strategy is not only the kind of expedient political compromise needed to sustain support for the reform effort in the IMF but also the kind of reform necessary to combine efficiency with equity and thereby enhance both the legitimacy and the effectiveness of the institution.

Viewing the network of individual international institutions and global governance groups together as a system should facilitate the reform process by making it possible to exploit synergies and reinforce elements of reform. It also may help further the understanding that not all values and objectives can be fulfilled in each part of the system. In a complex world, the combined effects of reforms throughout the system and the new interactions that they stimulate may provide more complete realization of the goals of reform than isolated intrainstitutional reforms. As Jack Boorman argues in chapter 1, pursuing principles for governance reform across the board—principles such as universality, legitimacy (fairness), subsidiarity, efficiency, and accountability— pushes those values forward in each institution and also helps ensure that the system as a whole maximizes their achievement.

Focusing on the nexus of institutional and global reforms also helps accentuate the potential gains to be had from reinforcing elements. For example, in the Per Jacobsson Lecture of September 2005, Michel Camdessus, former managing director of the IMF, argued that the International Monetary and Financial Committee (IMFC), the interministerial committee guiding the IMF, should be transformed from an advisory body to a decisionmaking group—from a committee to a council—with a membership that is more "congruent" with that of "a global governance group." Camdessus proposes a similar change in the World Bank's interministerial Development Committee. We would add to his proposals the recommendation that the two new councils be combined into one to add still greater "congruence" and efficiency in global financial and development leadership. Camdessus concluded by making an important point—that "far from leading to an undue politicization of the two institutions, this would place responsibilities squarely where they belong, namely, with governments."[1] According to Camdessus, the transformation of the IMFC and the Development Committee, accompanied by broadening of the country composition of the G-8 summits, "could be a good way to address properly the broader issue of world economic governance, far from the illusion of promoting some utopian world government, but with the more limited, but necessary, ambition of finding a global response to inescapable global problems."[2] These proposals illustrate the potential of simultaneous reforms in institutions and global groups to reinforce one another, making both more effective. They also illustrate the primacy of top-level national government authorities in giving strategic direction to the international institutions.

GLOBAL GOVERNANCE REFORMS AND NATIONAL LEADERSHIP

The central locus for democratic legitimacy is the people. The legitimacy to represent the people in an international forum—what we might refer to as representational legitimacy—is most clearly lodged in national political authorities, in particular in the head of state. While there are flaws in that formulation, no other criterion competes successfully with the legitimacy of national leaders based on the support of their people.[3] That is clearly the criterion underlying the Camdessus reforms, which are intended "to make more explicit the real political responsibility" of national leaders in the international system.[4] The secretary-general of the United Nations, the president of the World Bank, the managing director of the IMF, and other appointed leaders do not have the same degree or kind of legitimacy as do leaders of national governments. As a result, global governance reform cannot be based solely on empowering appointed leaders or on getting them to work more closely together.

The fate of the international system depends to a large degree on the vision and statesmanship of prominent national leaders. The Roosevelts and Churchill forged the United Nations; Truman pushed through the formation of the World Bank and the IMF; Valéry Giscard d'Estaing and Helmut Schmidt started the G-7 summits; and a long string of French leaders from Robert Schumann to Jacques Delors took the lead in the gradual formation of the European Union. Today, visionary leadership with respect to the international community is not evident among most of the current leaders of major countries. In any event, in our view it is not clear that making conceptual leaps to a new system with new institutions is the most desirable or necessary, let alone feasible, path to reform. But if the primary site for global reform is indeed the nexus between institutional and global reforms, then what is required now is a group of countries whose leaders are willing and able to push the global reform agenda across both venues. The key question then is this: Is there such a group?

Here are some of our impressions of the political scenario, derived from more than two years of research, consultation, and engagement with officials from major countries.[5] Two industrial countries stand out as the major advocates and practitioners of multilateralism: Canada and Australia. Canada has a long tradition, going back at least to former prime ministers Lester Pearson and Pierre Trudeau, of making multilateralism the centerpiece of Canadian diplomacy and foreign policy. Its most recent manifestations have been the leadership of former prime minister Paul Martin of the G-20 finance ministers in the group's early stages in the late 1990s and his more recent advocacy of broadening the G-8 by creating an L-20 leaders-level summit group modeled on the G-20 group of ten large emerging market economies and ten industrial countries. Canada continues to be vitally engaged in global reform.

Australia in the last two years has played an exemplary role in leading the IMF reform effort, in the G-20 finance ministers meeting in Beijing in 2005, and its own chairing of the G-20 in 2006; in its role in Singapore at the World Bank–IMF annual meetings, where the first steps toward an IMF reform sequence were taken; and in the annual meeting of the G-20 in Australia in November 2006. The troika leadership principle of the G-20 ensures that Australia will continue its efforts into 2007 at the very least. The Australians and Canadians are highly interested in G-8 summit reform, but their official positions currently are less specific than one might expect, given that the G-20/L-20 idea would give them both seats at the table, while other formulations well might not.

The strongest leading governments in the global "South" with respect to global governance reform appear to us to be Brazil and South Africa. Brazil has long conceived of its national identity and development within the framework of its role in the larger world and in the Latin American region. Its difficult experience in the late 1990s, when the repercussions of the Asian and Russian financial crises threatened its stability, strengthens the assertiveness and visibility of Brazil's finance ministry in discussions of the current pattern of global imbalances and the role of international financial institutions in the global economy. Brazil is also a major player in international trade negotiations and aspires to a seat on the UN Security Council. The October 2006 reelection of President Lula da Silva ensures continuity in Brazil's global leadership. South Africa takes its role as a leading African country extremely seriously; it is careful to present itself in international affairs as a country that attempts to articulate views on behalf of and with the agreement of its African neighbors. The success of the transition from apartheid under Mandela and the visibility of Trevor Manuel in global finance during his long tenure as chair of the Development Committee have strengthened South Africa's role as a leader in the international community. Its role as chair of the G-20 in 2007 will keep it in a visible leadership position for the foreseeable future.

Two Asian countries, Japan and China, have shown some interest in the international reform agenda. The future of Japan's role in world affairs depends on its new political leadership, but its professionalism and experience in international affairs and global finance give it continuing prominence. Japan aspires to a seat on the UN Security Council, and its positions on global financial institutions and summit reforms tend to favor the status quo, which already gives Japan substantial weight. China also exhibits significant interest and presence in global reform discussions, but it is more inclined to wait for an emerging consensus than to put forward concrete proposals or assert leadership. It is more active on security and UN affairs than on the international financial institutions (IFIs) and summits. China is reluctant to be brought into the G-8 by itself, which would put it in a minority position as the only non-industrial country and could possibly jeopardize its relations with the rest of the developing world. In sum, the two largest Asian economies are internationally engaged but not currently playing strong leadership roles. If anything, they have tended to look more toward the strengthening of Asian regional summits and organizations, including the possible creation of an Asian monetary fund.

Two other economic heavyweights, India and Germany, seem to have comparable positions on global reform. Both are significant players on most global issues, and their presence and political weight seem commensurate with their status. But both are more preoccupied with internal issues and governance than with global governance reform. They tend to be quiet and cautious rather than forthcoming and innovative in global discussions, despite the stake each has in its place in the international system. Both aspire to seats on the UN Security Council, but they are not trying to get there by taking a strong role on global issues and institutions in the way that, for example, Brazil and South Africa have. On the other hand, Germany and India seem more seriously attentive and engaged than Korea and Turkey, two countries that hold back even more in the international reform conversation. How Chancellor Angela Merkel manages Germany's leadership of the G-8 summit in 2007 will reveal her hand as a player in the global reform effort.

Weakened political leadership—whether because of expected leadership changes, impending elections, or other reasons—plays a significant role in a number of countries. In the United Kingdom, the transition from Tony Blair to Gordon Brown is under way. Both are prominent international reformers, but the tensions between them seem to have made even quite senior officials under each of them reluctant to engage fully in the global debate on reform, leaving it to their principals to articulate their own views and visions when and where they see fit. The dramatic decline in public support for Jacques Chirac in France has left his government distracted on the international front and reluctant to be fully forthcoming in pushing for reform, preferring instead to protect the position of France in the G-8 and in the IFIs. The election of former EC commissioner Romano Prodi as head of government in Italy is a hopeful sign in terms of global reform, but the delicate balance in his coalition government may weaken his potential on the international front. Indeed, the uncertainty regarding the fate of the constitution of the European Union following its defeat in referendums in France and the Netherlands in the spring of 2005 is a substantial obstacle in the formation of a strong European position and role in global reform.

Finally, there is the United States, undoubtedly the key player in international reform, especially as a gatekeeper in determining which options and issues have any chance of moving forward. Under the George W. Bush administration, the Treasury Department has been a strong and positive player in the IMF reform effort, assuming a noteworthy, important, and commendable role. However, the U.S. position and policy toward reform in the World Bank and the United Nations have been complicated by the difficult presidency so far of Paul Wolfowitz at the bank and the controversial role of John Bolton as U.S. ambassador at the UN. The Bush administration seems to be a reluctant reformer, at best, regarding summits, with the president not appearing to be an enthusiastic summiteer and seeming to prefer smaller, more manageable "coalitions of the willing" to discussions and negotiations in larger arenas involving partners with differing views. A full turn of U.S. foreign policy away from a more unilateralist approach to a fully engaged multilateral presence would seem to have to wait at least until the U.S. elections in November 2008. One of the factors that may be driving the United States to a more open acknowledgment of the need for governance reform is the fear that the Asian powers may begin to create their own strong regional institutions and forums as a reaction to their underrepresentation in global institutions, especially the IFIs. Such a trend could weaken the existing global governance structure even further and most likely would not be in the U.S. national interest, a fact that appears to be well understood in the current administration.

Other G-20 countries seem to be neutral observers, including Russia, which during the run-up to the St. Petersburg G-8 summit in July 2006 was unwilling or unable to focus on the longer-term institutional reform issues. Mexico has had a trying presidential election and aftermath, which have siphoned off its attention from the global arena. In our experience, Argentina, Indonesia, and Saudi Arabia have been relatively passive players.

Thus we see a mixed picture, with some significant countries showing leadership in pushing for reform while others evidently face constraints on the priority, innovative effort, and leadership that they can give to the reform agenda.

However, the global challenges are urgent, and the international institutions need support from member countries to move forward. The key to success seems to be to apply persistent pressure on multiple institutional fronts and on a variety of issues over time in order to exploit every opportunity for action and to leverage every opportunity for change. Given the fact that great leaps forward or breakthroughs are highly unlikely, the most feasible path to reform seems to call for steady effort by a variety of actors—current and former leaders, governments, think tanks, NGOs—on a variety of fronts to upgrade the international system to meet the challenges of the twenty-first century. As with many other areas of political and institutional reform, it may take a serious global crisis to shake the key players out of their current inertia. Certainly, the historic global governance initiatives that followed World War II were an example of crisis providing the impetus for reform. But we would hope that in the absence of visionary leadership, common sense will prevent crises and promote global governance reform at the same time.

NATIONAL POLITICS AND INTERNATIONAL BEHAVIOR

If the nexus of global reform is the link between institutional reform and global governance, the nexus of power in the new global age now seems to be between domestic politics and international engagement.[6] If national officials are the most legitimate source of political authority, the links of internal politics to foreign policy and international engagement are the nexus of power in international affairs. The different degrees to which individual countries exercise leadership in global reforms, just outlined above, clearly illustrate this nexus. The point we want to emphasize here is that if the essence of globalization is the interpenetration of societies rather than international relations between autonomous nations, then the grounds for domestic political discourse and decisionmaking shift and the links between internal and external issues and policies begin to fuse.

The proposal by IMF managing director Rodrigo de Rato to put financial surveillance of economic policies on a multilateral footing is an excellent example of these shifts in the terrain of international negotiations and their implications for national policymaking in the global context. De Rato's idea of multilateral surveillance envisions a group of countries sitting down with the

IMF to review the national economic policies of individual countries from a global perspective instead of continuing the current practice of surveillance, in which senior IMF officials and senior country economic policy officials engage in bilateral discussions.

The first trial run of this proposal is de Rato's initiative to bring five countries together to discuss the current pattern of global imbalances. At the moment, the United States (with its large fiscal and trade deficits) and China (with its large trade and capital account surpluses) are the major players. De Rato has invited the Eurozone, Japan, and Saudi Arabia to join the United States and China (and the IMF) to discuss the nature of global imbalances, different perspectives on their causes, alternative views of their consequences, and ideas for their resolution. This is an important new idea that, if taken seriously by all participants, could become an important mechanism for adjusting national economic policies to meet global requirements and could strengthen the role of the IMF in the global economy as a consequence. It deserves support from the key players, especially the United States and China. The idea might be improved by adding to the group a country, such as Brazil, that experienced the dramatic impact of global imbalances on its domestic economy and international position. Brazil could in effect represent the interests of the rest of the world, which could be significantly affected by how the imbalances between the United States and China are resolved.

The changing nature of the nexus of power between domestic and international policies fuses external and internal interests in a new way. The experiment in multilateral surveillance would be facilitated if countries, especially China and the United States in this case, were to incorporate into their policymaking process consideration of how the global impact of their economic policies affects their own national interests. That is far from standard practice today. Moreover, today debates typically are couched in terms of one country putting blame and pressure on the other—for example, the United States pushing China to move away from its fixed exchange rate and China pushing the United States to correct its fiscal and trade deficits. Instead, each country needs to articulate and execute policy adjustments in relation to its own domestic and international interests. That means that each country needs to base its policy adjustments on the argument that reducing global imbalances is in the domestic interest, enabling it to reap the benefits of sustainable monetary, fiscal, and structural policies and of integration into the global economy. Ultimately, that approach is more politically sustainable and analytically accurate than playing on national public perceptions by blaming or pressuring others.

A good example of unnecessary tensions leading to confrontation rather than coordination arose in the 1980s when, rather than trying to find domestic reasons for making internal adjustments, the United States and Japan blamed each other for the global imbalances prevailing at that time. In fact, in the 1990s, the United States eventually did reduce its fiscal deficit, not to satisfy Japan's interest in U.S. fiscal correction but to lessen pressure on capital markets, thereby lowering interest rates and fueling domestic growth through lower borrowing costs. At times, bashing and blaming others makes for good domestic politics in the short term, but it rarely generates the best policy mix in an interdependent global economy over the long term.

Another example of the need to maintain a delicate balance between domestic politics and international policies is the movement of European countries toward an increasingly integrated European Union. The defeat of the proposed European Constitution in referendums in the United Kingdom and the Netherlands in the spring of 2005 made it clear that reaching too far toward global integration could lead in a strong and decisive way to the reassertion of domestic political primacy over internationalization. The backlash that occurred reveals the critical need to conceptualize and articulate international policies in terms of domestic priorities and politics rather than purely as desiderata in their own right.

Two further specific examples of the interplay between domestic politics and international policies addressed in earlier chapters of this volume are the reforms needed in IFI governance and in the G-8 summit—by rebalancing shares and chairs in the former and by expanding the range of countries represented in the latter. In both cases, the main challenge is to overcome the resistance to reform of traditional domestic interests, which hope to maintain individual countries' or even individual ministries' influence in the IFIs and the G-8. They must be convinced that reform will improve the legitimacy—that is, the effectiveness and representativeness—of these institutions in a way that is in the long-term national interest even of the traditionally dominant countries, the United States and the European nations. In the remainder of this chapter we will briefly summarize our views on how reform of the IFIs and of the G-8 summit could be propelled forward in a substantive yet pragmatic manner.

REBALANCING THE SHARES AND CHAIRS IN THE
INTERNATIONAL FINANCIAL INSTITUTIONS

A core reform issue is the rebalancing of the weight of members in international institutions in light of members' changing economic and demographic weights since World War II and of changes forecast for the coming decades. Prime examples are the World Bank and the IMF, which traditionally are dominated by Europe and the United States. The main problem is twofold. On one hand, by any relevant measure the Europeans clearly are overrepresented in the IFIs, both in shares and chairs, relative to their share in the global economy (let alone population). But they are reluctant to give up any of their rights and privileges, especially since doing so would reduce the role in these institutions of individual countries and specific ministries and could make their continuing financial support of the IFIs more difficult to justify to domestic taxpayers. On the other hand, the United States, which frequently is seen as "the elephant in the room" because it is the largest single shareholder, wields an exceptional right to veto key decisions; moreover, the institutions' headquarters are located in the United States.[7] The United States also has been reluctant to reduce its dominant role in these institutions for fear of reducing its scope for using them as instruments of U.S. foreign policy and for fear of losing support for them in Congress. This preponderance of influence by the traditional powers is now being challenged by the newly emerging economic powers, especially in Asia, where initiatives to set up or strengthen regional financial institutions as alternatives to the traditional global financial institutions have been gaining momentum, partly as a reaction to the lack of progress until very recently in rebalancing shares and chairs within the IFIs.

Despite the extreme difficulty of getting ministries in individual European countries to give up their visibility and direct engagement on the executive boards, a good case actually can be made that the Europeans as a group would strengthen their position in the executive boards of the Bank and the IMF if they were to consolidate the eight chairs currently held by individual European countries and constituencies into a single chair with a combined voting share of more than 25 percent. That would give Europe the largest voting share and veto power, along with the United States. Such a move would also mark a major improvement in governance by reducing the number of seats at the table from twenty-four to as few as seventeen, thereby making the board a more effective decisionmaking body while enhancing European influence at the same time.[8]

To provide incentives for the Europeans to reduce their shares and consolidate their chairs into a single seat, we propose—in the spirit of striking a "grand bargain"—that the United States voluntarily give up its veto in both the IMF and the World Bank. If the United States voluntarily withdrew its right to veto major decisions in exchange for the Europeans consolidating their chairs into one and withdrawing the veto power that would then accrue to Europe, both sides would gain in terms of their key shared objective—making the IFIs more effective instruments of global financial and development policy. Doing so would also give the emerging market economies, especially those from Asia, a stronger voice and vote in the IFIs, thus reducing the pressure for fragmentation of the multilateral financial institutional system into regional blocs.

For the United States the key question is whether it wants to break the momentum of regionalization and support a move toward more effective, legitimate, and truly multilateral financial institutions. The fact is that the U.S. veto, which unilateralizes the U.S. role in the IFIs and creates resistance on the part of other countries, is inconsistent with the essential idea of a multilateral international institution. As IMF historian James Boughton writes in chapter 2 of this volume: "To borrow Thomas Friedman's phrase, the world economy has become a lot flatter since 1944, but to many people the IMF still looks like a steep mountain with the United States sitting at the summit." Worse still, as John Ikenberry recently pointed out, "the critical question for the future is: how will the United States respond to its lost legitimacy as a hegemonic leader?"[9] The unfortunate truth is that increasingly the United States itself is becoming a contentious issue in global affairs rather than the leader of the international community as a whole. For the United States to reduce its role as global lightening rod, it will need to take dramatic steps to modify its foreign policies and its role in international affairs. To regain its role as a leader of nations in a restructured international system, the United States will need to become a leader on behalf of the world. It must lead by virtue of its ability to reflect in its own behavior the values, interests, and views of others rather than to reinstall itself as hegemonic ruler by virtue of its power alone. Renouncing the U.S. veto in the IMF and the World Bank would be a small but significant step in the right direction. It would be an example of reconceptualizing American interests by redefining the U.S. presence in the world in a new way that incorporates the interests of others rather than seeks to prevail over them in both form and substance.

Such a grand bargain between the United States and Europe on chairs and vetoes would give real content and meaning to IFI governance reform. Along with other reforms under consideration, it could transform the spirit of IFI governance from one of resentment of the dominance of the two major powers into one of the multilateral bargaining, coalition building, and more democratic global governance needed for the twenty-first century.

REFORMING THE G-8 AS THE GLOBAL APEX INSTITUTION

The compelling logic for international institutional reform is that the legitimacy and effectiveness of these institutions are undermined by their twentieth-century governance structure, which does not recognize the economic transformations of the last fifty years or the increasing need for representational legitimacy to ensure their effectiveness in the twenty-first century. Extending that rationale to the G-8 summits, it is clear that the constellation of countries in the group are predominantly rich, industrial, Western countries in a world that is predominantly poor, nonindustrial, and non-Western. The G-8 embodies parochialism rather than universality as a principle of governance, to pick up on Jack Boorman's set of principles in chapter 1. It has no claim to represent the world or to be a steering committee for meeting global challenges—not in today's world of more than 6 billion people and much less in the world of 9 billion people anticipated for 2050, in which the additional 3 billion people will come from non-Western, nonindustrial, poorer countries. Therefore, the absence of a truly representative, globally inclusive steering group means that there is a void at the apex of the international system.

The international community is composed of a set of international institutions that have their own sectorial governance mechanisms, but there is no global governance group at the apex of the international system that has an overview of the system as a whole and of the interrelationships among the institutions. That may have been appropriate for the twentieth century, when problem solving and professions were based on specialization and expertise alone. The twenty-first century, in which globalization has become the dominant modality and motif of international relationships, is characterized by an interpenetration of domains in which the interconnections among challenges, sectors, and institutions are central rather than peripheral to the management of issues.

As a consequence, the void at the apex is now critical. The effectiveness of the international system depends on the relationships among the institutions that constitute it, which are crucial to addressing contemporary challenges.

These relationships present strategic guidance issues, not simple questions of interagency coordination or internal management. Therefore the annual meeting of the heads of international agencies and institutions at the Chief Executives Board (CEB), while welcome as a much-needed operational coordination mechanism, is an inadequate solution to the problem. The interrelationships among institutions are ultimately political problems because they entail determining relative priorities among the areas of health, education, gender equality, the environment, poverty, finance, trade, growth, and security—which in the end are determined by societal values, requiring societal input. Since national officials are the most legitimate source of political authority, heads of state and government are the most optimal representatives for public input and adjudication of cross-sector values, conflicts, and jurisdictions.

In addition, heads of state also are uniquely endowed among national authorities with intersectorial, interministerial, integrated responsibilities for public policy. They alone among political authorities can transcend the boundaries of sectors and bureaucracies to forge integrated strategies for dealing with problems whose essential character is increasingly multidimensional. Health governance issues cannot be resolved by health ministers alone, nor environmental problems by environment ministers alone, nor financial challenges by finance ministers alone. Today the global challenges in each domain are more fundamentally defined by their interaction with factors and forces outside each domain—so that overall strategic guidance is required to address their intersectorial and interinstitutional nature.

There is no better example for illustrating the integrated nature of global challenges than the Millennium Declaration and the Millennium Development Goals. The Millennium Declaration, promulgated by 183 heads of state at the Millennium Summit in September 2000, set out five major baskets of objectives in the areas of security, governance, human rights, poverty, and the environment, making clear their interconnectedness. At the Financing for Development (FFD) summit in Monterrey in March 2002, heads of state endorsed the eight Millennium Development Goals (MDGs) and quantitative indicators for tracking them. The MDGs are now the primary framework for multilateral and bilateral cooperation on development around the world. The MDGs consist of global goals to be achieved by 2015 in the areas of poverty, gender equality, universal education, mortality, infectious diseases, the environment, and international cooperation.

In addition to being specific goals to guide development efforts, the MDGs redefined the development paradigm as an interdependent, multidimensional set of actions, replacing the traditional focus of the development community, which was principally economic and financial in its orientation. The MDGs make clear that poverty reduction will not occur without action on gender, education, health, and environmental issues and that no action in those areas will be sustained unless direct actions are taken to reduce poverty, stimulate economic growth, and improve institutions and governance. The MDGs are one example of why the World Bank, the IMF, the World Trade Organization, the World Health Organization, and other specialized UN agencies need the strategic guidance that only heads of state can provide on how to relate to each other on behalf of a larger, multifaceted, and multi-institutional human agenda.

The void at the apex means that the MDGs and the Millennium Declaration have no steering group, no strategic guidance, and no focal point for implementation that can integrate individual institutional efforts into system-wide mobilization of resources and policy actions. That illustrates but does not exhaust the reasons why the G-8 summit needs to be reconstituted, in terms of both membership and stewardship, to fit the twenty-first century. Of course, one might wish to focus instead on reforming the economic, social, and environmental steering capacity of the UN and in particular aim for a fundamental redirection of the Economic and Social Council (ECOSOC) into an Economic Security Council of the UN. However, the painful experience with UN reform in recent decades, culminating most recently in the failure of the Millennium+5 UN summit in September 2005 to make any headway in UN governance reform (see also chapter 4), leads us to look to a revamped G-8 as the group to provide the necessary political forum for the major powers of the twenty-first century to discuss and, where possible, reach agreement on how to address some of the world's key challenges.

If it is to serve as a legitimate global apex institution, the G-8 needs to be enlarged to include the major emerging market economies in deliberations and decisions on issues that are global in scale and scope. We argue in chapter 5 that taking the ten industrial economies (including the EU) and the ten emerging market economies that are in the G-20 finance ministers group and creating an L-20 leaders-level group to replace the G-8 is one strong, pragmatic option that has salience and relevance. But it is not the only option. Many are convinced that the group should consist of a core consisting of the G-8 plus China, India, Brazil, and South Africa (and some say Mexico), thereby creating an L-12 or L-13. Others consider an L-12 or L-13 plus another half-dozen seats to be filled by different countries, depending on the issues being discussed ("variable geometry"), a better option because it is more inclusive and creates opportunities to bring countries that are neither large nor powerful to the table. Some find regional representation to be an attractive vehicle for inclusion. For us, the bottom line is that the current G-8 is condemned to irrelevance if its membership is not expanded. Some step forward on summit reform needs to be made, and made soon, and any of the alternatives mentioned above look to us substantially better than the status quo. The key requirement is that the new forum be substantially more inclusive, broader in its focus, and based on a new commitment to asserting stewardship of the international system by tackling a few major global challenges and pushing reform of the international institutions as a major priority.

THE WAY FORWARD FOR GLOBAL GOVERNANCE REFORM

The main point emerging from this volume is twofold. First, significant structural change in the country composition, mandates, and functions of international institutions and summits is vital to reflect the changing balance among the world's major economies and to address effectively the growing challenges facing our increasingly integrated and rapidly transforming globe. Second, each international institution is no longer able to deal effectively with its primary mandate without strategic guidance and well-defined relationships with other institutions that address related issues outside its primary mandate, mission, and capacity.

The central message of this book is therefore that there is a tight nexus between reform of individual international institutions and reform of the global governance system and its apex institution. Without progress on both fronts the international system will not have the capacity to provide the world's population with adequate responses to the issues of health, education, gender equality, environmental sustainability, poverty reduction, financial stability, economic growth, human rights, good governance, and personal security. If the international system does not develop the capacity to meet the challenges of the global age, it will fail to have "practical meaning," and it will falter and slip behind in meeting humanity's hopes and expectations.

This Summit's Promise

JAMES D. WOLFENSOHN

James D. Wolfensohn was president of the World Bank from 1995 to 2005. He is chairman of Wolfensohn and Co., an investment and advisory firm focused on emerging market economies.

Tomorrow's meeting of the Group of 20 leaders is a landmark in the evolution of global governance, one that I hope will create an opportunity to address a number of global issues. We have reached this point due to the perceived impotence of our initial response to the economic crisis. That response was led by members of the Group of Seven: the old boys' club of advanced countries that has traditionally taken the lead in tackling global crises.

The G-7's dominant role in international affairs over the past half-century was explained by its collective economic weight: Between 1965 and 2002, it accounted for a remarkably constant share of global output—about 65 percent. In recent years, however, the G-7 began an evanescence. Its share of global output has fallen to 52 percent. By 2030, it is likely to be down to 37 percent; by 2050, to a mere 25 percent.

The flip side of this coin is the rise of emerging markets. The International Monetary Fund forecasts that in 2009, as the advanced economies sink into their first collective recession since World War II, 100 percent of global growth will be attributable to developing nations. Against this backdrop, it is inconceiv-

Editors' Note: This op-ed was originally published on November 14, 2008, in the *Washington Post*.

able that today's global challenges could be addressed without the support of China, India, Brazil and other emerging powers. This is not simply a matter of fairness or generosity but one of efficacy and realism.

Thus the G-20 is the correct body to tackle a crisis of this magnitude. Its members account for 90 percent of global output and two-thirds of the world's population. It is diverse—with five countries from Asia, three from Latin America, two from the Middle East and one from Africa—and represents our rapidly globalizing world.

Western leaders must be careful not to slip into old habits in dealing with their new partners. The tendency to summon others to meetings or to see dialogue as an opportunity to educate others as to their best interests is a vestige of a bygone era. Instead, the West should listen to the expertise and concerns expressed by leaders of developing countries and treat them as full and equal partners, not as guests fortunate to be invited.

Behavior of this kind will improve the chances of a successful conclusion to the crisis talks. If, however, the recent history of global cooperation is anything to go by, achieving such an outcome will not be easy. Failure to deliver multilateral responses on key global issues has been a regrettable hallmark of the past decade: We have been unable to reach agreement at the global trade talks commenced some seven years ago at Doha; we neither reached a consensus on curbing greenhouse gas emissions nor designed a credible system for the enforcement of targets at Kyoto; we are failing to deliver on the aid pledges made at the Group of Eight meeting in Gleneagles, Scotland, in 2005 and are consequently in danger of missing the U.N. Millennium Development Goals. By no means is this list exhaustive; from nuclear nonproliferation to managing strategic oil reserves and food stockpiles, our efforts have fallen short.

Among these challenges, the financial crisis is unique in that it is unfolding directly before us: The foreclosures on our neighbors' mortgages, the plunging value of our retirement savings and rumors of sweeping layoffs are constant reminders of the costs of our inaction. But for two other of the world's most pressing challenges, the costs of inaction are hidden from view. The effects of climate change will be visible only in the future, when it will be too late to combat them, and the impoverishment of millions overseas is too far removed from our everyday lives.

Tomorrow's summit could be a watershed moment in overcoming crises that are both visible and less visible today. The financial crisis is stripping governments of the resources and energy they need to invest in green technologies and to scale up aid; until this crisis is meaningfully addressed on a global level, climate change and poverty will remain on the back burner. Eliminating the chaos being wreaked in their domestic economies is a sine qua non for restoring governments' powers to address these issues.

Moreover, progress at this summit can restore governments' faith in the fruits of global cooperation and renew their interest in tackling global issues that remain unresolved.

Our immediate charge is to deal with the crisis we can see. But it is my great hope that progress in addressing the financial crisis will open the door for progress on the world's other crises, which, though less visible, are no less important to securing our collective future.

Is the G-20 Summit a Step Toward a New Global Economic Order?

COLIN I. BRADFORD JR. and JOHANNES F. LINN

Colin I. Bradford is a nonresident senior fellow in Global Economy and Development.

Johannes F. Linn is the director of the Wolfensohn Center for Development and a former World Bank vice president for Europe and Central Asia.

In November 2008, President George W. Bush convened the first G-20 summit in Washington to address the worst global financial economic crisis since the Great Depression. This summit provided a long-overdue opportunity for a dramatic and lasting change in global governance. This was followed by the election of Barack Obama, who had campaigned on a distinctly different foreign policy platform compared with his Republican rival, Senator John McCain. These two events were no mere coincidence.

The global crisis has moved the United States, along with the rest of the world, toward a new global economic order, with the G-20 summit as one of the principal manifestations of the new global governance system. Of course, movement toward this new economic arrangement and progress toward reformed global governance are not inevitable. It will take a clear and sustained commit-

Editors' Note: This article was originally published as Policy Brief No. 170 by the Brookings Institution in September 2009.

ment to a new set of values and strong leadership, especially from President Obama and the United States, to ensure that the G-20 summit is not a short-lived exception to what had been a long-standing stalemate in global governance reform. The effectiveness of the G-20 in addressing the global economic crisis could lay the foundation for a new global order and provide the impetus for the many other necessary global governance reforms. Whether or not this happens will depend to a significant extent on the direction chosen by President Obama.

The president's vision of inclusion and openness and his approach to governing, which favors innovative and far-reaching pragmatic responses to key national and global challenges, make him a great candidate for this role. In due course the G- 20 summit can also serve as a platform for addressing other pressing global issues, including trade, climate change, energy and food security and reform of global institutions. To achieve such an outcome, President Obama and other world leaders need to demonstrate a clear vision and strong leadership starting at the G-20 Summit in Pittsburgh and beyond.

"OLD ECONOMIC ORDER" VERSUS "NEW ECONOMIC ORDER"

From recent debates on foreign policy and global governance, we have identified two different perspectives or sets of principles underlying the approaches toward U.S. and global foreign policy. Table 1 summarizes the key elements of what we call the "Old Economic Order" in juxtaposition to the "New Economic Order."

In the Old Order, the nation state is the point of departure, stressing the importance of sovereignty and national interest as the key principles driving a unilateral and assertive foreign policy. In contrast, the New Order's starting point considers that we live in a global society, where interdependency and recognition of common interests are the key principles to be pursued in reciprocal relations and with mutual respect across borders. Under the Old Order the rules of national power politics prevail, as competing blocs and fixed alliances strive for predominance, with "hard power" if necessary. Instead, the New Order operates on the basis of a new multilateralism, which builds on the prevalence of global networks in all spheres of life and multiple coalitions across borders, where bargaining for compromise and the tools of "soft power" prevail. Finally, the Old Order promotes the notion that a single economic and political

TABLE 1 Old versus New Economic Order

OLD ORDER	NEW ORDER
Nation-states	Global society
Severeignty	Interdependency
National Interest	Common Interest
Unilateralism	Reciprocity
Assertiveness	Respect
National Power Politics	New multilateralism
Competing Blocs	Global networks
Fixed alliances	Multiple coalitions
Predominance	Bargaining for compromise
Hard Power	Soft Power
Promotion of singular economic models and political values	Coexistence of diverse models of market economy and political systems

Note: This table is adapted from one first presented by the authors in a seminar at the IMF in June 2007. See: www.imf.org/external/np/seminars/eng/2007/glb/bl030607.pdf.

model should prevail, while the New Order accepts that different economic and political models coexist and compete side by side.

In the most simple terms, the Old Order broadly reflects the principles underlying the foreign policy agenda of the Bush administration and Senator John McCain's presidential platform, while the New Order approximates those underpinning the platform of Senator Barack Obama's presidential campaign and of his administration's foreign policy stance. Key elements of the Old Order (except the last one) have also been attributed to the current foreign policy approach of Russia, while New Order principles can be ascribed to the European Union.

In fact, what is reflected in these two approaches is the difference between twentieth-century principles of foreign policy versus principles appropriate to today's realities. We believe there are three interrelated sets of drivers of change that necessitate moving from the Old Order to the New Order. These drivers include the changing global demographic and economic balance, emerging global threats and the need for a more effective global governance system.

DRIVERS OF CHANGE

The first driver of change is the shifting global demographic and economic balance. By 2050, the world population is projected to reach 9.1 billion, up from 6.4 billion today, with the increase occurring almost entirely in today's developing countries. China is widely predicted to be the largest economy in the early 2040s, with the U.S. economy in second place and India's in third. Other emerging market economies, including Brazil, Indonesia and Russia, will be important economic players, while individual European countries will recede in importance. Continental Eurasia will be the new hub of global integration as China, India, Russia, the European Union and the Middle East's energy-producing countries knit their economies ever closer together. The United States will remain a superpower, but only one among others. Together, the major world powers will have to confront the fact that people in poorer and weaker states will feel left behind. Simultaneously, cross-border networks—economic and political, public and private, elite and grassroots, legitimate and illegitimate—will continue to grow and will weaken the traditional hold states have over the economic, financial, social and political actions of their citizens. These networks will create bonds that will either reinforce or undermine global stability.

The second driver of change is a set of emerging global threats:

- The current financial and economic crisis—triggered by poor macroeconomic management and lax financial regulation—reflects the realities of long-term financial imbalances among key economies. It proves the difficulties of managing a highly interdependent global financial system in the absence of agreed-upon global financial surveillance, supervision and regulation. It is likely that risks of global financial stress will continue in the coming decades.

- Global disparities will increase as the rich and the rapidly growing economies do well, while many poor and stagnating countries are left behind. There is potential for rising disparities within countries, too. These inequities will reinforce risks of domestic and cross-border conflict and terrorism. At the same time, the United States and other industrialized countries face a progressive loss of traditional industries, jobs and wages. Aging populations and overburdened pension systems will challenge their fiscal stability and may lead to groundswells of anti-globalization sentiments.

+ Rising food and energy prices, environmental threats and the risks of global epidemics—reinforced by population pressures—particularly affect the poorest countries.

+ Growing global interdependencies across borders and sectoral lines mean that individual countries can no longer address these threats alone and that a global response has to be coordinated across sectors.

The third driver of change is the growing and widespread recognition that the current system of global governance has become increasingly fragmented, ineffective, outdated and resistant to change. This systemic weakness is reflected in the persistent stalemate on many of the pressing global issues—most notably the Doha trade round—but also on global poverty, climate change and the risk of pandemics. Moreover, global institutions have become unrepresentative in the face of the changed global economic and political balances. Hence their legitimacy is suffering badly, and yet there is stalemate in the reform of individual international organizations.

Together, these three factors have made the principles of the Old Order irrelevant and strongly point in the direction of a New Order. They represent the new reality for governments, citizens and international institutions and force them to adopt new principles and reform existing institutions.

While the drivers are strong and the new global reality is seemingly unassailable, change is not inevitable. Old habits die hard. In the United States, traditions of self-reliance and "exceptionalism" continue to shape Americans' views of the rest of the world. At the same time, the widespread belief in the virtues of unfettered markets and low taxes, the influence of special interests for protection (agriculture, labor, old industry, banking) and the prevailing fractiousness of political decision-making may well undermine President Obama's efforts to move toward a new global paradigm. Compounding the entrenchment of the Old Order, new nations that are still recovering from centuries of colonialism—facing economic and political instability and wishing to catch up with the successful industrial countries—are lured to a strong sovereign nation state, unfettered control over their borders and their citizens, and a confrontational approach to foreign policy. Even the much admired willingness of the Europeans to give up sovereignty in favor of supranational institutions has its limits, not least when it comes to giving up their prerogatives of dominating the governing boards of the international financial institutions and other global forums.

Leadership, conviction and persistence will be required among many actors on the global stage to ensure there is progress toward effective reform of global institutions. This potential for change is exemplified by the recent emergence of the G-20 summit as a vehicle for global governance.

THE G-20 SUMMIT—ORIGINS, OPTIONS AND OBSTACLES

ORIGINS. The G-20 summit had its origins in the annual meetings of the G-7— the leaders of a group of seven major Western industrial countries who gathered annually starting in the 1970s, initially to enhance economic and financial policy coordination in reaction to a major financial crisis. After the break-up of the Soviet Union, the G-8 was formed by the addition of the Russian Federation. The G-8 increasingly became preoccupied with global economic and political issues— in effect assuming the role of a global steering group. But widespread criticism began to mount about its role. The G-8 summits were seen as ritualistic in process, ineffective in impact and increasingly unrepresentative in the face of global population and economic shifts, and hence lacking in legitimacy as a global steering group. The onset of the global financial crisis in mid-2008 pushed President George W. Bush into convening the G-20 Summit on November 15, 2008.

The ministerial-level G-20 was first created in the aftermath of the 1997–98 East Asia financial crisis. By convening representatives from 10 industrialized economies and 10 emerging market economies, the G-20 presented a much more geographically and culturally diverse group than the G-8. With about 90 percent of the world's economy and two thirds of the world's population, the G-20 is also much more representative than the G-8. Emerging market economies have been fully engaged in managing the proceedings of the meetings of G-20 finance ministers and central bank governors. It is therefore not surprising that there had been persistent calls by some experts and politicians for using the G-20 as a platform to replace the G-8. While moving from G-8 to G-20 summit might not create an optimal global steering group, it is a pragmatic and effective step, especially in response to crisis.

OPTIONS. Will the G-20 be a short-lived experiment or will it prove an effective tool of global governance? Various options are under debate among experts and practitioners. One possibility is to return to the G-8 summits like the one Italy hosted in 2009 and Canada plans to host in 2010. There is concern that the G-20 format is too unwieldy for effective exchanges among the key players. Hence, there will be continuing debates about reducing the size of the summit to somewhere between thirteen and sixteen members, as reflected in the recent proposal by the French president, Nicolas Sarkozy, to create a G-14. However, there are pressures to expand the number of participants to include more countries and to expand regional representation. Then there are proposals to develop a constituency-based approach to membership, with universal participation as in the case of the international financial institutions. Further, German chancellor Angela Merkel and a United Nations Commission chaired by Nobel laureate Joseph Stiglitz propose to establish an Economic Security Council at the UN.

None of these options will likely materialize in the foreseeable future. Instead there are two probable outcomes: The first is the continuation of the G-20 summit with a gradually expanding mandate beyond the current crisis. For this to be successful, it is critical that the G-20 format proves its effectiveness in the coming months and years. This outcome has three requirements: that the number of participants does not expand; that participants focus on a limited number of action items; and that a small but effective secretariat is established to support and monitor the G-20 summit with logistics and technical expertise.

The most likely alternative to the G-20 summit is what is frequently referred to as "variable geometry." Under this scenario, selected world leaders would convene on specific topics in shifting constellations, with participation of the most important actors decided separately for each topic. For example, the G-20 might continue to meet on global financial and economic matters for some time to come, while different groups would convene for action on climate change, nuclear proliferation or other topics. Support for this plan appears to be emerging from the Obama administration. It co-convened the summit on climate change at the tail-end of the 2009 G-8 summit, hosts the September 2009 G-20 economic summit in Pittsburgh and has called for a summit on nuclear nonproliferation in the spring of 2010. The challenge for summits of "variable geometry" is the ever-shifting number and composition of participants, the difficulty of systematic organization and follow-up and continuing debates about who would convene the summits, when, and with what participation.

OBSTACLES. As we look ahead, we see a number of challenges for the evolution of global summits beyond the G-8, whether toward an effective G-20 or some alternative, especially summits of variable geometry. These challenges emanate from the diverging interests of four sets of players: the United States, Europe, the new emerging powers and the rest of the world.

For the foreseeable future, active U.S. leadership is needed to overcome inertia and collective action problems in addressing global challenges and breaking the stalemate in global governance reform. The Obama administration appears to strongly support a paradigm shift toward a new global order, but so far has not announced its position on summit modalities.

Europe is a key player and has proven a major obstacle to global governance reform as it continues to claim far too many chairs at the G-20 (and in other global forums and institutions) for its economic and demographic weight. In effect, Europeans can either retain their over-representation, which gives them a fragmented voice and weakens their influence while also weakening the global institutions; or they can bundle their votes, chairs and voice for greater impact and to ensure more effective international organizations. Unfortunately, the current stalemate on internal EU governance reform blocks any new European approach to global governance reform.

The new emerging powers, especially China, India and Brazil, will face the challenge of moving beyond their traditional role of the "excluded" and "representatives of the South." They will need to accept co-responsibility for solving global problems and creating effective global governance institutions. They will have to look beyond issue-specific South-South coalitions to North-South coalitions where it is in their and the global interest (e.g., the push for international financial institution reform, for EU consolidation, for the completion of the Doha Round, etc.). There are hopeful signs that this is beginning to happen. South Korea's leadership of next year's G-20 represents a critical test of whether the new powers are ready to participate and conduct a G-20 forum at the leaders' level, not only ministerial.

Finally, there is the challenge of how to include the "excluded." The G-20 is much more inclusive than the G-8, but it still leaves out a majority of countries with a third of the world's population. Options for associating the rest of the world with the summit include ad hoc outreach (as the G-8 has done), expanding regional representation (as already practiced with the EU), introducing a constituency approach (as for the IFIs) and seeking a closer alignment with the UN (perhaps through an Economic Security Council). With the exception of the first two—which risk further expanding the number of participants at G-20 summits—none of the other options are likely to materialize soon. However, G-20 leaders will have to be sensitive to the needs of the "excluded" and ensure that the interests of the poorest countries are not neglected.

CONCLUSION

Great changes in the economic and political balance among countries, global threats and an antiquated global governance system confront the world community today. With the economic crisis as an immediate driver and a new U.S. president, the G-20 summit format has the potential to make a real shift in the global economic order in which a new set of values underpins the way countries and people cooperate across borders. To the extent that President Obama has articulated his vision of the global order and America's role in it, we believe he is headed in the direction that stresses common interests in a global society, the need for multilateral action and understanding for alternative approaches to economic and political development. This is very promising. The effectiveness of the G-20 in addressing the global economic crisis could lay the foundation for a new global order and provide the impetus for the many other necessary global governance reforms.

However, Europe, China and India are also critical for progress. Moreover, if President Obama is believed to fail the test of competence at home or a major shock hits the United States, a reversal is possible in the U.S. In any case, significant changes in global governance will take time to transpire. We may well see a long period of transition with only gradual improvement in current institutions. In the meantime, pressures for increased regionalism, bilateral deals among the big players, geopolitical competition among power blocs and growing instability and threats from the "excluded" will undermine international cooperation and the whole idea of a global order.

The G-20 summit forum represents a great opportunity for world leaders to begin to put into action the principles of a new global order. It will allow them to address the immediate global financial and economic crisis in a collaborative spirit. And in due course the G-20 summit can also serve as a platform for addressing other pressing global issues, including trade, climate change, energy and food security, and reform of global institutions. To achieve such an outcome, President Obama and other world leaders need to demonstrate a clear vision and strong leadership at the G-20 summit in Pittsburgh and beyond.

Epilogue

HOMI KHARAS *and* GEOFFREY GERTZ

The Wolfensohn Center for Development was founded in 2006 with a simple but ambitious mission, to create knowledge that leads to action with real, scaled-up, and lasting development impact. In its five years of activity, it helped build within the Brookings Institution a critical mass of scholars, scholarship, and institutional linkages and partnerships with other development stakeholders. As the chapters here have demonstrated, the idea was to focus on a few critical areas that were not receiving adequate attention in the rest of the world, as well as to bring the understanding of what was going on in developing countries to bear on Brookings' work on domestic issues.

Any "start-up" such as the Wolfensohn Center needs to show some concrete achievements as well as lay a basis for future growth and sustainability. With the benefit of a half-dozen years of hindsight, it is possible to begin to put the achievements of the Center in perspective.

Since 2008 the University of Pennsylvania has produced annual rankings of think tanks around the world.[1] Brookings ranked first in the category of "International Development" every year until 2016, when it fell to third place globally, while retaining top position among U.S. think tanks working on this topic. While such rankings are of course only one incomplete means of evaluating a research institute, they suggest that the work being done at Brookings on international development has been, and continues to be, well regarded by outside observers.

What is perhaps more surprising is how work streams that were developed over a decade ago in the Wolfensohn Center remain the focus of Brookings's development work today. Indeed, the original bet to identify topics that were at the time under the radar but likely to grow in importance, such as global governance reform and youth exclusion in the Middle East, has clearly paid off: the Center's priority areas are now at the core of the international development agenda. In this epilogue, we provide an overview of how this agenda has evolved in recent years, highlighting how the institution's contemporary contributions to this research and actions are rooted in the earlier work of the Wolfensohn Center.

For those engaged in international development, 2015 was a watershed year. In that year three major international conferences—the Addis Ababa financing for development forum, the Sustainable Development Goals (SDGs) Summit, and the Paris Climate Summit—all resulted in major international agreements, which are likely to define the global development landscape for the coming years.[2] Brookings scholars working on development effectiveness were active in the preparations for, and activities in, each of these conferences. And the origins of their engagement can be found in work started at the Center.

The Addis Ababa Action Agenda gave shape to the financing for development agenda—what came to be known as the "billions to trillions" issue.[3] The point was simple: Official aid was being measured in billions of dollars (about 100 billion net disbursements per year going to developing countries). Yet even the most conservative assessments of the cost of investments necessary to achieve the SDGs put the tab at upwards of a trillion dollars of incremental financing.[4] The development financing question, therefore, has become where can new resources be found and how can they be allocated or programmed toward projects that serve to advance the SDGs?

Raising more resources for development will only be feasible if aid becomes more catalytic. That is the main message of the Wolfensohn Center book *Catalyzing Development: A New Vision for Aid*, published in 2011. More recent work at Brookings has gone into detail about how to operationalize this concept and make it more tangible.

A catalyst can initiate or speed up change. At Brookings, there are now three areas where the catalytic properties of public development assistance are being explored. One is speeding up the transition to universally accessible and sustainable infrastructure, especially in energy and transport, where projects tend to be large and take many years to design and execute. Current mechanisms for speeding up access to infrastructure are not working. The multilateral development banks themselves do not have the resources to scale up investments to the degree required. Early enthusiasm at the World Bank and among other development agencies for infrastructure funded by private means has not led to the breakthrough needed, and the volume of such projects has flattened out.[5] Today Brookings scholars are exploring new ways of developing scalable platforms for sustainable infrastructure financing to deliver a higher volume and better quality of investments. This work is being done through a consortium of experts supporting the Global Commission on the Economy and Climate,[6] as well as through efforts to support the multi-stakeholder Global Infrastructure Forum and related international platforms.

A second area of catalytic change is through leveraging donor budgetary resources. Brookings scholars have engaged with multilateral development institutions themselves, researching options for optimizing balance sheets and convening senior officials of the agencies (and their shareholders) to discuss mandates and resources.[7] They have also engaged with the Organization for Economic Cooperation and Development on new concepts for development financing, currently called Total Official Support for Sustainable Development, to document the extent of non-aid flows oriented toward development projects.

A third area of catalytic change is the growing realization that private business can contribute to development—jobs, innovation, efficiency—even in the poorest countries. Until now, the small scale of low-income country markets had made it difficult for foreign investors to realize good commercial returns from investments in low-income countries. But growth and expansion of markets, along with technology that has reduced the cost of market entry and of information, have made private investment a more viable option. There are a number of instruments development institutions can use to help de-risk private investment, including guarantees, first-loss provisions, up-front financing of studies or other initial project costs, subsidies for experts to make projects bankable or for marketing new products, and strengthening of regulatory practices and institutions. Brookings scholars were called on to advise the Business Commission on Sustainable Development, and, through membership in the World Economic Forum's Global Agenda Council, they continue to explore mechanisms through which private and public finances can be blended.

The world has also changed with the passage of the SDGs, the second major agreement of 2015. Achieving a global consensus on the SDGs was no easy feat. Some countries wanted to keep to a narrow focus on extreme poverty reduction, finishing the job begun with the Millennium Development Goals. Others, however, wanted a more expansive agenda. Brookings scholars weighed in on this debate. Homi Kharas was selected to be the executive secretary and lead author of the report of the High Level Panel advising then–secretary general Ban Ki-Moon on the post-2015 agenda. This panel, cochaired by President Ellen Johnson Sirleaf of Liberia, President Susilo Bambang Yudhoyono of Indonesia, and Prime Minister David Cameron of Great Britain, elaborated a vision of an ambitious, integrated, and universal agenda, a scope that was reflected in the final agreement reached by UN member states.[8]

A sense of the controversy around the development goals emerged in editorials, such as that in *The Economist* magazine, calling the post-2015 vision "Stupid Development Goals" and "worse than useless."[9] These critics missed a key insight that had been central to the worldview of James Wolfensohn and the Wolfensohn Center: developing countries could no longer be viewed as a single homogeneous group. They differed significantly in context, prospects, and challenges for the future. With such diversity of needs and aspirations, it was inevitable that a global agenda would need to be expansive. Had the agenda been boiled down to a few issues salient to low-income countries only, it would have been relevant to a minority of the nations in the world, rather than presaging a universal and global transformation of production and consumption patterns to achieve a more sustainable world.

Brookings scholars continue to work on ideas to implement the SDGs more effectively. Building off the Center's work on global governance and international summits, they have argued for bringing development more fully into the discussions of finance ministers and leaders at G-20 meetings. They have engaged with academics in the T20 process, a grouping of think tanks from each of the G-20 countries. They have engaged with senior management of global institutions: the MDBs, of course, but also the International Fund for Agricultural Development, the Global Partnership for Education, the Global Fund for the Fight against AIDS, Tuberculosis, and Malaria, and the Global Partnership for Sustainable Development Data. They have become involved in numerous global commissions and panels.

The third major agreement of 2015, the Paris Agreement on Climate Change, has spawned a major body of work at Brookings. Climate change was not a direct focus area of the Wolfensohn Center, but preserving the earth's natural resources was one of the core development challenges espoused by James Wolfensohn. The Center conducted some early work on the distribution of water resources from the Jordan River. Over time, however, climate has become so closely intertwined with other development issues—finance, sustainable infrastructure, global governance—that it was inevitable that research on this would grow.

The legacy of the Wolfensohn Center, however, goes beyond the topic areas currently covered by Brookings scholars. It has also embedded core principles into the work of the Global Economy and Development program. One principle of the Center, "giving voice to developing countries with high-level policy engagement and broad networking," is fundamental to the operations of the Africa Growth Initiative, a program within Brookings's Global Economy and Development division. Staffed by African scholars, and connected to networks tied in with African think tanks, the Africa Growth Initiative brings the voice of Africa to the policy establishment in Washington, D.C.

Another core principle of the Wolfensohn Center was to link development theory and practice, to bring about more effective action. This also continues in Brookings work on development today. Engagements with policymakers and senior managers of international institutions systematically expose Brookings scholars to what is happening on the ground, giving new insights to research. Scholars have actively engaged with the Global Fund, UNESCO, the Global Partnership for Education, IFAD, and other project agencies, as well as the multilateral development banks. Moreover, a number of practical innovations have followed out of Brookings's work. Specific projects, such as the case studies conducted under the Ending Rural Hunger project, and the Learning Metrics Task Force and Millions Learning programs organized by Brookings's Center for Universal Education, have allowed for extensive dialogue with policymakers.[10] This two-way interaction between research and practice remains a guiding axiom for the Global Economy and Development program at Brookings.

A third principle of the Wolfensohn Center was to approach issues from a universal perspective, proxied by the four-tier world framework. All work at Global, including beyond-GDP metrics of well-being, determinants of productivity growth, urban planning, trade, and financial and monetary stability also have significant implications for development. The converse is now also true. The lessons of what is working in developing countries are being brought back to inform policies in advanced countries. Developing countries are leapfrogging ahead in renewable energy, in green finance, in mobile banking, in digitized forms of social assistance provision, and in thinking about access to infrastructure in backward regions. The middle class in developing countries is flourishing at the same time as it stagnates in advanced economies. Correlation or causation? Are policy lessons transferable across countries? These questions have become part of the research agenda, not least because they have become institutionalized by the adoption of a universal set of goals through the SDGs. Development is no longer seen as something for rich countries to finance in poor countries, but as a journey being taken by all countries learning together how to build prosperity in a sustainable way.

The original decision to create the Wolfensohn Center for Development was a calculated gamble. It was a bet that a small research center could fill a niche in an already crowded development space, helping to shape a forward-looking agenda on understudied development challenges. And it was a bet that investments in rigorous, policy-oriented research could reap long-term dividends, as the initial ideas nurtured in the Center could evolve and expand over time, delivering impact for years to come.

Today, the Wolfensohn Center's principles and priorities now permeate the Global Economy and Development program, and it is fair to say that it is the Wolfensohn Center itself that has been scaled up. The Wolfensohn Center's legacy is a dynamic research program at the heart of international development debates, continuing the search for effective solutions to create a more prosperous and stable world.

About the Contributors

Colin Bradford is a nonresident senior fellow in the Global Economy and Development program at Brookings.

Raj Desai is a visiting fellow in the Global Economy and Development program at Brookings and associate professor of international development in the Edmund A. Walsh School of Foreign Service at Georgetown University. From 2006 to 2008 he was a visiting fellow at the Wolfensohn Center for Development.

Jacques van der Gaag is a nonresident senior fellow at the Center for Universal Education at Brookings and a professor emeritus of development economics at the Faculty of Economics and Business of the University of Amsterdam (UvA).

Geoffrey Gertz is a postdoctoral research fellow in the Global Economy and Development program at Brookings. From 2008 to 2011 he was a research analyst at the Wolfensohn Center for Development.

HOMI KHARAS is a senior fellow and codirector in the Global Economy and Development program at Brookings. From 2007 to 2011 he was a senior fellow at the Wolfensohn Center for Development.

JOHANNES F. LINN is a nonresident senior fellow in the Global Economy and Development program at Brookings, distinguished resident scholar of the Emerging Markets Forum, and senior adviser at the Results for Development Institute (R4D). From 2006 to 2010 he was the director of the Wolfensohn Center for Development.

Wolfensohn Center for Development Publications

Books

The following books are available for purchase from www.brookings.edu/press/.

Getting to Scale: How to Bring Development Solutions to Millions of Poor People, edited by Laurence Chandy, Akio Hosono, Homi Kharas, and Johannes F. Linn, 2013

Catalyzing Development: A New Vision for Aid, edited by Homi Kharas, Koji Makino, and Woojin Jung, 2011

Global Leadership in Transition: Making the G20 More Effective and Responsive, edited by Colin I. Bradford and Wonhyuk Lim, 2011

Delivering Aid Differently: Lessons from the Field, edited by Wolfgang Fengler and Homi Kharas, 2010

Generation in Waiting: The Unfulfilled Promise of Young People in the Middle East, edited by Navtej Dhillon and Tarik M. Yousef, 2009

Tournament Approaches to Policy Reform: Making Development Assistance More Effective, by Clifford F. Zinnes, 2009

Good Intentions, Bad Outcomes: Social Policy, Informality, and Economic Growth in Mexico, by Santiago Levy, 2008

Global Governance Reform: Breaking the Stalemate, edited by Colin I. Bradford and Johannes F. Linn, 2007

Progress against Poverty: Sustaining Mexico's Progresa-Oportunidades Program, by Santiago Levy, 2006

Working Papers

The following working papers can be downloaded from www.brookings.edu/series/ wolfensohn-center-for-development-working-papers/.

"The Political Economy of Urban Poverty in Developing Countries," Raj M. Desai, 2010

"Urban Poverty in Developing Countries: A Scoping Study for Future Research," Johannes F. Linn, 2010

"Municipal Finance of Urban Infrastructure: Knowns and Unknowns," James Alm, 2010

"Land Markets, Government Interventions, and Housing Affordability," Alain Bertaud, 2010

"Scaling-Up Early Child Development in South Africa: Introducing a Reception Year (Grade R) for Children Aged Five Years as the First Year of Schooling," Linda Biersteker, 2010

"Scaling-Up Early Child Development in Cuba—Cuba's Educate Your Child Program: Strategies and Lessons from the Expansion Process," Alfredo R. Tinajero, 2010

"External Assistance for Urban Development: A Scoping Study for Further Research," Homi Kharas, Laurence Chandy, and Joshua Hermias, 2010

"Case Study on Aid Effectiveness in Tajikistan," Firuz Kataev, Matin Kholmatov, and Rustam Aminjanov, 2009

"Do Philanthropic Citizens Behave Like Governments? Internet-Based Platforms and the Diffusion of International Private Aid," Raj M. Desai and Homi Kharas, 2009

"Quality and Coordination of Official Development Aid in Pakistan," Abdul Malik, 2009

"Aid Coordination on the Ground: Are Joint Country Assistance Strategies the Answer?," Johannes F. Linn, 2009

"A Case Study of Aid Effectiveness in Ethiopia: Analysis of the Health Sector

Aid Architecture," Getnet Alemu, 2009

"A Case Study of Aid Effectiveness in Kenya: Volatility and Fragmentation of Foreign Aid, with a Focus on Health," Francis M. Mwega, 2009

"Aid Effectiveness in Cambodia," Ek Chanboreth and Sok Hach, 2008

"Post-Tsunami Aid Effectiveness in Aceh: Proliferation and Coordination in Reconstruction," Harry Masyrafah and Jock MJA McKeon, 2008

"The Experience with Regional Economic Cooperation Organizations: Lessons for Central Asia," Johannes F. Linn and Oksana Pidufala, 2008

"Scaling Up: A Framework and Lessons for Development Effectiveness from Literature and Practice," Arntraud Hartmann and Johannes F. Linn, 2008

"Measuring the Cost of Aid Volatility," Homi Kharas, 2008

"The Political Economy of Poverty Reduction," Raj M. Desai, 2007

"Trends and Issues in Development Aid," Homi Kharas, 2007

Notes

1 Introduction

1. The $10 million commitment was in addition to an initial $1 million that James Wolfensohn had pledged to Brookings in 2005 to fund preparatory work for the Center.

2 Meeting the Challenge of Development

1. The methodology is spelled out in the appendix in H. Kharas, "The Emerging Middle Class in Developing Countries," OECD Development Center Working Paper 285, Organization for Economic Cooperation and Development, 2010.

2. Speech to students at Peking University, May 2002 (www.china.org.cn/english /2002/May/33449.htm).

3. H. Kharas and G. Gertz, "The New Global Middle Class: A Cross-Over from West to East," 2010 (www.brookings.edu/wp-content/uploads/2016/06/03_china_middle _class_kharas.pdf).

4. OECD, "Perspectives on Global Development: Shifting Wealth," 2011 (www. oecd.org/dev/pgd/).

5. J. Wolfensohn, "Farewell to Development's Old Divides," Project Syndicate, 2007 (www.project-syndicate.org/commentary/farewell-to-development-s-old-divides).

6. For example, see "Towards the End of Poverty," *The Economist,* June 1, 2013.

7. See L. Chandy and G. T. Gertz, "Poverty in Numbers: The Changing State of World Poverty from 2005 to 2015," 2011 (www.brookings.edu/research/poverty-in-numbers-the-changing-state-of-global-poverty-from-2005-to-2015/).

8. H. Kharas, "The Unprecedented Expansion of the Global Middle Class," 2017 (www.brookings.edu/wp-content/uploads/2017/02/global_20170228_global-middle-class.pdf).

3   Scaling Up Development Impact

1. Blanca Moreno-Dotson, ed., *Reducing Poverty on a Global Scale: Findings from the Shanghai Global Learning Initiative* (Washington, D.C.: World Bank, 2005). In addition, the World Bank published a volume of case studies: *Reducing Poverty, Sustaining Growth: Scaling Up Poverty Reduction. Case Study Summaries.* A Global Learning Process and Conference in Shanghai, May 25–27, 2004 (http://documents.worldbank.org/curated/en/799211468314992503/pdf/307590Scaling1Up1Poverty0Reduction.pdf).

2. Wolfensohn Center for Development (no date). *Brochure.*

3. Santiago Levy, *Progress against Poverty: Sustaining Mexico's Progresa-Oportunidades Program* (Brookings Institution Press, 2007).

4. Raj Desai, "The Political Economy of Poverty Reduction: Scaling Up Antipoverty Programs in the Developing World," Working Paper No. 2, Wolfensohn Center for Development, Brookings, 2007.

5. Clifford Zinnes, *Tournament Approaches to Policy Reform* (Brookings Institution Press, 2009) (www.brookings.edu/research/books/2009/tournamentapproachestopolicyreform) and www.brookings.edu/research/papers/2009/07/aid-zinnes.

6. See, for example, Claudia Pompa, "Understanding Challenge Funds," Overseas Development Report, October 2003 (www.odi.org/sites/odi.org.uk/files/odi-assets/publications-opinion-files/9086.pdf).

7. Arntraud Hartmann and Johannes F. Linn, "Scaling Up: A Framework and Lessons for Development Effectiveness from Literature and Practice," Working Paper No. 5, Wolfensohn Center for Development, Brookings, 2008 (www.brookings.edu/research/papers/2008/10/scaling-up-aid-linn).

8. Arntraud Hartmann and Johannes F. Linn, "Scaling Up Through Aid: The Real Challenge," Global Views No. 7, 2008 (www.brookings.edu/research/papers/2008/10/scaling-up-linn).

9. Johannes F. Linn, Arntraud Hartmann, Homi Kharas, Richard Kohl, and Barbara Massler, "Scaling Up the Fight Against Rural Poverty: An Institutional Review of IFAD's Approach," Working Paper No. 39, Wolfensohn Center for Development, Brookings, 2010 (www.brookings.edu/research/papers/2010/10/ifad-linn-kharas).

10. Arntraud Hartmann, Homi Kharas, Richard Kohl, Johannes F. Linn, Barbara Massler, and Cheikh Sourang, "Scaling Up Programs for the Rural Poor: IFAD's Experience, Lessons and Prospects (Phase II)," Working Paper 54, Wolfensohn Center for Development, Brookings, 2013 (www.brookings.edu/research/papers/2013/01/ifad-rural-poor-kharas-linn).

11. IFAD, "Evaluation Synthesis Report on IFAD's Support to Scaling up of Results," Independent Office of Evaluation, Rome, 2017. The evaluation notes the inputs provided by the Wolfensohn Center to IFAD's scaling agenda.

12. Johannes F. Linn, "Scaling Up with Aid: The Institutional Dimension," in *Catalyzing Development: A New Vision for Aid*, edited by H. Kharas, K. Makino, and W. Jung (Brookings Institution Press, 2011).

13. OECD, Busan Partnership for Effective Development Co-Operation, December 1, 2011 (www.oecd.org/development/effectiveness/49650173.pdf).

14. Laurence Chandy and Johannes F. Linn, "Taking Development Activities to Scale

in Fragile and Low Capacity Environments," Global Working Paper No. 41, Brookings, 2011 (www.brookings.edu/research/papers/2011/09/development-activities-chandy-linn).

15. AusAID, "Guidelines: Scaling Up," Portfolio Planning and Development Section, Australian Government, June 2012.

16. Laurence Chandy, Akio Hosono, Homi Kharas, and Johannes F. Linn, eds., *Getting to Scale: How to Bring Development Solutions to Millions of Poor People* (Brookings Institution Press, 2013).

17. Natalia Agapitova and Johannes F. Linn, "Scaling Up Social Enterprise Innovations," Working Paper No. 95, Global Economy and Development, Brookings, 2016 (www.brookings.edu/research/scaling-up-social-enterprise-innovations-approaches-and-lessons/).

18. Eileen McGivney, Jenny Perlman Robinson, and Rebecca Winthrop, "Millions Learning: Scaling up Quality Education in Developing Countries," report, April 13, 2016 (www.brookings.edu/research/millions-learning-scaling-up-quality-education-in-developing-countries/).

19. Johannes F. Linn, "Scaling Up in the Country Program Strategies of Aid Agencies: An Assessment of the African Development Bank's Country Strategy Papers," *Global Journal of Emerging Market Economies* 7, no. 3 (2015), pp. 236–56 (http://eme.sagepub.com/content/7/3/236.abstract).

20. Miliça Begovic, Johannes F. Linn, and Rastislav Vrbenski, "Scaling up the Impact of Development Interventions: A Review of UNDP Country Programs," Working Paper No. 101, Global Economy and Development, Brookings, March 2017 (www.brookings.edu/wp-content/uploads/2017/03/global-20170315-undp.pdf).

21. Global Delivery Initiative, "Guidelines for Delivery Case Studies. Annex XII," World Bank, 2016 (www.globaldeliveryinitiative.org/sites/default/files/pages/delivery_case_study_guidelines_-_english.pdf).

22. Tamara Giltsoff, "The 'Scale' Elephant in the Room at IDIA," DFID, 2016 (https://medium.com/@InnovateDFID/the-scale-elephant-in-the-room-at-idia-c7c470cf1bdc).

23. Johannes F. Linn, ed., "Scaling Up in Agriculture, Rural Development and Nutrition," *2020 Focus Briefs*, IFPRI, 2012 (www.brookings.edu/research/articles/2012/06/scaling-up-development).

24. Lawrence Cooley and Johannes F. Linn, "Taking Innovations to Scale: Methods, Applications and Lessons" Results for Development Institute, 2014 (http://r4d.org/about-us/press-room/taking-innovations-scale).

25. OECD, The DAC Prize 2015 (www.oecd.org/dac/dacprize.htm).

26. Management Systems International, "Scaling-Up Community of Practice Launched," February 27, 2015 (www.msiworldwide.com/2015/02/scaling-up-community-of-practice-launched/).

The Challenge of Reaching Scale

1. This is not to imply that developed countries are entirely harmonious societies; no country is without its unique socioeconomic problems and political failings. The point, rather, is that the challenges of development represent a unique kind of problem.

2. Pritchett, Woolcock, and Andrews (2010).

3. Levy (2006).

4. Duffy (2010).

5. World Bank (2011).

6. One exception is the study by Hartmann and Linn (2008).

7. The phrase *mission critical* is borrowed from the International Fund for Agricultural Development, which provides a rare example of an aid agency that has made scaling up an integral and explicit part of its modus operandi.

8. Busan Partnership for Effective Development Cooperation (2011, p. 2ff).

9. Miguel and Kremer (2004).

10. Mullins and Komisar (2009).

11. Prahalad (2004).

12. Figures represent total HIV/AIDS spending, not just expenditure on antiretroviral therapy.

13. UNAIDS (2012).

14. For instance, see World Bank (2012).

15. Quote by Bunker Roy in Bishop and Green (2010).

16. Lewin (2008); Kenny (2010).

17. Devarajan (2010).

18. UK DFID (2008).

19. Woolcock, Szreter, and Rao (2011).

20. Kubzansky (2010).

21. Worthington and Pipa (2011); Bishop and Green (2010).

22. Oxfam (2012).

23. ActionAid (2011).

24. Stabile (2010); Saltuk and others (2013).

25. J. P. Morgan (2010).

26. Isenman and Shakow (2010).

4 The Effectiveness of Development Assistance

1. OECD, "The High Level Fora on Aid Effectiveness: A History" (www.oecd.org/dac/effectiveness/thehighlevelforaonaideffectivenessahistory.htm).

2. The first Wolfensohn Center working paper was on the topic of aid effectiveness. See H. Kharas, "Trends and Issues in Development Aid," 2007 (www.brookings.edu/wp-content/uploads/2016/06/11_development_aid_kharas.pdf).

3. See figure 5 in H. Kharas, "Development Assistance in the 21st Century," contribution to the VIII Salamanca Forum on the Fight against Hunger and Poverty, 2009.

4. H. Kharas, "Measuring the Cost of Aid Volatility," Working Paper 3, Wolfensohn Center for Development, Brookings, 2008.

5. N. Birdsall and H. Kharas, 2010, "The Quality of Official Development Assistance Assessment" (www.cgdev.org/sites/default/files/1424481_file_CGD_QuODA_web.pdf).

6. L. Chandy and G. Gertz, "Poverty in Numbers," 2011 (www.brookings.edu/wp-content/uploads/2016/06/01_global_poverty_chandy.pdf).

7. H. Kharas, K. Makino, and W. Jung, eds., *Catalyzing Development: A New Vision for Aid* (Brookings Institution Press, 2011).

Measuring the Quality of Aid

1. The first edition of QuODA was released in October 2010. N. Birdsall and H. Kharas, "Quality of Official Development Assistance Assessment," www.cgdev.org/quoda.

2. For most of our indicators, 2009 is the latest year of data available. Indicators based on the Paris Declaration Monitoring Survey use 2010 data.

3. This summary focuses on the findings of the QuODA country-level analysis. The forthcoming report will also separately assess individual agencies in the 23 countries, comparing them to multilaterals, for a total of 113 agencies in the agency-level analysis.

4. Further detail on methods and findings will be available in our forthcoming full report and on our website, www.cgdev.org/quoda.

5. The average change in the three dimensions where significant change occurred is about 8 percent. To determine percent change in donors' performance between the first and second editions of QuODA, we cannot directly compare 2009 to 2008 scores; in some cases, donors' performance improved but their score on a particular indicator fell because the performance of others improved even more. We measure absolute improvement by computing a 2009 score that is directly comparable to a 2008 score that has been adjusted for methodological changes. We find that the magnitude of the change for the three dimensions where significant change occurred is about .2 standard deviations.

6. OECD (Organisation for Economic Co-operation and Development), Aid Effectiveness 2005–10: *Progress in Implementing the Paris Declaration* (Paris, 2011).

7. A possible vehicle for donors and recipients to agree on evaluation and learning standards is the *International Initiative for Impact Evaluation*. However, only 11 official donor agencies and 5 developing countries are 3IE members. Contributions by donors to 3IE are included in the global public goods indicator in the maximizing efficiency dimension.

An Agenda for the Busan High-Level Forum on Aid Effectiveness

1. See chapter 6, this volume, for the definition of fragility and the classification methodology used in this chapter.

2. Severino and Ray (2009).

3. World Bank (2008).

4. Arndt, Jones, and Tarp (2010).

5. Cumulative net ODA disbursements in 2007 constant dollars.

6. OECD/DAC (various years); chapters 2 and 3, this volume.

7. OECD/DAC (various years).

8. OECD/DAC (2010).

9. Rogerson (2010).

10. OECD (2008).

11. See note 1.

12. About 54 percent of aid is country programmable. OECD/DAC (2010).

13. Technical cooperation is used as a proxy, albeit a highly imperfect one, for capacity development—for which unfortunately time-series data do not exist. In comparing the volume of aid for various types of capacity development in the Creditor Reporting System for 2008, we find it is close to the volume for technical cooperation reported by the DAC.

14. While not all aspects of this changing environment are strictly new—for instance, China has been providing aid to other countries since the 1950s, and capacity building has long been an objective of aid—they nevertheless represent a range of issues that have come to prominence in recent years and that demand greater attention in the evolving aid effectiveness agenda.

15. While this chapter focuses on flows from developed to developing countries, it is important to note that local NGOs and civil society organizations are beginning to raise sums from individual donors in developing countries. Many local NGOs also get significant amounts of in-kind assistance from citizens of developing countries.

16. Hudson Institute (2010).

17. InterAction (2009).

18. Long (2008).

19. In meetings with U.S. officials in 2009, InterAction members said that their staff in Afghanistan numbered 11,000, with 98 percent being local hires.

20. See, for example, McKinsey and Co. (2010); Tuan (2008); Grantmakers (2009).

21. Many INGOs routinely plan to spend private development assistance as ten-plus-year investments into a particular program area or civil society organization.

22. This case is articulated by Alesina and Dollar (1998).

23. Monitor Institute (2009).

24. The easiest way of cooperating is through multinational institutions. Yet even traditional donors are channeling a smaller share of their resources through multilaterals, showing the practical limits to cooperation in today's world.

25. Collier and others (2003).

26. Of the respondents who were aware of CDCs in 2009, 78 percent expressed their satisfaction with the performance of their local CDCs. Furthermore, 81 percent believed that their CDCs are capable of representing their interests before the provincial authorities, while 62 percent believed that they are capable of doing so before the national government. Rennie, Sharma, and Sen (2009, pp. 80–84).

27. As of June 2010 fast-start commitments were about $28 billion, but it is unclear if

these are additional to prior development assistance. The question is the credibility of these commitments. This year marks the end point for achievement of the Gleneagles targets of increasing aid to Africa by $25 billion. Only half that target is likely to be achieved.

28. IPCC (2007).

29. Even successful projects may not be appropriate for scaling up. Some projects are "gold-plated" to ensure their success, but the cost is so high that scaling up becomes infeasible or would entail too high an opportunity cost in terms of forgone development in other areas. One World Bank evaluation summarizes the problem as follows: "By and large, what is being scaled up has not been locally evaluated." Ainsworth, Vaillancourt, and Gaubatze (2005, p. 62).

30. The International Fund for Agricultural Development is the only identified agency to have conducted such a review.

31. The Alliance for Financial Inclusion, for example, funded by the Bill and Melinda Gates Foundation and GTZ, operates a program to share South experiences with microfinance.

5   Youth Inclusion in the Middle East

1. "Arab Youth: Look Forward in Anger," *The Economist*, August 6, 2016.

2. See, for example, Ivo H. Daalder, Nicole Gnesotto, and Philip H. Gordon, eds. *Crescent of Crisis: US-European Strategy for the Greater Middle East* (Brookings Institution Press, 2006); James A. Piazza, "Draining the Swamp: Democracy Promotion, State Failure, and Terrorism in 19 Middle Eastern Countries," *Studies in Conflict & Terrorism* 30, no. 6 (2007): 521–39; Richard N. Haass, "The New Middle East," *Foreign Affairs* 85 (2006): 2; Barry Rubin, *The Long War for Freedom: The Arab Struggle for Democracy in the Middle East* (New York: John Wiley & Sons, 2006).

3. In 2009 Silatech began supporting this effort through Taqeem (Arabic for "evaluation"), a program aimed at promoting the use of impact evaluation across the Middle East in the critical areas of employment and entrepreneurship to ensure more effective youth policy and program development.

4. These working papers are archived at www.meyi.org/publications.html.

5. Navtej Dhillon and Tarik Yousef, eds., *Generation in Waiting: The Unfulfilled Promise of Young People in the Middle East* (Brookings Institution Press, 2011).

6. Thomas L. Friedman, "Up With Egypt," *New York Times*, February 8, 2011.

7. www.rand.org/international/cmepp/imey.html

8. www.youthpolicy.org/mappings/regionalyouthscenes/mena/facts/

9. www.mercycorps.org/research-resources/civic-engagement-youth-middle-east-and-north-africa

10. www.cmimarseille.org/programs/arab-youth-initiative

11. www.clintonfoundation.org/clinton-global-initiative/commitments/first-jobs-then-futures-mena-youth

12. World Bank, *Building Effective Employment Programs for Unemployed Youth in the Middle East and North Africa* (Washington, D.C., 2013).

13. "Text: Obama's Speech in Cairo," *New York Times*, June 4, 2009 (www.nytimes.com/2009/06/04/us/politics/04obama.text.html).

14. Nader Kabbani, "Why Young Syrians Prefer Public Sector Jobs," Wolfensohn Center for Development, Brookings, 2009.

15. "Vocational Priorities," *Forward Syria*, July 2010, p. 36.

16. "Egypt Moves to Recapture its Recent Economic Growth," *Wall Street Journal*, March 10, 2010, p. A19.

17. Ehaab Abdou, Amina Fahmy, Diana Greenwald, and Jane Nelson, "Social Entrepreneurship in the Middle East: Toward Sustainable Development for the Next Generation," Middle East Youth Initiative Working Paper No. 10, Wolfensohn Center for Development, Brookings, 2010.

18. Hillary Clinton, "Closing Remarks at the Presidential Summit on Entrepreneurship," Washington, D.C., April 27, 2010 (https://2009-2017.state.gov/secretary/20092013clinton/rm/2010/04/140968.htm).

19. Aziza Osman, "Arab World's Pioneers of Social Entrepreneurship," *Arabian Business*, March 16, 2016 (www.arabianbusiness.com/arab-world-s-pioneers-of-social-entrepreneurship-625018.html).

20. Bassam Haddad, "The Syrian Regime's Business Backbone," *Middle East Report* 42, no. 262, Middle East Research and Information Project, 2012.

21. Edward A. Sayre and Tarik M. Yousef, eds. *Young Generation Awakening: Economics, Society, and Policy on the Eve of the Arab Spring* (Oxford University Press, 2016).

22. Anne Case and Angus S. Deaton, "Mortality and Morbidity in the 21st Century," Brookings Panel on Economic Activity, March 23–24, 2017, Brookings Institution, Washington, D.C.

Generation in Waiting

1. Alan Richards and John Waterbury, *A Political Economy of the Middle East* (Boulder, Colo.: Westview Press, 2007).

2. Hilary Silver, "Social Exclusion: Comparative Analysis of Europe and Middle East Youth," Middle East Youth Initiative Working Paper No. 1, Wolfensohn Center for Development at the Brookings Institution and the Dubai School of Government, 2007.

3. Glen H. Elder Jr., Monica Kirkpatrick Johnson, and Robert Crosnoe, "The Emergence and Development of Life Course Theory," in *Handbook of the Life Course*, edited by Jeylan T. Mortimer and Michael J. Shanahan (New York: Springer, 2004).

4. Silver, "Social Exclusion: Comparative Analysis of Europe and Middle East Youth."

5. World Bank, *World Development Report 2007: Development and the Next Generation* (Washington: 2006).

6. Cynthia Lloyd, ed., *Growing Up Global: The Changing Transitions to Adulthood in Developing Countries* (Washington: National Academies Press, 2005).

6 Investing in Early Child Development

I benefited greatly from comments and input by E. Gustafsson-Wright, M. E. Young, and G. T. Gertz.

1. See M. E. Young, ed., *From Early Child Development to Human Development* (Washington, D.C.: World Bank, 2002).

2. The late Fraser Mustard, a prominent Canadian physician and scientist who specialized in ECD (especially brain development), often accompanied her.

3. Many countries have some form of private sector provision of ECD, but there is little or no involvement of the corporate sector in large-scale ECD operations.

4. The event was held in cooperation with the Committee for Economic Development.

5. Sophie Gardiner and Emily Gustafsson-Wright, "Updates from the Field on Costing Early Childhood Development," Brookings Institution, September 22, 2016 (www.brookings.edu/blog/education-plus-development/2016/09/22/updates-from-the-field-on-costing-early-childhood-development/).

6. See Emily Gustafsson-Wright, Sophie Gardiner, and Vidya Putcha, "The Potential and Limitations of Impact Bonds," Brookings Institution, July 2015; Emily Gustafsson and Sophie Gardiner, "Using Impact Bonds to Achieve Early Child Development Outcomes in Low- and Middle-Income Countries," Brookings Institution, January 2016; and Emily Gustafsson-Wright, Sophie Gardiner, and Katie Smith, "Ensuring Effective Outcome-Based Financing in Early Childhood Development: Recommendations to the International Commission on Financing Global Education Opportunity," Brookings Institution, December 2016.

Scaling Up Early Childhood Development in South Africa

1. Regulations governing school admission were amended by the Educational Laws Amendment Act 50 of 2002. In 2000–01 children were only permitted to attend formal schooling in the year they turned seven. This was amended in 2002 to the year they turn six, enabling children to access Grade 1 if they turn six before June 30 of that year. This in turn permits the admission of children to Grade R if they turn five before the end of June. Grade 1 onwards is compulsory.

2. Children at targeted public schools benefit from the School Nutrition Programme, but this is not a health intervention—it is a snack aimed at alleviating the effects of hunger on capacity to learn.

3. DET was the education department serving African children within South Africa (not the "homelands"). At this time there were several education departments serving different "race" and ethnic groups.

4. A serious problem prior to the introduction of Grade R—underage enrollments were encouraged by

    1. Principals of bigger schools getting a higher salary, allowable staff complement and other resources
    2. Lower cost to parents in fees and access to food at primary schools compared with community ECD sites (Department of Education 2001c)

5. While the contribution of advocacy and political clout seems to have been an important factor in the inclusion of an ECD commission, specialist education informants interviewed indicated that the fact that NEPI was a comprehensive study of an education system including basic, tertiary, adult education, teacher education, and that many developed countries had preschool systems, was reason enough for its inclusion.

6. South Africa's governance and budget system is such that once the total revenue has been shared across the three spheres (national, provincial, and local), each has discretion over how to divide its slice across the different programs and services for which it has responsibility. The only exception is when a decision has been taken to use the conditional grant mechanism to fund a program, service, or infrastructure. Then money sourced from the National Revenue Fund is "ring-fenced" for provincial departments to spend on a particular purpose. Treasury does not favor the conditional grant mechanism because experience has shown that it runs the risk of provinces underspending due to limited implementation capacity (Streak & Norushe, 2008).

7. The ECD and Teacher Education Directorates in the national department of education have been in discussion about streamlining and incorporating Grade R into the formal teaching system (SAIDE Grade R Research Terms of Reference document, 2009).

8. A recent school sanitation audit of primary schools in Metropolitan Cape Town found about 25 percent of schools had learner to toilet ratios greater than 40:1. The researchers expressed concern that Grade R learners were being phased in to schools without addressing these sanitation issues. Minimum standards for ECD centers (Department of Social Development, 2006) stipulate a ratio of 20 children per toilet, and there is no reason why this should not be a benchmark for schools. Personal communication, L. Lake, October 2008.

9. According to Naidoo (2007) analysis of the 2007 Community Survey, there were 569,970 children aged five attending educational institutions in 2007, which gives an additional 82,445 children in some form of community-based ECD provision, but not necessarily a registered Grade R class. Some children aged four and some aged six are also eligible for Grade R, which would increase numbers. In the Western Cape alone there are 20,000 children in this age group in community-based sites registered by Department of Social Development.

10. Speech by the minister of education, Professor Kader Asmal, at the colloquium marking the launch of the Foundation Phase Systemic Evaluation, June 2003, accessible at www.info.gov.za/speeches/2003/.

11. Address by the minister of education, Naledi Pandor, at the Foundation Phase Conference, September 30, 2008.

7 Global Governance for Development

1. Colin Bradford and Johannes F. Linn, "Reform of Global Governance: Priorities for Action," Brookings Policy Brief No.163 (Washington, D.C.: Brookings, 2007), p. 6.

2. Bradford and Linn had first explored the G-20 summit option in April 2004 in Brookings Policy Brief No. 131, and then again in April 2006 in Policy Brief No. 152, and in October 2007 in Policy Brief No. 163.

3. Paul Martin had joined Bradford and Linn in December 2008 in praising the first G-20 summit and laying out an agenda for future summits in Brookings Policy Brief No. 168: "Global Governance Breakthrough: The G-20 Summit and the Future Agenda."

4. Colin Bradford and Johannes F. Linn, "Is the G-20 Summit a Step Toward a New Global Economic Order?," Brookings Policy Brief No. 170 (Washington, D.C.: Brookings, 2009).

Global Governance Reform

1. Michel Camdessus, "International Financial Institutions: Dealing with New Global Challenges," Per Jacobsson Lecture, Washington, September 25, 2005 (www.perjacobsson.org/lectures.htm), p. 10.

2. Ibid., p. 12.

3. One obvious flaw is that it fails to deal with the problem of autocratic regimes, whose democratic legitimacy is at best weak. That also weakens the representational legitimacy of their heads of state in international forums.

4. Camdessus, "International Financial Institutions," p. 5.

5. We consulted principally, but not exclusively, with officials and think tank representatives in the G-20 countries.

6. For a definition of the "global age" as an era distinct from the modern age, see Martin Albrow, *The Global Age* (Stanford University Press, 1997).

7. The U.S. veto right derives from the fact that the threshold for passage of major decisions—such as quota increases, changes in the Articles of Agreement, and so forth—is a supermajority of 85 percent and the United States has more than 17 percent of the voting power.

8. An interim step would be to unify only the Eurozone chairs, which would be justified especially in view of their common currency and common monetary and exchange rate policy.

9. G. John Ikenberry, "America and the Reform of Global Institutions," CIGI '06, Centre for International Governance Innovation, Waterloo, Ontario, Canada, July 29, 2006, p. 18.

Epilogue

1. Annual rankings are available from www.gotothinktank.com/.

2. See, for further information on the three meetings, Third International Conference on Financing for Development, "Addis Ababa Action Agenda," 2015 (www.un.org/esa/ffd/wp-content/uploads/2015/08/AAAA_Outcome.pdf); United Nations, "Transforming our World: the 2030 Agenda for Sustainable Development," 2015 (https://sustainabledevelopment.un.org/content/documents/21252030%20Agenda%20for%20Sustainable%20Development%20web.pdf); UNFCCC, "The Paris Agreement," 2015 (http://unfccc.int/files/essential_background/convention/application/pdf/english_paris_agreement.pdf).

3. World Bank, "From Billions to Trillions: Transforming Development Finance," 2015 (http://siteresources.worldbank.org/DEVCOMMINT/Documentation/236 59446/DC2015-0002(E)FinancingforDevelopment.pdf).

4. UNCTAD, "Investing in the SDGs: An Action Plan," 2014, http://unctad.org/ en/PublicationsLibrary/wir2014_en.pdf

5. The Private Provision of Infrastructure Database (https://ppiaf.org/documents/ 2973?ref_site=ppiaf).

6. Global Commission on the Economy and Climate, "Better Growth, Better Climate," 2015 (http://static.newclimateeconomy.report/wp-content/uploads/2014/08/NCE_SynthesisReport.pdf).

7. A. Bhattacharya and H. Kharas, "A New Global Agenda: Implications for the Role of the World Bank," 2016 (www.brookings.edu/wp-content/uploads/2016/10/ global_20161005_new-global-agenda.pdf).

8. Report of the High-Level Panel of Eminent Persons on the Post-2015 Development Agenda, 2013, "A New Global Partnership: Eradicate Poverty and Transform Economies through Sustainable Development" (www.post2015hlp.org/wp-content/ uploads/2013/05/UN-Report.pdf).

9. "The 169 Commandments," *The Economist*, March 26 2015 (www.economist. com/news/leaders/21647286-proposed-sustainable-development-goals-would-be-worse-useless-169-commandments).

10. For further information on these programs, see www.endingruralhunger.org, www.brookings.edu/learning-metrics-task-force-2-0/about-the-lmtf/, and www.brookings .edu/research/millions-learning-scaling-up-quality-education-in-developing-countries/.

Index

Lightning Source UK Ltd.
Milton Keynes UK
UKOW04n2158051017
310477UK00003B/34/P